THE SEAGULL READER

Poems

W. W. Norton & Company, Inc., also publishes

THE SEAGULL READER: STORIES • edited by Joseph Kelly

THE SEAGULL READER: ESSAYS • edited by Joseph Kelly

THE SEAGULL READER

Poems

edited by Joseph Kelly

College of Charleston

W. W. Norton & Company • New York • London

The text of this book is composed in Adobe Garamond
with the display set in Bernhard Modern.
Composition by PennSet, Inc.
Manufacturing by Haddon Craftsmen.
Book design by Chris Welch.

Library of Congress Cataloging-in-Publication Data

The seagull reader. Poems / edited by Joseph Kelly.
        p.   cm.
Includes index.

ISBN 0-393-97631-9 (pbk.)

    1. English poetry. 2. American poetry. I. Kelly, Joseph, 1962–

PR1175.S388 2000
821.008—dc21

                                                        00-061638

W. W. Norton & Company, Inc., 500 Fifth Avenue, New York, N.Y. 10110
www.wwnorton.com
W. W. Norton & Company Ltd., Castle House, 75/76 Wells Street,
London W1T 3QT

5 6 7 8 9 0

*

Contents

*

Acknowledgments

I owe a great debt to John Ruszkiewicz, which this acknowledgment barely begins to discharge. I want to thank Susan Farrell for her help and kindness. And I must mention also Scott Dupree, who first taught me much of what I have contributed to this book.

Along with the publisher, I am happy to thank the following for their assistance during various stages of this project:

Jay Adler (Los Angeles Southwest College); Thomas Austenfeld (Drury College); Paul Aviles (Onondaga Community College); Leslie G. Bailey (Saint Martin's College); G. R. Benzinger (Duquesne University); David Bergman (Towson University); Stephen Bernstein (University of Michigan at Flint); Martin Bickman (University of Colorado); Eric Birdsall (University of Akron); George Bishop (D'Youville College); Jenny Brantley (University of Wisconsin at River Falls); Edward H. Brodie, Jr. (University of South Carolina); William Carpenter (College of the Atlantic); Tom Chandler (Bryant College); Kevin Clark (California Polytechnic State University at San Luis Obispo); Patricia Clark (Grand Valley State University); Bruce Clarke (Texas Tech University); Seamus Cooney (Western Michigan University); Carolyn M. Craft (Longwood College); Virginia Crank (Rock Valley College); Koos Daley (Adams State College); Robert Darling (Keuka College); Charles L. Darr (University of Pittsburgh at Johnstown); John Dick (The University of Texas at El Paso); Paul B. Diehl (University of Iowa); William Doreski (Keene University); Gregory Eiselein (Kansas State University); S. K. Eisiminger (Clemson University); Shir Filler (North County Community College); Marilyn Fontane (Saint Louis College of Pharmacy); Chris Forhan (Trident Technical College); Robert Fuhrel (Community College of Southern Nevada);

Victoria Gaydosik (Southwestern Oklahoma State University); Len Gougeon (University of Scranton); Carol Harding (Western Oregon University); Clarinda Harris (Towson University); Lois Head (Saint Cloud State University); John Healy (Baker University); John Hildebidle (Massachusetts Institute of Technology); Charles Hood (Antelope Valley College); Shari Horner (Shippensburg); George Hudson (Colgate University); Jefferson Hunter (Smith College); James D. Johnson (Humboldt State University); Richard Kelly; Christopher B. Kennedy (Duke University); Millie M. Kidd (Mount Saint Mary's College, Los Angeles); Herbert W. Kitson (University of Pittsburgh at Titusville); Linda Kittell (Washington State University); Steve Klepetar (Saint Cloud State University); Stanley Krohmer (Grand Valley State University); Dennis Leavens (Truman State University); Michael Leddy (Eastern Illinois University); and Carol de Saint Victor (University of Iowa).

Note on Dates

After each poem, we cite the date of first book publication on the right; in some instances, this date is followed by the date of a revised version for which the author was responsible. In a few instances (when the information may be relevant to the reading of a poem), we cite the date of composition on the left.

What Is Poetry?

When we turn on the radio or put on a CD, we hear poetry's most popular form: song. In fact, lyrics that are set to music might be considered the most *poetic* of all **poems**, because anything written in meter is poetry, and we can best define meter as music. In the lines of poetry, stressed and unstressed syllables rise and fall with a musical lilt. These rhythms are most obvious in songs: we've all sometimes felt the spell, the almost physical power, in the music of our favorite lyrics. When we replay the lyrics of a favorite song in our heads, we often remember the band's music and the singer's voice. And if we say the lines aloud, we often even mimic the rhythms given to them by the band and singer. If you're familiar with Bruce Springsteen's "The River," when you read his lyrics on page 174, the music of the recording probably will invade your mind. The song's power will reach you through the tones of the harmonica or through your memory of Springsteen's unique singing style.

Literary poems, including those printed here, have this disadvantage: no instruments play the rhythm and no singer conveys the phrasing. The music can come to you through your own voice only. Try reading aloud these lines from the end of Alfred Tennyson's "Ulysses":

> *Though much is taken, much abides; and though*
> *We are not now that strength which in old days*
> *Moved earth and heaven; that which we are, we are,*
> *One equal temper of heroic hearts,*
> *Made weak by time and fate, but strong in will*
> *To strive, to seek, to find, and not to yield.*

Read it two or three more times, slowly, letting the rhythms settle themselves in your speech. Leaving aside any consideration of the words' meaning, their sound has a pleasure and a musical power. The meter directs you to say the lines a certain way. We can hear the difference from prose, even literary prose. Consider this passage for comparison:

> The *Nellie*, a cruising yawl, swung to her anchor without a flutter of the sails and was at rest. The flood had made, the wind was nearly calm, and being bound down the river the only thing for it was to come to and wait for the turn of the tide.

These lines, from the opening of Joseph Conrad's *Heart of Darkness*, capture the elegance and pleasure of natural speech at its best. But they are not musical, not in the way Tennyson's are.

If ever you've been moved to tears by a song, or if you have a favorite tape you blast in the car with the windows rolled down in the sun, if listening to a good song can change your mood, then you have a talent for poetry. And who does not? No matter how educated or unsophisticated, we all know the pleasure of listening to song. The root of that pleasure may be a mystery, but we all know it's true: that words wrestled into music have a charm and power ordinary language does not.

Like most descriptions of literary genres, this definition is fuzzy. Some prose writers do write in an almost musical style, while some poets consciously suppress the music in their poems. But roughly speaking, the definition will serve our needs: poetry is writing that sounds musical. A **lyric poem** is a short poem. There's no specific length requirement. We call a poem a lyric if it's about the size of a song. Of course, some songs are longer than others, so the division between lyrics and narratives can blur. And we can divide lyric poetry into more genres, like the **sonnet, dramatic monologue, elegy, ode,** and **ballad.** These special genres are defined in the section devoted to the structure of poetry.

How Do You Read Poems?

The literary forms that you know well, whether they're movies or TV shows or novels or popular songs, have laid the groundwork for reading poems. Songs, whose conventions you probably have been internalizing your whole life, are especially close to the poems in this volume. You're not learning new skills so much as becoming more aware of what you already can do pretty well. But as you become more aware, you'll find yourself able to handle these analytical tools with more precision and confidence.

Speaker

Every lyric poem has a **speaker**. You should imagine that every poem is a little speech by a real person: the speaker. Sometimes, the speaker's identity is a total mystery, but usually a poem will give you some clues. More often than not, it will tell you a lot about the speaker. The first thing to do when you analyze a poem is define the speaker as precisely as you can. For example, take this poem by William Wordsworth:

> She dwelt among the untrodden ways
>   Beside the springs of Dove,
> A Maid whom there were none to praise
>   And very few to love;
>
> A violet by a mossy stone
>   Half hidden from the eye!
> —Fair as a star, when only one
>   Is shining in the sky.

She lived unknown, and few could know
When Lucy ceased to be;
But she is in her grave, and, oh,
The difference to me.

The speaker tells very little about himself, but we can speculate about him. In fact, it's really speculation to say the speaker is male. He sounds like he was in love with Lucy and perhaps was courting her. From the way he describes Lucy we might further guess that he was a little older than she was, perhaps he is a bit cosmopolitan, probably he has seen some of the world. But even if he's seen some of the world, we also might assume that he's lived near the Dove River or that he's had a reason to spend some time on the "untrodden ways," or he never would have discovered Lucy himself.

We are often tempted to associate the speaker with the singer or poet, and sometimes this works. Some poems are obviously autobiographical. Poems from the Romantic era especially often invite us to equate the speaker with the poet. But it is good practice to assume that the speaker is a fictional persona unless you have evidence to prove otherwise. In other words, don't say, "William Wordsworth loved a girl named Lucy, but she died before he ever married her." In this case, though Wordsworth is a Romantic poet and did write many autobiographical poems, "She Dwelt Among Untrodden Ways" does not tell a "true" story. We should always begin by assuming the poet is playing a role.

Audience and Rhetorical Situation

If every poem has a speaker, you might logically assume that every poem also has a listener or **audience**. Ultimately, of course, anyone who reads the poem is the audience, just as anyone who hears a song in concert or on a CD is the singer's audience. But as a literary term, "audience" has a specialized meaning. It is the character(s) or persona(e) whom the speaker is addressing.

In Wordworth's poem, we have a much tougher time defining the audience than the speaker. This is not always the case. Most love poems, for example, are addressed to the speaker's lover. Turn to page 12 and look at Matthew Arnold's "Dover Beach." From clues in the poem we can guess that the audience is the speaker's beloved.

We can also determine the **rhetorical situation** of "Dover Beach," what occasions the speaker to address the audience in these words. We might guess that the speaker and his audience are newlyweds, because many English couples in the nineteenth century spent their wedding night at Dover and then took the ferry to the Continent for their honeymoon. Whether the speaker and his lover are embarking on a honeymoon or not, they seem to be on a vacation, because the speaker marvels at the seascape in a way that a local probably wouldn't. He and his lover may be in a cottage or house or a hotel room. We can't be sure, but we know they are inside some building, because they are looking out a window at the ocean.

In Wordsworth's poem, we don't have many clues about the rhetorical situation. The speaker's audience doesn't know Lucy, but he or she seems to be on fairly intimate terms with the speaker, since the speaker is unburdening his grief. Perhaps the audience is the speaker's close friend, someone from the city far from Lucy's home near Dove River. But where are they? Are they talking late at night before a hearth fire? Are they old men recounting their youth and their regrets? We don't really know.

The first couple of times you read a poem, you should focus on these three elements: speaker, audience, and rhetorical situation. Try to figure out the story of the poem, who is speaking to whom on what occasion. If you read a poem that confuses you, guess who the speaker is. Then try out your hypothesis by rereading the poem. You'll probably have to adjust your idea. That's normal. Even professional critics have to reread poems to understand them. Keep rereading until you're confident you know who the speaker is and to whom he or she is talking.

Paraphrase

The next thing you should do is make sure you understand the literal level of the poem: the basic meaning of the speaker's words. Some poems, like Wordsworth's, are so clear that you don't have to paraphrase at all. But most poems have at least a few lines that are challenging to figure out even on the literal level. Let's look again at Matthew Arnold's "Dover Beach," for example. The first eight lines are straightforward. If you read them slowly and carefully, you will probably understand the literal level. The following lines are a little more difficult:

> *Listen! you hear the grating roar*
> *Of pebbles which the waves draw back, and fling,*
> *At their return, up the high strand,*
> *Begin, and cease, and then again begin,*
> *With tremulous cadence slow, and bring*
> *The eternal note of sadness in.*

Arnold is taxing our sense of grammar to its limits. It helps, of course, to know that "strand" is an English word for "beach." A good dictionary would tell you that, and a good dictionary is an indispensable tool for reading poetry. But even knowing the meaning of "strand" doesn't clear things up totally. Where does that "Begin, and cease" belong, for example? Is the speaker telling his lover to begin and cease and then again begin?

By translating these lines into your own language, you can usually clear up those grammatical confusions. Here's one paraphrase of Arnold's lines:

> Listen to the loud noise of the pebbles. When the waves go out they drag the pebbles out to sea, and when the waves come crashing back they throw the pebbles up on the beach. You can hear the noise of the pebbles begin and stop and begin again, almost like they are beating out a slow rhythm. The sound they make makes me feel sad.

A paraphrase should be as straightforward as this. You should be able to read it aloud to your roommate, and your roommate should understand perfectly, without the slightest confusion, everything you say. If something in your paraphrase sounds a little unclear, then you should try again.

Note that this paraphrase used sixty-six words to express in prose what Arnold said in forty-one words of poetry. That's typical. Poetry is economical. In a paraphrase, you should expect to use at least one and a half times as many words as the poet, and you should suspect you've omitted some important details if you use fewer. Notice also that this paraphrase broke Arnold's single sentence into four sentences. This technique of separating out the details can help you see the big picture. For instance, after paraphrasing the second and third lines of the selection from Arnold's poem you may be able to see that "Begin, and cease" were not commands. They simply complete the thought that begins with these words: "you hear the grating roar / Of pebbles." Everything in between is an interruption. When you skip the interruption, the sentence makes more sense: "Listen! you can hear the grating roar / Of pebbles . . . / Begin, and cease, and then again begin."

You don't need to paraphrase every line of a poem. When you read through a poem, you should mark the parts that don't seem to make sense to you grammatically. Then go back and spend some time paraphrasing those lines. You don't have to actually write them down, but you should work them out in your head. When verbs seem to dangle by themselves, hunt down their subjects. When you see descriptive phrases, find out what thing they describe. Fill the margins of your book with the results, so you'll remember them.

Sometimes you'll find that you do have to write down the paraphrase. Sometimes, only by taking a pen to a blank piece of paper can you unravel the **syntax** of unclear lines. You should do this for any poem that you're writing a paper about, just to make sure that you understand the literal level perfectly, because the success of your interpretation hinges on accurately reading the poem's literal level. For example, to say that the speaker in "Dover Beach" is standing on the beach along the *French* coast rather than the *English* coast is just dead wrong. It would set your interpretation off in the wrong direction, and you would never get back on the right track.

After you've mastered the literal level of a poem, you should begin examining the **figurative levels**. As you read the poem over and over again, you'll begin to recognize how it communicates much more than what is conveyed by the literal meaning. Through metaphors and patterns of images and symbols, even through the physical sound of the words, a poem conveys meanings that deepen and amplify the literal level. What might have seemed a flat piece of writing suddenly explodes into a third dimension, and you'll find your emotions and your intellect caught up in the complexities. The following sections should help you see, understand, and feel this dimension.

Tone

Tone in a poem is the same as tone in speech. When someone is talking to you, you unconsciously determine the tone of their voice. By visual clues, like facial expression, you determine their emotion, and that information helps you to fully appreciate the meaning of their words. Take this dialogue, for example:

> "How are you doing?"
> "I'm doing all right, I guess."

Compare it to this version, which includes tonal clues:

> "How are you doing?" he asked lightly.
> "I'm doing all right," she said slowly, with a resigned look
> on her face. "I guess."

Sometimes, tone does not just contribute to the meaning of the words: it reverses the literal meaning. Someone asks you how you are doing, and you answer sarcastically, "I'm doing all right," and they know that you are *not* doing all right. You convey the sarcasm through tonal qualities in your voice, and maybe by rolling your eyes.

The text of a poem, of course, can use neither facial expression nor voice. Therefore, the tone of a poem is harder to detect than the tone of someone speaking to you. Nevertheless, with some careful attention, you should be able to determine the tone of the speaker in a poem, even though you cannot hear him or her.

Sometimes you might notice a difference between the speaker's tone and the poet's tone. In a poem like Gwendolyn Brooks's "We Real Cool," for example, we get a strong sense that the poet does not entirely approve of the speakers' swagger, especially when they nonchalantly conclude, "We / Die soon." Brooks's attitude is more knowing and more critical than the speakers'. When you recognize such a difference, you have detected **irony**. What the poet means is different than what the speaker means. Often the degree of irony in a poem is a matter of interpretation and debate. Does Ulysses speak for Tennyson in that dramatic monologue? Is Poe critical of the hypersensitive narrator in "The Raven"? These are matters that cannot be decided with finality, but it is nearly always useful to entertain the possibility that the speaker is ironized.

Imagery

An **image** is anything you see, hear, smell, touch, or taste in a poem. Anything "concrete" (to use a familiar metaphor) as opposed to "abstract" is an image. Images are the basic building blocks of just about any poem.

Consider these two poems, the first by A. E. Housman and the second by W. B. Yeats:

When I Was One-and-Twenty

When I was one and twenty
I heard a wise man say
"Give crowns and pounds and guineas
But not your heart away;
Give pearls away and rubies
But keep your fancy free."
But I was one-and-twenty,
No use to talk to me.

When I was one-and-twenty
I heard him say again,
"The heart out of the bosom
Was never given in vain;
'Tis paid with sighs a plenty
And sold for endless rue."
And I am two-and-twenty,
And oh, 'tis true, 'tis true.

Down by the Salley Gardens

Down by the salley gardens my love and I did meet;
She passed the salley gardens with little snow-white feet.
She bid me take love easy, as the leaves grow on the tree;
But I, being young and foolish, with her would not agree.

In a field by the river my love and I did stand,
And on my leaning shoulder she laid her snow-white hand.
She bid me take life easy, as the grass grows on the weirs;
But I was young and foolish, and now am full of tears.

The first poem doesn't give us many vivid images. Some vague pictures might come to your mind when you read them. You might picture a wise man speaking to a young man, though even that rhetorical situation is hardly described. There are some concrete nouns (currency and coins, hearts and bosoms) but for the most part the poem functions in the abstract. The lines do convey information (love leads to heartache), but they don't engage our imagination.

The second poem delivers the same information, but it conveys it through a series of evocative images: two young lovers meeting under willow trees; the woman is small, perhaps even frail in stature, with very white skin; we see the two argue, perhaps playfully; we see them by a river; we see the girl leaning her head on the speaker's shoulder; we see the speaker weeping. The final lines of the two poems will drive this point home: " 'The heart . . . / [is] sold for endless rue.' / And I am two-and-twenty, / And oh, 'tis true, 'tis true," compared to "But I was young and foolish, and now am full of tears." *Rue* is an abstraction; *tears* are an image.

If you read the two poems over and over again, you'll probably find yourself more attracted to the second. Housman's poem is pithy and witty, and, though it's light verse, perhaps it is laced with serious undertones. Yeats's poem conveys the same information about young lovers, but it interests us more. It excites our imagination and draws out our emotions. That's why poets use images more than abstractions.

Most poems lay out their images in a pattern. Take this poem by Robert Browning:

Home-Thoughts, from Abroad

I

Oh, to be in England
Now that April's there,
And whoever wakes in England
Sees, some morning, unaware,
That the lowest boughs and the brushwood sheaf
Round the elm-tree bole are in tiny leaf,
While the chaffinch sings on the orchard bough
In England—now!

2

And after April, when May follows,
And the whitethroat builds, and all the swallows!
Hark, where my blossomed peartree in the hedge
Leans to the field and scatters on the clover
Blossoms and dewdrops—at the bent spray's edge—
That's the wise thrush; he sings each song twice over,
Lest you should think he never could recapture
The first fine careless rapture!
And though the fields look rough with hoary dew,
All will be gay when noontide wakes anew
The buttercups, the little children's dower
—Far brighter than this gaudy melon flower!

The speaker, living or vacationing abroad, feels nostalgia for the springtime sights and sounds of his native country. It is a sentiment *anyone* from *anywhere* might feel when abroad for a long time, and it could be summed up by this short sentence: I miss home. But if we examine the images in this poem—the details the speaker chooses to mention—we can begin to see that the poem communicates much more than this universal statement of homesickness. We can detect a moral judgment about England.

Here are the images:

low branches with tiny new leaves
dense underbrush with tiny leaves surrounding the trunk of an
    elm
a chaffinch singing from the branch of a tree in a (pear?)
    orchard
a whitethroat building a nest
many swallows
the little white blossoms of a pear tree
a hedge
clover, sprinkled with pear blossoms
dewdrops on clover
a thrush singing
fields all white with dew
buttercups in a yard reserved for children

When we list these images, we can begin to see some commonalities among them. All of the images are natural, and nearly all are small. Buttercups, pear blossoms, and clover blossoms are all tiny flowers, yellow and white. We see small young leaves. The animals—a chaffinch, a whitethroat, swallows, and a thrush—are small song-birds. The only big image is an elm tree, and all we see of this is its trunk surrounded by bushes and its branches that hang down low. The combination of these images makes us feel as if England is a place where everything is on a small scale, unthreatening, and com-fortable. The only humans mentioned are children, and they along with the white flowers and young leaves and the little birds suggest an innocence, as if life in England were free of the complexities that plague grown-up life.

    Contrasted to all of these images is the "gaudy melon flower" that concludes the poem. From what we know of Robert Brown-ing's life, that flower is probably in Italy, but even without that knowledge we could guess that the speaker is in a semitropical lo-cale where colors are brilliant, noises are loud, and the sun is blaz-ing hot. If we think of the small, white pear blossom next to the colorful, big melon flower, we might even detect some sexual con-notations. If England is the place of childhood's prepubescent inno-cence, the semitropical place abroad is associated in the speaker's mind with sexual knowledge, perhaps even promiscuity. The tropics themselves tend to have these connotations to people in colder climes, and Italy has long figured in the English imagination as a place where the staid, respectable English citizen can enjoy sensual pleasures. So the pattern of these concrete images—the generalizations that tie the specific images to each other—reveals an otherwise obscured theme in the poem.

It is especially important that you learn to track such patterns, because they're working on your unconscious mind whether you know it or not. Even if you had not recognized the qualities that the images in "Home-Thoughts, from Abroad" have in common, on some level you would have been *feeling* England's innocence and youthful wholesomeness, and you would have sensed the corruption of the locale abroad. It is good to be able to recognize consciously these manipulations of your unconscious mind. Certainly if you want to articulate how a poem affects you, you need to trace these patterns.

If you analyze the imagery of almost any poem, you're bound to find patterns like this. Obviously, you don't want to write out a column of images for every poem you read, nor should you. That would ruin the pleasure. But you should foster the habit of looking for these patterns. And for any poem you write about in an English class, you probably should actually write the images down.

Metaphors

A **metaphor** is a comparison. For example, *the ship plowed through the water* is a metaphor: a ship does not literally plow through water. The expression is a **figure of speech** that compares the way the ship's prow moves through water to the way a plow moves through soil. To interpret the metaphor, we imagine to ourselves the work a plow does: it throws the earth up to the side in long ridges as it digs a straight shallow furrow. The prow of the ship, then, must have been rolling up the water on either side in ridges higher than the level sea. And it must have left behind a shallow trough like a furrow in a plowed field.

Without even knowing it, your mind went through a shorthand version of this process when you first read the words *plowed through the water*. In an instant you pictured the water spurting up on either side of the ship's nose. More than likely, you skipped the step of picturing the plow in the earth. We've seen this metaphor so often in our lives that it has lost its ability to conjure up any comparison. The verb "plow" seems to have taken on a second literal meaning, so that it refers not only to what plows do but also to what prows do.

When a metaphor becomes so overused that it brings to our mind only one image rather than two, we call it a "dead metaphor" or a "cliché." You could hardly utter a dozen words without using one. *The Yankees got slaughtered last night* and *I was just cruising home when out of nowhere this ambulance flies through a red light* and *I'm dying to get those tickets* all use metaphors. A baseball team's loss is compared to the butchering of cattle or swine; a car is compared to a boat; an ambulance is compared to an airplane; and a person's eagerness is compared to a fatal illness. But these metaphors might as well be literal, because they don't conjure up any figurative images anymore. To be slaughtered now literally means to be beaten badly in a game. To beat someone is itself a dead metaphor: no one pictures one team punching or clubbing the other team into submission.

But new, fresh metaphors will conjure up *two* images in your mind. Take these famous lines from T. S. Eliot's "The Love Song of J. Alfred Prufrock":

> *Let us go then, you and I,*
> *When the evening is spread out against the sky*
> *Like a patient etherized upon a table.*

We see two images here. One is the evening sky (which is *literally* there in the poem). The other is a body anesthetized and awaiting surgery (which is there in the poem *figuratively* but not literally). You might wonder how these two things could be compared. How can an evening be like a surgery patient? They seem to have nothing in common. By answering that question you interpret the metaphor. Remember to ask the correct question: we're not interested in how a patient can be like a sky, but in how a sky can be like a patient. The metaphor is about the literal term in the comparison, not about the figurative term.

So the first step is to think about the figurative image. What is an etherized patient like? An etherized patient is senseless, dulled to pain, horizontal, apparently lifeless though living, completely still though slightly breathing. Many of these ideas might apply to the evening sky. Perhaps the air is so still that there is only the slightest breath of wind, or no wind at all. The clouds and the colors of twilight might stretch horizontally just above the horizon. There might not be any motion, not even a single bird, to suggest life.

We could develop the comparison even further by thinking about our associative responses to the image of the patient, even the emotions it arouses in us. We might recoil slightly from the image of the etherized patient as if it were something creepy. If we imagine the patient's cool, clammy, bloodless skin that's hardly more animate than a corpse's, we may get a difficult-to-define, unsavory feeling. Those are the feelings that the evening sky arouses in the speaker.

Some metaphors are easy to spot. Eliot's comparison is a **simile**, which is a metaphor that announces itself with the word "like" or "as" and is hard to miss. But some metaphors are so subtle that half the work of interpreting them is recognizing them in the first place. Take these lines from Eliot's poem: "And I have known the eyes already, known them all— / The eyes that fix you in a formulated phrase[.]" The speaker is remembering the way women look at him at tea parties: they "fix" him, which we know cannot be literally true. Even so, we might forget to ask, *To what, exactly, are the eyes being compared?* Have the eyes *repaired* the speaker? Have they *put him in a fix?* Or have they *fastened* him to something? In this case, the following lines leave no doubt: "And when I am formulated, sprawling on a pin, / When I am pinned and wriggling on the wall . . ." The eyes, then, are like a scientist fixing an insect specimen to a display with a needle. The woman's clever, withering phrase is the pin. And Prufrock, the speaker, is the not-yet-dead insect under scrutiny. This particular example is an **extended metaphor**, because Eliot draws out the comparison over a few lines.

Symbols

A **symbol** is an object that represents something else, sometimes another object but more often an abstraction. For example, consider General Robert E. Lee's surrender to Ulysses S. Grant at Appomattox. One object represented another: Lee stood for the defeated Army of Northern Virginia, and by surrendering himself to Grant he surrendered his entire command. So he dressed in his last clean uniform and belted on his sword in order to present his ragtag army in the best possible light. Grant might have taken Lee prisoner, but he didn't. He refused, even, to confiscate Lee's sword. In this context, the sword represented a number of abstractions, not the least of which was Lee's honor. Grant's refusal to take the sword communicated his esteem for Lee and for the soldiers who had until that minute been his enemies.

Some things seem to carry the same symbolic meaning in just about any culture. The sunrise will probably call to mind birth or new beginnings no matter where you go, just as the sunset seems to naturally represent death or ending. They are the same in Bali as they are in Belgium. Ferocious predators might represent evil in many different cultures. A dense forest might symbolize the unknown. These are **universal symbols**, and typically they are drawn from the natural world that every culture experiences.

Poets use universal symbols. Look at Yeats's "The Lake Isle of Innisfree," for example. The island represents isolation, but Yeats did not invent this symbol himself. Whether you are in Ireland or in Argentina, an island seems to naturally represent isolation and seclusion. Other objects carry meaning only in the context of a particular culture. The rose is a good example. In North America and Great Britain, a red rose symbolizes love. But if you went to a town whose inhabitants never read Western literature, saw Hollywood movies, or heard of Valentine's Day, the citizens might look at a rose as they do a daffodil or tulip. The symbol is not universal: it is a convention contrived by a particular population of people. The rose, then, is a **conventional symbol**.

Sometimes, it is obvious that the symbolic meanings of conventional symbols are contrived. Consider the regalia of clubs and political organizations: the mascot of a sports team is chosen by the team's owner or by a committee of professional marketers, and thereafter the Major League baseball team in Arizona is symbolized by a rattlesnake. A flag is sewn by Betsy Ross and adopted by a committee, and instantly it symbolizes a nation.

But most conventional symbols have a mysterious pedigree. It is impossible to say who invented them, as if they arose anonymously out of the culture itself. Who can say when apple pie came to symbolize the values of middle America? Did anyone decide that the Midwest would represent wholesomeness and näiveté? Or that the American West would symbolize rugged individualism? Show a picture of John Wayne on a horse in a Western landscape to people raised in North America, and they will understand the symbolism. In fact, most people in Europe would recognize it too, for the icon of the American cowboy, and the notions of self-reliance and freedom and violence that he represents, is one of America's cultural exports. But show the picture of John Wayne to farmers in China, and they would see just a man on a horse. No one person or committee decided that these objects would convey symbolic meaning in our culture; nevertheless, they do. And outside our culture they are often meaningless.

William Blake's "The Sick Rose" provides a good example. Most of us probably would jump to the conclusion that the flower represents love, and this connection does yield a coherent interpretation of the whole poem. In our post-Freudian culture, we might even guess the worm in the poem represents a penis. The rose, then, would symbolize not only love but also a woman's virginity. Both of these interpretations are provided by our culture. (Some might argue that the symbols Freud interpreted are *universal*, not *conventional*, and perhaps they'd be right.) But most North Americans would miss something obvious to most British: the rose is a symbol of England.

Your ability to recognize conventional symbols is exactly proportional to your familiarity with a culture. You are probably adept at recognizing symbols that arise out of general North American culture, but the symbols of particular subcultures in America might escape your notice. And many of the poems in this book come from outside North America—many from England, a few from South America, Africa, Wales, and Ireland. Certainly North Americans share a lot of culture with these continents and countries, but there might be some things that are symbols in, say, England that are not symbols in North America. For example, Dover means something to the English, as discussed above. It brings to mind newlyweds the way Niagara Falls might for Americans, and its tall chalk cliffs symbolize England the way the Statue of Liberty, which greets people arriving in New York harbor, symbolizes the United States. Dover may not mean anything to you. Likewise, quite a few of these poems were written generations ago, and objects that might have carried symbolic meaning three hundred years ago no longer do. In this case, only familiarity with the culture will help you to recognize conventional symbols and their meanings. If you haven't lived in a culture, you might have seen enough movies or TV programs or read enough books or listened to enough music to recognize its symbols. Or you might study the culture, or learn about it in a footnote. Otherwise, you'll need to treat these conventional symbols as if they were literary symbols.

A **literary symbol** is an object that represents something else only within the very narrow context of a particular work of literature. Outside the poem the object does not mean what it does inside the poem. A literary symbol, then, is authored neither by nature nor by a culture, but by a writer. As with a conventional symbol, when you take a literary symbol out of its original context, it stops being a symbol.

You need a good deal of ingenuity to recognize that an object in a poem not only is its literal self but also represents something else. There are a few clues you can count on to help you. If the title of a poem is a literal object in the poem, you can assume it also symbolizes something. That was the case in "Dover Beach" (Dover represented something), and it's true in most poems. For instance, the title to Elizabeth Bishop's poem "The Fish" tips us off to the fish's importance. We should expect the fish to carry meaning beyond the literal level of the poem. Right away you should be asking yourself, *what could the fish represent?* William Blake's "The Tyger" and "The Lamb" also call attention to important symbols.

For the most part, it is impossible to teach someone how to recognize which objects are symbolic and which are not. You have to trust your own gut feelings. If you find your attention drawn to an object, if you suspect that something might have more than literal significance, you're probably right. The text itself will call attention to its literary symbols: Listen to what the poem tells you. For example, "Dover Beach" tells us that the sea is a symbol. It appears in the first line of the poem ("The sea is calm tonight"), we hear its sound throughout the first stanza, and it figures again in the second stanza. The poem calls so much attention to the sea that, in a second or third read through the poem, we should guess that the sea is there to represent something other than its literal self. But what?

The second task in interpreting a literary symbol is to figure out what the object represents. Again, you have to trust your instincts. Read the poem a few times and an idea will more than likely come to you: the object represents the speaker's love; it represents death; it represents the American dream; it represents hope. Usually, a symbol represents abstractions: love, death, dreams, hopes. And often it represents a range of things, not just one.

To come back to the "Dover Beach" example: we wonder, *what could the sea represent?* The speaker makes it easy for us when he says, "The Sea of Faith / Was once, too, at the full, and round earth's shore[.]" We know that it represents "faith." But we might further ask, *faith in what?* Some possibilities: faith in God; faith in political institutions; faith in traditional mores and values; perhaps all of these. We'll have to see if any or all of these abstractions work in the poem.

Be prepared to revise your hypotheses. If you try to interpret an object symbolically and it just does not seem to work, maybe you were wrong. To paraphrase Sigmund Freud, sometimes a cigar is just a cigar. Or maybe you were wrong about what the object represents. Keep revising and refining your ideas always until you think you get it exactly right.

You can tell if you got it right by interpreting the **symbolic action**. Look at what happens to the symbol in the poem; the same thing happens to what the symbol represents. Think of the symbol of the rose again. The morning after two college sophomores' first date, the young man gets up at dawn to bring a dozen roses to the apartment door of the woman. He knocks on the door and runs downstairs and around to the parking lot where he can see without being seen. The young woman opens the door, finds the roses at her feet, picks them up, smells them. She knows that roses symbolize love, so she can interpret the symbolic action: the guy likes her a lot. By leaving these flowers at her door, he is offering his esteem, his affection, even his love. In short, he has given her his heart. Now the young man, from the parking lot, watches her pick up the flowers, smell them, think for a moment about what they mean. He sees her toss them on the ground. He watches in horror as she stomps them. She grinds the petals with her heel. She's grinding more than the flowers: she's stomping his love into the ground. And we know that he won't be calling her for a second date.

So interpreting a literary symbol takes three steps (the first two steps are automatic with universal and conventional symbols):

1. identify which object(s) you think might be symbols;
2. establish what the object(s) represent(s);
3. interpret the symbolic action.

For example, let's consider the symbolic action of the sea in "Dover Beach." The tide is going out, and the speaker hears a note of sadness in its "long withdrawing roar." Similarly, then, faith is withdrawing from Europe, and its departure leaves people in misery. All of the earlier possibilities—faith in God, in political institutions, in traditional values—work in this context. According to Arnold, periods of faith and faithlessness go in cycles, like the tides, and the mid-nineteenth century was a low point in the cycle.

Structure

Prosody

Prosody is the study of poetry's **rhythms**. We can describe the rhythms of a poem by scanning its **meter**. To **scan** a poem, first read it aloud two or three times, until you can feel yourself using the rhythm dictated by the words. Then mark the stressed syllables by putting an ictus (´) above them. Mark the unstressed syllables with a mora (˘). A scanned line might look like this one from Shakespeare's Sonnet 73:

That time of year thou mayst in me behold

Once you've identified where the stresses fall, you should see a pattern. In this case, the pattern is unstressed/stressed. This repeated unit of unstressed/stressed syllables is called a **foot**. Feet are marked with slashes (/):

$$\text{ˇ}\quad\text{ʹ}\ /\ \text{ˇ}\quad\text{ʹ}\ /\ \text{ˇ}\quad\quad\text{ʹ}\ /\ \text{ˇ}\quad\text{ʹ}\ /\ \text{ˇ}\quad\text{ʹ}$$

That time / of year / thou mayst / in me / behold

You can scan just about any line of poetry in English if you know six different kinds of feet:

iamb: (ˇ ʹ)   as in "the book"
trochee: (ʹ ˇ)   as in "printer"
anapest: (ˇ ˇ ʹ)   as in "intercede"
dactyl: (ʹ ˇ ˇ)   as in "willowy"
spondee: (ʹ ʹ)   as in "big truck"
pyrrhic: (ˇ ˇ)   as in "of the"

So the line from Sonnet 73 has five **iambs**. Our shorthand designation for lines of five iambs is "iambic pentameter." If the stresses had been reversed, the line would have been "trochaic pentameter." The names for the line lengths are

one foot: monometer
two feet: dimeter
three feet: trimeter
four feet: tetrameter
five feet: pentameter
six feet: hexameter
seven feet: heptameter

By combining the names of the feet and the line lengths, you can describe the rhythm—the meter—of just about any line of poetry.

But don't get the idea that poets are thinking about spondees and iambs and heptameter when they compose their poems. Nearly all good poets know how to measure their own lines, just as carpenters know how to measure the wood they work with. Yet poetry is unlike carpentry in this way: you do not measure the lines before you put them together. You do not work from a plan. Poets don't sit down and say to themselves, "All right, to complete this line I need three more iambs." Poets trust their own ears to get the line to sound right. In revision, they might scan their lines and tinker with the stresses with some conscious purpose. But for the most part, they just listen to the music. Prosody is a way of measuring lines *after* they have been composed.

Further, poetry violates regular rhythm all the time. For example, you will never find a poem written entirely in iambic pentameter. If you ever came across such a poem, say a sonnet, with fourteen lines of iambic pentameter, you'd be reading a hundred and forty straight syllables with the unstressed/stressed rhythm. It would sound like a metronome. Its music would be the unrelenting, steady beat of a drum, which is fine if you're marching, but otherwise it's pretty boring. Instead, the poet will substitute a spondee or a trochee or a pyrrhic here and there, or maybe an anapest, for a few iambs. For example, here is how we might scan the first four lines of Shakespeare's sonnet:

That time / of year / thou mayst / in me / behold

When yel / low leaves, / or none, / or few, / do hang

Upon / those boughs / which shake / against / the cold,

Bare ru / ined choirs, / where late / the sweet / birds sang.

Depending on how you read the poem, some of these lines could be scanned differently. Does "those boughs" have two stressed syllables? Is "which shake" a spondee? It's not certain. But the first and last feet of the fourth line are definitely spondees. It is completely unnatural to say "bare" without stressing it, just as it is impossible to say "birds" without a stress. By the fourth line of the poem, Shakespeare has disrupted the rhythm he laid down in the first two lines.

Usually, the disruptions happen much sooner. Sometimes a poet disrupts the rhythm so often that it's hard to find a single line with a string of perfectly regular feet.

With so many disruptions to the rhythm, you might at first find it hard to scan poetry. Consider this tip. Most monosyllabic nouns will take a stress, just as most articles ("a," "an," "the") and one-syllable prepositions ("of," "in," "on," etc.) will be unstressed. After scanning a few poems, you'll begin to get a feel for such shortcuts. But the best advice is to read the poem aloud again and again, and mark where you find yourself giving stresses. Listen for the rhythm. Mark where the stresses are trying to fall, even if it doesn't quite work. More than likely, you'll find a lot of iambs. At least four out of five poems written in English use iambs as the basic foot. But whether you discover that the underlying rhythm is iambs or trochees or anapests, mark the whole poem as if it were perfectly regular. (Note: some poems might combine types of feet. The basic rhythm of a poem might begin each line with three iambs and con-clude with an anapest.) Your goal at this stage is to recognize such regularities.

Then go back and find the spots that disrupt the rhythmic pat-tern. Properly mark those feet. The point to scanning a poem is not to figure out what the underlying rhythm is. Knowing that a poem is written in iambic pentameter doesn't help us understand it at all. We analyze a poem's regular rhythm only so we can figure out where it breaks the rhythm. In other words, we scan Shakespeare's sonnet not to see the iambs, which are all over the place, but to find the spondees.

What's the point of finding those irregularities? That's the tough-est question to answer. It is not always possible to link such rhyth-mic irregularities to the meaning of a poem. Who can say with any confidence what is the effect on a reader of the spondee opening line 4 of Shakespeare's Sonnet 73?

$$\acute{}\quad\acute{}\quad\breve{}\quad\acute{}\quad\breve{}\quad\acute{}\quad\breve{}\quad\acute{}\quad\acute{}\quad\acute{}$$

Bare ru / ined choirs, / where late / the sweet / birds sang.

All we can say for sure is that such irregularities call attention to themselves. They add a bit of "umph" to the feet that contain them.

The barrenness of those choirs might stick in our mind a little more emphatically than if we heard about them in another iamb.

Surely the rhythms of a poem contribute to its tone, but, again, it is a delicate business to claim something like this: *the two spondees of line 4, following as they do on three lines of regular iambic pentameter, give us a sense of the echoing hollowness of the silent church ruins described in the line.* The images convey this melancholic tone more ably than the rhythm. As you begin your study of poetry, then, you should make only the slightest claims about how the meter of a poem contributes to its meaning. Probably the best use of prosody is to help you compose your own poetry. It is the basic tools of the art—the brushstrokes and paints, if you will, of poetry. It is the most physical part of poetry.

Rhyme and Stanzas

Rhyme is the repetition of sound in different words. Usually, the repeated sound is in the end of the word. "Round," "sound," "ground," and "profound" all rhyme. If a rhyme is in the middle of a line, it's called an **internal rhyme.**

Poets often use end rhymes to group the lines of their poems. We use a simple system of letters to describe the rhymes. The last sound of the first line is assigned the letter *a*, as are all subsequent lines ending with the same sound. Each line that introduces a new end-sound is assigned the next letter of the alphabet. So the rhyme scheme for the opening of Emily Dickinson's "Because I Could Not Stop for Death—" looks like this:

Because I could not stop for Death—	a
He kindly stopped for me—	b
The Carriage held but just Ourselves	c
And Immortality.	b
We slowly drove—He knew no haste	d
And I had put away	e
My labor and my leisure too,	f
For His Civility—	e

"Away" is not an exact rhyme for "civility," so it's called an *off rhyme.*
A **feminine rhyme** is a two-syllable rhyme with the stress falling on
the next-to-last syllable, as in these lines from Anne Bradstreet's "A
Letter to Her Husband":

> *So many steps, head from the heart to sever,*
> *If but a neck, soon should we be together.*

The end rhymes give a poem structure by dividing it into groups of
lines, which are typically called **stanzas.** Notice in Dickinson's poem
that the rhymes gather the lines into groups of four. Poets usually
indicate the divisions between stanzas with a blank line on the page,
but even if you don't see the text of a poem, when you hear it read
aloud, the rhymes will tell you where each stanza ends. Like meter,
rhymes establish a rhythm in our minds.

Often, the literal meaning of the poem will divide into sections
just as the stanzas do. It is not surprising, for example, that each of
the stanzas in Dickinson's poem ends by finishing a sentence. In this
way, the rhyme scheme will help you analyze a poem because it di-
vides the poem into smaller coherent parts. Each stanza usually de-
velops a single thought. Likewise, the rhyming end of each line
usually mirrors a strong grammatical pause, as the ends do in Brad-
street's poems.

Just as with meter, you should be especially interested in rhyme
irregularities. In Dickinson's poem, for example, the rhyme suggests
that we ought to pause after "away" in the sixth line, but the gram-
mar of the sentence compels us to hurry on to line 7. Poets often
use this technique. For example, Shakespeare disrupts our expecta-
tions in the opening lines of Sonnet 73:

> *That time of year thou mayst in me behold*
> *When yellow leaves, or none, or few, do hang*
> *Upon those boughs which shake against the cold,*

The first time you read the poem, you expect the rhyme at the end
of the third line to mirror a strong grammatical pause. In that case,
"cold" seems to be a noun rounding out the clause concerned with
the tree boughs: the boughs seem to shake against the cold of win-

ter. But the next line indicates that "cold" is merely an adjective describing "choirs":

> *Upon those boughs which shake against the cold,*
> *Bare ruined choirs, where late the sweet birds sang.*

The rhyme misled us: it does not designate a significant grammatical pause. When a line seems to pour over its natural boundary this way and spill into the next line, we call it **enjambment**. The confusion caused by this enjambment draws our attention to the image of the ruined choir, just as the spondee did.

Some subgenres of lyric poetry have fairly strict rules about rhyme schemes. By convention, certain rhyme schemes and certain stanzaic patterns have come to be associated with particular subjects. So stanzaic forms are linked to a poem's meaning by convention. Ballads, sonnets, and odes, each of which has a set of standard subjects, are defined by their stanzaic form.

Subgenres

Some poems have so many elements in common that they have created their own genres within the larger **genre** of lyric poems. Each of these **subgenres** calls up in the reader's mind certain expectations, just as the opening credits of a TV show will usually indicate if you're watching a sitcom or a drama. When you recognize the subgenre, you expect certain things. The ballad, for example, has its own grammar, its own conventions. Below are descriptions of the subgenres that appear in this anthology, accompanied by some of the elements you should expect when you encounter each one.

Ballads

Ballads are the most popular form of lyric poetry. They were first sung in the city streets, at folk gatherings in the country, and at the fire's side. Now, most popular styles of music use ballads: rock, blues, pop, and particularly country. Ballads tell stories in short, terse narratives. The classic **ballad stanza** is four lines long with a rhyme scheme of *abab*; the *a* lines are tetrameter, and the *b* lines are trimeter. But just about any narrative lyric with four-line stanzas would be called a ballad today.

Dramatic Monologues

A **dramatic monologue** is a poem that seems as if it is a speech lifted right out of a play. These generally have one or a few long stanzas, usually unrhymed or in couplets, though the rhyme schemes can vary. Almost always, the poet's beliefs do not exactly correspond to the speaker's beliefs in a dramatic monologue. Robert Browning's "My Last Duchess" is a dramatic monologue, as is Alfred, Lord Tennyson's "Ulysses."

Elegies

Elegy used to designate poems written in alternating lines of hexameter and pentameter, usually on the theme of love. But a few hundred years ago the genre began to deal exclusively with death. Sometimes an elegy might be a lament for a particular dead person, sometimes a complaint about mortality in general, often both. Though today elegies have no particular meter or rhyme, typically they are longish, meditative poems. Thomas Gray's "Elegy Written in a Country Churchyard" fits this description, as does W. H. Auden's "In Memory of W. B. Yeats," though that poem's stanzaic form suggests that it is an irregular ode. Ben Jonson's two poems, "On My First Son" and "On My First Daughter," which are short enough to be engraved on tombstones, are epitaphs rather than elegies.

Occasional Poems

An **occasional poem** is any poem written in response to a specific event: a death, an inauguration, a military victory or defeat, a marriage, etc. Lynn Bryer's "The Way," which commemorates Nelson Mandela's release from prison, is an occasional poem.

Odes

John Keats's **odes** in this volume are modeled on the odes of the Roman poet Horace. These Horatian odes usually meditate on fairly abstract concepts or on objects that symbolize something abstract.

They use colloquial diction, and, typically, they are calm statements of praise or judgment. The stanzas can follow any invention of the poet, but every stanza must have the same meter and rhyme scheme.

Auden's "In Memory of W. B. Yeats" is an irregular ode: a meditation on some serious subject in stanzas of irregular length and rhyme scheme. This irregularity allows the tone of each stanza to mimic the varying mood and thoughts of the speaker, as if he were spontaneously thinking aloud in the poem.

Sonnets

Traditionally, the **sonnet** has been used to express the feelings that a beloved arouses in the speaker. Often, sonnets come in sequences or "cycles" that chronicle the speaker's varying emotions. The sentiment expressed in one poem might be contradicted in the very next poem, just as the moods of love can change quickly. Often the speaker's love is unrequited. William Shakespeare's, Elizabeth Barrett Browning's, and Edna St. Vincent Millay's sonnets in this anthology are from cycles of love poems.

In the Romantic era especially, but also in other ages, the sonnet has been used for different purposes, such as political commentary. Sonnets on such themes are usually not part of a sequence but stand alone.

There are two types of sonnets: the **Italian** (or **Petrarchan**) **sonnet**, and the **English** (or **Shakespearean**) **sonnet**. They each have fourteen lines, but the rhyme schemes divide the lines differently. An English sonnet has this rhyme scheme: *ababcdcdefefgg*. As a result, the poem is divided into four sections: three **quatrains** (four lines) and a concluding **couplet** (two lines). An Italian sonnet has this rhyme scheme: *abbaabbacdecde*. As a result, the poem divides into an **octave** (eight lines) and a **sestet** (six lines). Sometimes the rhyme scheme of the sestet will vary, but an Italian sonnet always divides in two between the eighth and ninth lines. Recognizing these divisions, whether in an English or in an Italian sonnet, will help you interpret the poem: analyze it section by section.

Conclusion

After this long discussion of the parts of poems, of stanzaic forms and feminine rhymes and iambs, you may find yourself wondering if the pleasure of poetry has been ruined for you. Does analyzing poetry mean you can't enjoy it anymore? In a sense Wordsworth *was* right: we do murder to dissect. The casual fan enjoys a figure skater's grace and agility with a simplicity and awe that the afficionado can only remember. The unlearned ear listens to a jazz ensemble with an innocence that the trained ear can never recapture. It is the same with poetry. As you discover how poems work, as you grow more adept at analysis, as you master the art of interpretation, something is lost.

But the loss is more than recovered by a different pleasure. The afficionado recognizes a thousand subtleties the casual observer can never notice, and each of those subtleties might occasion some analysis. The casual fan views a skater's jump, and her appreciation amounts to the awestruck phrase: *How can they do that?* The afficionado, who *knows* how the skater can do that, who knows the names of particular jumps, who knows the strength each requires and the technique, who can recognize the slight defect in the landing and notice the skater's smooth recovery, can appreciate each subtlety in the performance and the sum of them all. The learned observer's reaction is, perhaps, less pure, certainly less complex, but more profound.

But the most ardent claims on this regard cannot convince you of anything. Study, analyze, reread, recite like an afficionado of poetry and confirm it for yourself.

THE SEAGULL READER

Poems

Anonymous

"Western Wind" and "Sir Patrick Spens," two anonymous poems, were written in the early-sixteenth and mid-seventeenth centuries, respectively. "Western Wind," a short lyric, was originally set to music and was later incorporated into Mass services, despite its seemingly secular subject matter. "Sir Patrick Spens" is a ballad, a subgenre of lyric poetry that tells a story in a compact, yet detailed narrative. It recounts what may be the true experience of Spens, a Scottish nobleman sent against his will by the king to deliver a princess to her bridegroom in Norway. All members of the escort party drowned on the way home.

Western Wind

Western wind, when will thou blow,
    The small rain down can rain?
Christ, if my love were in my arms
    And I in my bed again!

Sir Patrick Spens

1

The king sits in Dumferling town,
    Drinking the blude-reid wine:
"O whar will I get guid sailor,
    To sail this ship of mine?"

2

Up and spak an eldern knicht,   5
    Sat at the king's richt knee:
"Sir Patrick Spens is the best sailor
    That sails upon the sea."

3

The king has written a braid[1] letter
    And signed it wi' his hand,
And sent it to Sir Patrick Spens,   10
    Was walking on the sand.

4

The first line that Sir Patrick read,
    A loud lauch lauched he;
The next line that Sir Patrick read,   15
    The tear blinded his ee.

5

"O wha is this has done this deed,
    This ill deed done to me,
To send me out this time o' the year,
    To sail upon the sea?   20

6

"Mak haste, mak haste, my mirry men all,
    Our guid ship sails the morn."
"O say na sae, my master dear,
    For I fear a deadly storm.

7

"Late, late yestre'en I saw the new moon   25
    Wi' the auld moon in hir arm,
And I fear, I fear, my dear master,
    That we will come to harm."

1. Broad, i.e., long.

8

O our Scots nobles were richt laith
　　To weet their cork-heeled shoon,   30
But lang or a' the play were played
　　Their hats they swam aboon.[2]

9

O lang, lang may their ladies sit,
　　Wi' their fans into their hand,
Or ere they see Sir Patrick Spens   35
　　Come sailing to the land.

10

O lang, lang may the ladies stand
　　Wi' their gold kems in their hair,
Waiting for their ain dear lords,
　　For they'll see them na mair.   40

11

Half o'er, half o'er to Aberdour
　　It's fifty fadom deep,
And there lies guid Sir Patrick Spens
　　Wi' the Scots lords at his feet.

1765

2. I.e., their hats swam above (them).

John Agard
1945–

> Agard was born in Guyana, which was once a British colony on the
> Caribbean coast of South America. Like most Guyanans, Agard de-
> scended from black slaves imported by whites to work the rich
> mines and plantations. In this poem, Agard writes in the local cre-
> ole dialect, and you might consider the degree to which the speaker
> is "putting it on," so to speak.

Palm Tree King

Because I come from the West Indies
certain people in England seem to think
I is a expert on palm trees

So not wanting to sever dis link
with me native roots (know what ah mean?)   5
or to disappoint dese culture vulture
I does smile cool as seabreeze

and say to dem
which specimen
you interested in   10
cause you talking
to the right man
I is palm tree king
I know palm tree history
like de palm o me hand   15
In fact me navel string
bury under a palm tree

If you think de queen could wave
you ain't see nothing yet
till you see the Roystonea Regia   20
—that is the royal palm—
with she crown of leaves

waving calm-calm
over the blue Caribbean carpet
nearly 100 feet of royal highness   25

But let we get down to business
Tell me what you want to know
How tall a palm tree does grow?
What is the biggest coconut I ever see?
What is the average length of the leaf?   30

Don't expect me to be brief
cause palm tree history
is a long-long story

Anyway why you so interested
in length and circumference?   35
That kind of talk so ordinary
That don't touch the essence
of palm tree mystery
That is no challenge
to a palm tree historian like me   40

If you insist on statistics
why you don't pose a question
with some mathematical profundity?

Ask me something more tricky
like if a American tourist with a camera   45
take 9 minutes to climb a coconut tree
how long a English tourist without a camera
would take to climb the same coconut tree?

That is problem pardner
Now ah coming harder   50

If 6 straw hat
and half a dozen bikini
multiply by the same number of coconut tree

equal one postcard
how many square miles of straw hat   55
you need to make a tourist industry?

That is problem pardner
Find the solution
and you got a revolution

But before you say anything   60
let I palm tree king
give you dis warning
Ah want de answer in metric
it kind of rhyme with tropic
Besides it sound more exotic   65

                    1985

Paul Allen
1945–

> "The Man with the Hardest Belly" is a narrative poem, so we read
> it with some of the same tools we use to read a story, looking for a
> conflict and resolution. It is also a study in irony. Readers, as well as
> the characters in the poem, view the preacher and his sermon dif-
> ferently than he expects to be viewed. Thus his similarities to Christ
> are undercut. But in the last three lines of the poem we discover a
> possible conflict and the role the preacher played in resolving the
> conflict. With these last three lines in mind, you might reread the
> poem and consider the irony once again.

The Man with the Hardest Belly

I

THE MAN WITH THE HARDEST BELLY knows God
compensates his loss of limbs—legs

to knee, nub arms—with a gift
to titillate the congregations when he is delivered
from Ocala in his motor home to call us to Christ.   5
This handsome chunk of what was left
after he'd been shucked, he says, at 14
found God by serving himself on our tables
if we had canned corn at all in 19 and 55.

We are not members here. As Dad said, we   10
have our own faith. But someone spirit-filled
made Mother promise. So we're here cross-legged
on the cool ground at the river,
and my father is chosen. The Youth Director
is chosen. The man high up in Amway   15
is chosen. The three of them hang
THE MAN WITH THE HARDEST BELLY over the first branch
of the maple like a sandbag on the levee.
He pops his torso, flips, chins
to the next branch, flips, grabs a limb   20
with his thighs. Left nub for leverage,
he hooks another V with the back
of his head, walks on stumps up the trunk
to the next limb, flips to his belly, bends,
flips, holds with his teeth. He maneuvers   25
like something stained and mating
toward the top of our slide in godless biology,
or like the little dots we see inside our own eyes
on days we're morose. The thing
we've come to watch we can't watch   30
directly as he works toward the sun. The higher
he goes, the more we must look down to save
our eyes. We pull grass, look up and squint
to check his progress, kill an ant climbing our shoe.
Some stand to change the angle,   35
to keep him closer to the shaded cars.
Settling high, balanced and swaying, he preaches
from the texts painted on his motor home
under the faded "DOUBT AND DELIVERY."

II

. . . so look with me now at Genesis, whole people, Genesis 15:1–6.   40
Abram. Abram was a cripple in bed, had no standing among
men. Listen to me, had no standing among men, praise God, and
Moses, who said no, not me, not me, God gave Moses what he
needed. And Joshua at their first real trial? Joshua didn't think he
could do nothing. Joshua 7:1–10. I thank God my arms and legs   45
went to your soft tummies in '55. I was born again in that
shucking machine, look at my belly, my hard and strong belly, you
could park a truck on my belly praise God, God gives you what
you need. I need a strong belly and a lithe neck to climb trees and
show you the Holy Spirit at work, and show you the   50
compensations of our precious Lord. Praise you, Lord. The Holy
Spirit turns my pages for me. Look at Joshua splashing dirt up in
his face. I'm here to tell you people there's no dirt in my face, no
Lord. And Gideon. It's right there in your book. Judges 6:1–14.
What does God say to that worthless garment of feces? (Excuse me,   55
ladies, but the compensations of God is nothing to be delicate
about.) Says to Gideon, go in your power. Go in your power.
Listen to me now: Go in your power and save my people. Read it.
Isn't that what it says? Your power. Don't look at me, I know I'm
pretty. Look at your book, look at your own Holy Word. Now   60
examine, if you will, First Corinthians 10:13. See? God won't give
you nothing wrong without a correlational power to get out of it.
. . . Jesus himself, his wonderment self, take this cup from my lips,
listen now, take this cup from my lips, take this cup. . . .

III

We pull off the road to let the other cars by.   65
The Youth Director finds a wide place.
And the man high up in Amway finds a wide place.
The three of us wait, our hazard lights blinking,
while the born again wave and the kids shout
from their windows that Jesus is the One   70
and fathers honk (Honk If You Love Jesus).

My father nods occasionally. My sister starts
it. We are arguing about whether
THE MAN WITH THE HARDEST BELLY crawls on all
four nubs around the rooms of his scriptural   75
motor home, or slithers like something run over.
Crawls. Slithers. My father hushes us. My sister hits
me, says, "For unto you is born *a child*." I hit
my sister: "Let the women keep silent
in the Chevrolet." My mother has had enough.   80
She separates us. We aren't to speak. We aren't
to utter a peep. Each of us must look out our own window.

IV

The cars are thinning. We can hear the hazards now.
The road is dark and the dust is settling.
"I told her we'd go, and we went," my mother says.   85
"I told you we'd come, and we came," my father says.
"I thought it a bit much, though," she says, "when
he stood on his perch, spread those arms
and screamed, 'Nail me. Nail me.' "
"Me too," my father says, "nails wouldn't work."   90
My mother is looking at him. He says,
"Toggle bolts might work."
"Go help him down," my mother says, "and let's go home."

My father joins the other two on the road. They walk
back toward the river. My mother tells us it will   95
turn cool; we don't need to bathe when we get home,
but we do need to wash our feet. My father appears.
He eases us between the Youth Director and the man
high up in Amway. When we're on the main road
and the others have turned off, my mother says,   100
"I thought we'd have your mother over tomorrow.
Remind me to get a ham out when we get home."
"And corn?" my father says. "Whatever," she says.

V

Tonight down the cold upstairs hall we hear
them laughing, my mother and father.   105
Tonight we hear them making love again.

1997

Matthew Arnold
1822–1888

> *Because Dover is the spot on the English coast closest to France,*
> *newlyweds often would spend their wedding night there before sail-*
> *ing for the Continent, and some evidence indicates that Arnold first*
> *drafted this poem on his honeymoon in 1851. The poem was not*
> *published until 1867, so it made its debut in the midst of the reli-*
> *gious doubts fomented by Darwin's* Origin of Species *(1859). In the*
> *wake of what he considered religion's failure, Arnold imagined that*
> *poetry would do the work religion no longer could.*

Dover Beach

The sea is calm tonight.
The tide is full, the moon lies fair
Upon the straits; on the French coast the light
Gleams and is gone; the cliffs of England stand,
Glimmering and vast, out in the tranquil bay.   5
Come to the window, sweet is the night-air!
Only, from the long line of spray
Where the sea meets the moon-blanched land,
Listen! you hear the grating roar
Of pebbles which the waves draw back, and fling,   10
At their return, up the high strand,
Begin, and cease, and then again begin,
With tremulous cadence slow, and bring
The eternal note of sadness in.

Sophocles long ago   15
Heard it on the Aegean, and it brought
Into his mind the turbid ebb and flow
Of human misery; we
Find also in the sound a thought,
Hearing it by this distant northern sea.   20

The Sea of Faith
Was once, too, at the full, and round earth's shore
Lay like the folds of a bright girdle furled.
But now I only hear
Its melancholy, long withdrawing roar,   25
Retreating, to the breath
Of the night-wind, down the vast edges drear
And naked shingles[1] of the world.

Ah, love, let us be true
To one another! for the world, which seems   30
To lie before us like a land of dreams,
So various, so beautiful, so new,
Hath really neither joy, nor love, nor light,
Nor certitude, nor peace, nor help for pain;
And we are here as on a darkling plain   35
Swept with confused alarms of struggle and flight,
Where ignorant armies clash by night.

                                        1867

---

1. Beaches of smooth pebbles.

Margaret Atwood
1939–

"You Fit into Me" is the first poem in Atwood's Power Politics *(1971). This book tells the story of a relationship between a female speaker and her male lover, who is the audience. As it follows the pair going to the movies, going out to dinner, doing all the things courting couples do,* Power Politics *demythologizes the romance of domestic love. The book's title echoes that of Kate Millett's* Sexual Politics *(1970), a landmark volume that demonstrates that political power is exercised through domestic and romantic relations between men and women.*

You Fit into Me

you fit into me
like a hook into an eye

a fish hook
an open eye

1971

W. H. (Wystan Hugh) Auden
1907–1973

Auden, a political liberal and homosexual, wrote "Musée des Beaux Arts" (Museum of Fine Arts) while staying in Paris in December 1938. He believed that Western democracies were doing nothing as fascists in Spain, Germany, and Italy violently oppressed communists, homosexuals, Jews, and others. The first stanza describes Pieter Brueghel's painting The Massacre of the Innocents, *which depicts Herod's attempt to kill the infant Jesus by slaughtering all young Jewish children. The second stanza refers to Brueghel's* The Fall of Icarus, *in which that mythical figure, who flew too near the sun wearing wings of feathers and wax, falls from the sky in a corner of the painting, almost unnoticed. In early 1939, Auden wrote "In Memory of W. B. Yeats" to commemorate the death of the Irish poet. The poem surprised Auden's contemporaries because it seems to declare that poetry cannot change society.*

Musée des Beaux Arts

[handwritten: Ekphrastic — artistic medium w/in another]

About suffering they were never wrong,
The Old Masters: how well they understood
Its human position; how it takes place
While someone else is eating or opening a window or just
    walking dully along;
How, when the aged are reverently, passionately waiting   5
For the miraculous birth, there always must be
Children who did not specially want it to happen, skating
On a pond at the edge of the wood:
They never forgot
That even the dreadful martyrdom must run its course   10
Anyhow in a corner, some untidy spot
Where the dogs go on with their doggy life and the torturer's
    horse
Scratches its innocent behind on a tree.

In Brueghel's *Icarus*, for instance: how everything turns away
Quite leisurely from the disaster; the ploughman may   15
Have heard the splash, the forsaken cry,
But for him it was not an important failure; the sun shone
As it had to on the white legs disappearing into the green
Water; and the expensive delicate ship that must have seen
Something amazing, a boy falling out of the sky,
Had somewhere to get to and sailed calmly on.

1938

In Memory of W. B. Yeats

(d. Jan. 1939)

I

He disappeared in the dead of winter:
The brooks were frozen, the airports almost deserted,
And snow disfigured the public statues;

The mercury sank in the mouth of the dying day.
What instruments we have agree   5
The day of his death was a dark cold day.

Far from his illness
The wolves ran on through the evergreen forests,
The peasant river was untempted by the fashionable quays;
By mourning tongues   10
The death of the poet was kept from his poems.

But for him it was his last afternoon as himself,
An afternoon of nurses and rumours;
The provinces of his body revolted,
The squares of his mind were empty,   15
Silence invaded the suburbs,
The current of his feeling failed: he became his admirers.

Now he is scattered among a hundred cities
And wholly given over to unfamiliar affections;
To find his happiness in another kind of wood   20
And be punished under a foreign code of conscience.
The words of a dead man
Are modified in the guts of the living.[1]

But in the importance and noise of to-morrow
When the brokers are roaring like beasts on the floor of the
    Bourse,[2]   25
And the poor have the sufferings to which they are fairly
    accustomed,
And each in the cell of himself is almost convinced of his
    freedom,
A few thousand will think of this day
As one thinks of a day when one did something slightly
    unusual.

---

1. Auden suggests here that after death poets live only through their poems; Yeats, whose politics approached fascism, might suffer from this condition.
2. Stock exchange.

What instruments we have agree   30
The day of his death was a dark cold day.

2

You were silly like us: your gift survived it all:
The parish of rich women,³ physical decay,
Yourself. Mad Ireland hurt you into poetry.
Now Ireland has her madness and her weather still,   35
For poetry makes nothing happen: it survives
In the valley of its making where executives
Would never want to tamper, flows on south
From ranches of isolation and the busy griefs,
Raw towns that we believe and die in; it survives,   40
A way of happening, a mouth.

3

Earth, receive an honoured guest:
William Yeats is laid to rest.
Let the Irish vessel lie
Emptied of its poetry.⁴   45

In the nightmare of the dark
All the dogs of Europe bark,⁵
And the living nations wait,
Each sequestered in its hate;

---

3. Yeats was often supported by rich women, especially Lady Augusta Gregory (1851–1932), the owner of an estate in the west of Ireland.

4. Three stanzas that originally followed this were omitted in the 1966 edition of Auden's *Collected Shorter Poems* and thereafter: "Time that is intolerant / Of the brave and innocent, / And indifferent in a week / To a beautiful physique, // Worships language and forgives / Everyone by whom it lives; / Pardons cowardice, conceit, / Lays its honours at their feet. // Time that with this strange excuse / Pardoned Kipling and his views, / And will pardon Paul Claudel, / Pardons him for writing well." Rudyard Kipling's views were imperialistic. Paul Claudel (1868–1955), French poet, dramatist, and diplomat, was extremely right-wing in his political ideas. Yeats's own politics were at times antidemocratic and appeared to favor dictatorship.

5. Perhaps a reference to the heated political rhetoric that preceded World War II.

Intellectual disgrace   50
Stares from every human face,
And the seas of pity lie
Locked and frozen in each eye.

Follow, poet, follow right
To the bottom of the night,   55
With your unconstraining voice
Still persuade us to rejoice;

With the farming of a verse
Make a vineyard of the curse,
Sing of human unsuccess   60
In a rapture of distress;

In the deserts of the heart
Let the healing fountain start,
In the prison of his days
Teach the free man how to praise.   65

Feb. 1939   *1940, 1966*

Elizabeth Bishop

1911–1979

> *Bishop spent most of 1940 in Key West, where she caught a giant Caribbean jewfish, the subject of "The Fish."* Partisan Review *published the poem in March 1940 and launched Bishop's career. Readers often take the speakers in Bishop's poems to be the poet herself. In "Sestina" Bishop writes about her own childhood, just as "One Art," a villanelle written in 1975, was inspired by her battle with alcohol. When reading Bishop, consider whether the strict formal requirements of the sestina and villanelle increase or diminish the emotions expressed in her poems.*

The Fish

I caught a tremendous fish
and held him beside the boat
half out of water, with my hook
fast in a corner of his mouth.
He didn't fight.   5
He hadn't fought at all.
He hung a grunting weight,
battered and venerable
and homely. Here and there
his brown skin hung in strips   10
like ancient wallpaper,
and its pattern of darker brown
was like wallpaper:
shapes like full-blown roses
stained and lost through age.   15
He was speckled with barnacles,
fine rosettes of lime,
and infested
with tiny white sea-lice,
and underneath two or three   20
rags of green weed hung down.
While his gills were breathing in
the terrible oxygen
—the frightening gills,
fresh and crisp with blood,   25
that can cut so badly—
I thought of the coarse white flesh
packed in like feathers,
the big bones and the little bones,
the dramatic reds and blacks   30
of his shiny entrails,
and the pink swim-bladder
like a big peony.
I looked into his eyes
which were far larger than mine   35

but shallower, and yellowed,
the irises backed and packed
with tarnished tinfoil
seen through the lenses
of old scratched isinglass.[1]   40
They shifted a little, but not
to return my stare.
—It was more like the tipping
of an object toward the light.
I admired his sullen face,   45
the mechanism of his jaw,
and then I saw
that from his lower lip
—if you could call it a lip—
grim, wet, and weaponlike,   50
hung five old pieces of fish-line,
or four and a wire leader
with the swivel still attached,
with all their five big hooks
grown firmly in his mouth.   55
A green line, frayed at the end
where he broke it, two heavier lines,
and a fine black thread
still crimped from the strain and snap
when it broke and he got away.   60
Like medals with their ribbons
frayed and wavering,
a five-haired beard of wisdom
trailing from his aching jaw.
I stared and stared   65
and victory filled up
the little rented boat,
from the pool of bilge
where oil had spread a rainbow
around the rusted engine   70
to the bailer rusted orange,

1. A transparent gelatin made from the air bladders of some fish.

the sun-cracked thwarts,
the oarlocks on their strings,
the gunnels—until everything
was rainbow, rainbow, rainbow!   75
And I let the fish go.

                    1946

Sestina

September rain falls on the house.
In the failing light, the old grandmother
sits in the kitchen with the child
beside the Little Marvel Stove,
reading the jokes from the almanac,   5
laughing and talking to hide her tears.

She thinks that her equinoctial tears
and the rain that beats on the roof of the house
were both foretold by the almanac,
but only known to a grandmother.   10
The iron kettle sings on the stove.
She cuts some bread and says to the child,

It's time for tea now; but the child
is watching the teakettle's small hard tears
dance like mad on the hot black stove,   15
the way the rain must dance on the house.
Tidying up, the old grandmother
hangs up the clever almanac

on its string. Birdlike, the almanac
hovers half open above the child,   20
hovers above the old grandmother
and her teacup full of dark brown tears.
She shivers and says she thinks the house
feels chilly, and puts more wood in the stove.

It was to be, says the Marvel Stove.   25
I know what I know, says the almanac.
With crayons the child draws a rigid house
and a winding pathway. Then the child
puts in a man with buttons like tears
and shows it proudly to the grandmother.   30

But secretly, while the grandmother
busies herself about the stove,
the little moons fall down like tears
from between the pages of the almanac
into the flower bed the child   35
has carefully placed in the front of the house.

Time to plant tears, says the almanac.
The grandmother sings to the marvelous stove
and the child draws another inscrutable house.

1965

One Art

The art of losing isn't hard to master;
so many things seem filled with the intent
to be lost that their loss is no disaster.

Lose something every day. Accept the fluster
of lost door keys, the hour badly spent.   5
The art of losing isn't hard to master.

Then practice losing farther, losing faster:
places, and names, and where it was you meant
to travel. None of these will bring disaster.

I lost my mother's watch. And look! my last, or   10
next-to-last, of three loved houses went.
The art of losing isn't hard to master.

I lost two cities, lovely ones. And, vaster,
some realms I owned, two rivers, a continent,
I miss them, but it wasn't a disaster.   15

—Even losing you (the joking voice, a gesture
I love) I shan't have lied. It's evident
the art of losing's not too hard to master
though it may look like (*Write* it!) like disaster.

1976

William Blake
1757–1827

> *Blake, an Englishman sympathetic to political and social revolution, was an engraver, and his books included his own illustrations. In 1789, the year of the French Revolution, Blake published* Songs of Innocence, *which he expanded five years later to include his* Songs of Experience. *The two sections of this book were meant to display "the two Contrary States of the Human Soul," as his title page announces. The "innocent" poems are prefaced by a picture of an angelic child and a rustic musician. The child asks the musician to "Pipe a song about a Lamb," and the musician sings the "songs of innocence" in response. Of the six poems here, "The Lamb" and the first "The Chimney Sweeper" come from the* Songs of Innocence. *The poems of "experience," "The Sick Rose," "The Tyger," "London," and the second "The Chimney Sweeper," are "earth's answer" to the heavenly "innocence."*

The Lamb

Little Lamb, who made thee?
  Dost thou know who made thee?
Gave thee life & bid thee feed,
By the stream & o'er the mead;
Gave thee clothing of delight,   5

Softest clothing wooly bright;
Gave thee such a tender voice,
Making all the vales rejoice!
    Little Lamb who made thee?
    Dost thou know who made thee?   10

    Little Lamb I'll tell thee,
    Little Lamb I'll tell thee!
He is calléd by thy name,
For he calls himself a Lamb:
He is meek & he is mild,   15
He became a little child:
I a child & thou a lamb,
We are calléd by his name.
    Little Lamb God bless thee.
    Little Lamb God bless thee.   20

1789

The Chimney Sweeper

When my mother died I was very young,
And my father sold me while yet my tongue,
Could scarcely cry weep weep weep weep.
So your chimneys I sweep & in soot I sleep.

Theres little Tom Dacre, who cried when his head   5
That curl'd like a lambs back, was shav'd, so I said.
Hush Tom never mind it, for when your head's bare,
You know that the soot cannot spoil your white hair.

And so he was quiet, & that very night,
As Tom was a sleeping he had such a sight,   10
That thousands of sweepers Dick, Joe, Ned & Jack
Were all of them lock'd up in coffins of black,

And by came an Angel who had a bright key,
And he open'd the coffins & set them all free.

Then down a green plain leaping laughing they run   15
And wash in a river and shine in the Sun.

Then naked & white, all their bags left behind,
They rise upon clouds, and sport in the wind.
And the Angel told Tom if he'd be a good boy,
He'd have God for his father & never want joy.   20

And so Tom awoke and we rose in the dark
And got with our bags & our brushes to work.
Tho' the morning was cold, Tom was happy & warm,
So if all do their duty, they need not fear harm.

1789

The Sick Rose

O Rose, thou art sick.
The invisible worm
That flies in the night
In the howling storm

Has found out thy bed   5
Of crimson joy,
And his dark secret love
Does thy life destroy.

1794

The Tyger

Tyger! Tyger! burning bright
In the forests of the night,
What immortal hand or eye
Could frame thy fearful symmetry?

In what distant deeps or skies   5
Burnt the fire of thine eyes?

On what wings dare he aspire?
What the hand, dare seize the fire?

And what shoulder, & what art,
Could twist the sinews of thy heart?   10
And when thy heart began to beat,
What dread hand? & what dread feet?

What the hammer? what the chain?
In what furnace was thy brain?
What the anvil? what dread grasp   15
Dare its deadly terrors clasp?

When the stars threw down their spears,
And water'd heaven with their tears,
Did he smile his work to see?
Did he who made the Lamb make thee?   20

Tyger! Tyger! burning bright
In the forests of the night,
What immortal hand or eye
Dare frame thy fearful symmetry?

                                           1794

London

I wander thro' each charter'd¹ street,
Near where the charter'd Thames does flow,
And mark in every face I meet
Marks of weakness, marks of woe.

In every cry of every man,   5
In every Infant's cry of fear,
In every voice, in every ban,²
The mind-forg'd manacles I hear.

---

1. Within the city limits of London.
2. A law or notice commanding or forbidding; a published penalty.

How the Chimney-sweeper's cry
Every blackning Church appalls;   10
And the hapless Soldier's sigh
Runs in blood down Palace walls.

But most thro' midnight streets I hear
How the youthful Harlot's curse
Blasts the new-born Infant's tear,   15
And blights with plagues the Marriage hearse.

1794

The Chimney Sweeper

A little black thing among the snow:
Crying weep, weep, in notes of woe!
Where are thy father & mother? say?
They are both gone up to the church to pray.

Because I was happy upon the heath,   5
And smil'd among the winter's snow:
They clothed me in the clothes of death,
And taught me to sing the notes of woe.

And because I am happy, & dance & sing,
They think they have done me no injury: 10
And are gone to praise God & his Priest & King
Who make up a heaven of our misery.

1794

Anne Bradstreet
1612 or 1613–1672

> *The primitive conditions of colonial America contrasted with the*
> *delicacy of Bradstreet's life in England, but she prospered and raised*
> *eight children, all the while writing poetry. These two love poems to*
> *her husband were not published until the posthumous, second edi-*

tion of her one book, The Tenth Muse, *in 1678. They were written after she settled in Andover in a comfortable, three-story house, the privations of pioneering behind her. In these poems, Bradstreet addresses her husband, Simon, who was once governor of the colony and ambassador to the court of England. In many interesting ways, Bradstreet contradicts the stereotype we have of the Puritan ethic of fleshly denial.*

To My Dear and Loving Husband

If ever two were one, then surely we.
If ever man were loved by wife, then thee;
If ever wife was happy in a man,
Compare with me, ye women, if you can.
I prize thy love more than whole mines of gold   5
Or all the riches that the East doth hold.
My love is such that rivers cannot quench,
Nor ought but love from thee, give recompense.
Thy love is such I can no way repay,
The heavens reward thee manifold, I pray.   10
Then while we live, in love let's so persevere
That when we live no more, we may live ever.

                                        1678

A Letter to Her Husband, Absent upon Public Employment

My head, my heart, mine eyes, my life, nay, more,
My joy, my magazine[1] of earthly store,
If two be one, as surely thou and I,
How stayest thou there, whilst I at Ipswich lie?
So many steps, head from the heart to sever,   5
If but a neck, soon should we be together.
I, like the Earth this season, mourn in black,

---

1. Warehouse, storehouse.

My Sun is gone so far in's zodiac,
Whom whilst I 'joyed, nor storms, nor frost I felt,
His warmth such frigid colds did cause to melt.   10
My chilled limbs now numbed lie forlorn;
Return, return, sweet Sol, from Capricorn;[2]
In this dead time, alas, what can I more
Than view those fruits which through thy heat I bore?
Which sweet contentment yield me for a space,   15
True living pictures of their father's face.
O strange effect! now thou art southward gone,
I weary grow the tedious day so long;
But when thou northward to me shalt return,
I wish my Sun may never set, but burn   20
Within the Cancer[3] of my glowing breast,
The welcome house of him my dearest guest.
Where ever, ever stay, and go not thence,
Till nature's sad decree shall call thee hence;
Flesh of thy flesh, bone of thy bone,   25
I here, thou there, yet both but one.

                                            1678

Gwendolyn Brooks

1917–2000

Though Brooks's early poems dealt with racial injustice, her work was initially recognized more for its fine craftmanship. "The Mother" is from her first book of poems, A Street in Bronzeville *(1945), which recorded in realistic detail some of the experiences of Chicago's African American community. Brooks won the Pulitzer Prize in 1950, the first African American to do so, which expanded her audience considerably. "We Real Cool" and "The Bean Eaters" were published in* The Bean Eaters *(1960), which overtly criticized racial discrimination in America. Some critics attacked Brooks for abandoning the lyricism of her earlier work in favor of political rhetoric. The dropouts in "We*

2. Capricorn, the tenth sign of the zodiac, represents winter. "Sol": sun.
3. Cancer, the fourth sign of the zodiac, represents summer.

Real Cool," she explained, "are people who are essentially saying, 'Kilroy is here. We are.' But they're a little uncertain of the strength of their identity. . . . I want to represent their basic uncertainty."

the mother

Abortions will not let you forget.
You remember the children you got that you did not get,
The damp small pulps with a little or with no hair,
The singers and workers that never handled the air.
You will never neglect or beat   5
Them, or silence or buy with a sweet.
You will never wind up the sucking-thumb
Or scuttle off ghosts that come.
You will never leave them, controlling your luscious sigh,
Return for a snack of them, with gobbling mother-eye.   10

I have heard in the voices of the wind the voices of my dim
     killed children.
I have contracted. I have eased
My dim dears at the breasts they could never suck.
I have said, Sweets, if I sinned, if I seized
Your luck   15
And your lives from your unfinished reach,
If I stole your births and your names,
Your straight baby tears and your games,
Your stilted or lovely loves, your tumults, your marriages,
     aches, and your deaths,
If I poisoned the beginnings of your breaths,   20
Believe that even in my deliberateness I was not deliberate.
Though why should I whine,
Whine that the crime was other than mine?—
Since anyhow you are dead.
Or rather, or instead,   25
You were never made.
But that too, I am afraid,
Is faulty: oh, what shall I say, how is the truth to be said?

You were born, you had body, you died.
It is just that you never giggled or planned or cried.   30

Believe me, I loved you all.
Believe me, I knew you, though faintly, and I loved, I loved
    you
All.

1945

We Real Cool

THE POOL PLAYERS.
SEVEN AT THE GOLDEN SHOVEL.

We real cool. We
Left school. We

Lurk late. We
Strike straight. We

Sing sin. We   5
Thin gin. We

Jazz June. We
Die soon.

1960

The Bean Eaters

They eat beans mostly, this old yellow pair.
Dinner is a casual affair.
Plain chipware on a plain and creaking wood,
Tin flatware.

Two who are Mostly Good.   5
Two who have lived their day,

But keep on putting on their clothes
And putting things away.

And remembering . . .
Remembering, with twinklings and twinges,   10
As they lean over the beans in their rented back room that is
    full of beads and receipts and dolls and clothes, tobacco
    crumbs, vases and fringes.

                                                    1960

Elizabeth Barrett Browning
1806–1861

> *Barrett was a famous poet and invalid when, in 1846, the young*
> *playwright, Robert Browning, secretly courted her. Barrett recorded*
> *her feelings of excitement, doubt, and ecstasy in a series of forty-four*
> *sonnets. "How Do I Love Thee" is the penultimate poem in the se-*
> *quence. The curious title,* Sonnets from the Portuguese, *was*
> *meant to disguise the autobiographical nature of the poems, but to-*
> *day they are considered an accurate portrait of Barrett's feelings for*
> *Browning. Though it is tempting to dismiss this poem as sentimen-*
> *tal, in the context of the great religious doubts of the nineteenth*
> *century, assigning one's lover the role of savior was provocative*
> *rather than conventional.*

Sonnets from the Portuguese

43

How do I love thee? Let me count the ways.
I love thee to the depth and breadth and height
My soul can reach, when feeling out of sight
For the ends of Being and ideal Grace.
I love thee to the level of everyday's   5
Most quiet need, by sun and candle-light.

I love thee freely, as men strive for Right;
I love thee purely, as they turn from Praise.
I love thee with the passion put to use
In my old griefs, and with my childhood's faith.   10
I love thee with a love I seemed to lose
With my lost saints—I love thee with the breath,
Smiles, tears, of all my life!—and, if God choose,
I shall but love thee better after death.

1850

Robert Browning
1816–1889

> *"My Last Duchess" was first published in the collection* Dramatic
> Lyrics *in 1842. It breaks with the Romantic tendency to equate the
> speaker in the poem with the poet. Rather, "My Last Duchess" is a
> dramatic monologue: the situation of the poem is a fiction, and the
> speaker and his listener are characters. Though the Duke was sug-
> gested to Browning by a real, historical figure, this poem says as
> much about gender relations in Victorian England as in sixteenth-
> century Italy.*

My Last Duchess[1]

Ferrara

That's my last duchess painted on the wall,
Looking as if she were alive. I call
That piece a wonder, now: Frà Pandolf's hands
Worked busily a day, and there she stands.
Will't please you sit and look at her? I said   5

---

1. Alfonso II d'Este, the duke of Ferrara in the sixteenth century, married the fourteen-
year-old daughter of the duke of Florence in 1558. Three years later she died suspiciously, and
Alfonso soon began negotiating for the daughter of the count of Tyrol.

"Frà Pandolf" by design, for never read
Strangers like you that pictured countenance,
The depth and passion of its earnest glance,
But to myself they turned (since none puts by
The curtain I have drawn for you, but I)　　　　　　　10
And seemed as they would ask me, if they durst,
How such a glance came there; so, not the first
Are you to turn and ask thus. Sir, 'twas not
Her husband's presence only, called that spot
Of joy into the Duchess' cheek: perhaps　　　　　　　15
Frà Pandolf chanced to say "Her mantle laps
Over my lady's wrist too much," or "Paint
Must never hope to reproduce the faint
Half-flush that dies along her throat": such stuff
Was courtesy, she thought, and cause enough　　　　　20
For calling up that spot of joy. She had
A heart—how shall I say?—too soon made glad,
Too easily impressed; she liked whate'er
She looked on, and her looks went everywhere.
Sir, 'twas all one! My favor at her breast,　　　　　　25
The dropping of the daylight in the West,
The bough of cherries some officious fool
Broke in the orchard for her, the white mule
She rode with round the terrace—all and each
Would draw from her alike the approving speech,　　　30
Or blush, at least. She thanked men—good! but thanked
Somehow—I know not how—as if she ranked
My gift of a nine-hundred-years-old name
With anybody's gift. Who'd stoop to blame
This sort of trifling? Even had you skill　　　　　　　35
In speech—(which I have not)—to make your will
Quite clear to such an one, and say, "Just this
Or that in you disgusts me; here you miss,
Or there exceed the mark"—and if she let
Herself be lessoned so, nor plainly set　　　　　　　40
Her wits to yours, forsooth, and made excuse,
—E'en then would be some stooping; and I choose
Never to stoop. Oh sir, she smiled, no doubt,

Whene'er I passed her; but who passed without
Much the same smile? This grew; I gave commands;   45
Then all smiles stopped together. There she stands
As if alive. Will 't please you rise? We'll meet
The company below, then. I repeat,
The Count your master's known munificence
Is ample warrant that no just pretense   50
Of mine for dowry will be disallowed;
Though his fair daughter's self, as I avowed
At starting, is my object. Nay, we'll go
Together down, sir. Notice Neptune, though,
Taming a sea-horse, thought a rarity,   55
Which Claus of Innsbruck cast in bronze for me!

1842

Lynne Bryer
1946–1994

"The Way" was first published in Illuminations, *an international
magazine of contemporary writing. Later, when Bryer republished
it in a popular anthology of South African poets, she changed the
title to "Release, February 1990," making no doubt that the subject
of the poem is Nelson Mandela. The speaker, like Bryer herself, is
white. Note the allusion to Zecchaeus, the tax collector in Luke's
Gospel, who climbed a tree to catch a glimpse of Christ walking by.*

The Way

He came out, walked free
looking like an ordinary, sweet grandfather
from the Eastern Cape:
those lovely old men we children knew
were wise and saintly   5
when we saw them walking down the streets
in ancient suits, greatcoats
from the First World War. We always

greeted, an exchange both
courteous and right.   10

So now, grown older, we salute
Mandela. Not the bogeyman whose face
was a forbidden sight (abroad,
we looked in libraries): nor charismatic
warrior, giving tongue in blood and flame.   15
The heavens did not fall.
But then, for days before, the mountain
(struck by lightning) burned,
the dark alive with crimson snakes
writhing on air, black elevation of the night.   20

Omens alone foretold the change.
And confirmation came
less from our eyes, watching the images that flew
about the world, than from the way we felt:
elated, cool, not doubting this was true,   25
the destined time and place.

This is the way messiahs come—
when time can stand no more delay,
and people walk the streets, mill in the square,
climb trees to see. Even the soldiers,   30
nervous in the mob (since they alone are armed,
and hence not free) are part of the rightness,
the dislocated, sudden calm of knowing:
This was the way it had to be.

                                                         1990

Lewis Carroll [*Charles Lutwidge Dodgson*]
1832–1898

> *Carroll is remembered today for his pair of challenging children's books,* Alice in Wonderland *(1865) and* Through the Looking-Glass *(1871). Alice reads "Jabberwocky" in the first chapter of the second book, but Carroll began writing the poem much earlier and even published the first stanza, with his own glosses, in 1855. Humpty Dumpty explains to Alice that "slithy" is a combination of "slimy" and "lithe," and thus the "toves" have slick, limber, nimble bodies. But what is a "tove"? According to Humpty Dumpty, a tove is a type of badger with long back legs and horns and a hunger for cheese. And "bryllyg," Humpty explains, comes from the verb "broiling" and means late afternoon, that time of day when dinner is broiled. Obviously, we cannot even guess the meaning of some words—they exist only in Carroll's imagination. Nevertheless, as this poem demonstrates, even nonsense syllables have connotations for readers and listeners.*

Jabberwocky

'Twas brillig, and the slithy toves
   Did gyre and gimble in the wabe:
All mimsy were the borogoves,
   And the mome raths outgrabe.

"Beware the Jabberwock, my son!   5
   The jaws that bite, the claws that catch!
Beware the Jubjub bird, and shun
   The frumious Bandersnatch!"

He took his vorpal sword in hand:
   Long time the manxome foe he sought—   10
So rested he by the Tumtum tree,
   And stood awhile in thought.

And, as in uffish thought he stood,
   The Jabberwock, with eyes of flame,
Came whiffling through the tulgey wood,   15
   And burbled as it came!

One, two! One, two! And through and through
   The vorpal blade went snicker-snack!
He left it dead, and with its head
   He went galumphing back.   20

"And hast thou slain the Jabberwock?
   Come to my arms, my beamish boy!
O frabjous day! Callooh! Callay!"
   He chortled in his joy.

'Twas brillig, and the slithy toves   25
   Did gyre and gimble in the wabe:
All mimsy were the borogoves,
   And the mome raths outgrabe.

1871

Samuel Taylor Coleridge
1772–1834

> *In his preface to "Kubla Khan," Coleridge describes how he composed two or three hundred lines of the poem in an opium reverie, writing them down upon waking until he was interrupted. Coleridge was habituated to opium by October 1797, but his claims about his method of composition are part of the fiction of the poem itself. In fact, his pose is characteristic of that of Romantic poets, who abhorred artifice and believed poetry should flow naturally from the artist. Probably, Coleridge labored long over the poem, and even if he dreamed the images in 1797, most likely he did not write the poem until much later. He did not publish it until 1816. Likewise, his claim to have no special understanding of the symbolism in the poem, as if it originated in something other than his own consciousness, is Romantic. In modern terms, we might say that Coleridge's subconscious authored the symbols.*

Kubla Khan

In Xanadu did Kubla Khan
A stately pleasure-dome decree:
Where Alph, the sacred river, ran
Through caverns measureless to man
   Down to a sunless sea.   5
So twice five miles of fertile ground
With walls and towers were girdled round:
And there were gardens bright with sinuous rills
Where blossomed many an incense-bearing tree;
And here were forests ancient as the hills,   10
Enfolding sunny spots of greenery.

But oh! that deep romantic chasm which slanted
Down the green hill athwart a cedarn cover!
A savage place! as holy and enchanted
As e'er beneath a waning moon was haunted   15
By woman wailing for her demon-lover!
And from this chasm, with ceaseless turmoil seething,
As if this earth in fast thick pants were breathing,
A mighty fountain momently was forced:
Amid whose swift half-intermitted burst   20
Huge fragments vaulted like rebounding hail,
Or chaffy grain beneath the thresher's flail:
And 'mid these dancing rocks at once and ever
It flung up momently the sacred river.
Five miles meandering with a mazy motion   25
Through wood and dale the sacred river ran,
Then reached the caverns measureless to man,
And sank in tumult to a lifeless ocean:
And 'mid this tumult Kubla heard from far
Ancestral voices prophesying war!   30

   The shadow of the dome of pleasure
   Floated midway on the waves;
   Where was heard the mingled measure

From the fountain and the caves.
It was a miracle of rare device, 35
A sunny pleasure-dome with caves of ice!
   A damsel with a dulcimer
   In a vision once I saw:
   It was an Abyssinian maid,
   And on her dulcimer she played, 40
   Singing of Mount Abora.
   Could I revive within me
   Her symphony and song,
   To such a deep delight 'twould win me,
That with music loud and long, 45
I would build that dome in air,
That sunny dome! those caves of ice!
And all who heard should see them there,
And all should cry, Beware! Beware!
His flashing eyes, his floating hair! 50
Weave a circle round him thrice,[1]
And close your eyes with holy dread,
For he on honey-dew hath fed,
And drunk the milk of Paradise.

                 1816

Billy Collins

1941–

> *To understand "Picnic, Lightning," you might find it useful to compare it to Philip Larkin's "Aubade." Both consider the inescapable truth that we all will someday die, but the effect that this knowledge has on Collins's speaker is quite different than the effect it has on Larkin's. "On Turning Ten" comically alludes to Shelley's "Ode to the West Wind" in its last lines (Shelley's statement, meant to be taken quite seriously, reads "I fall upon the thorns of life! I bleed!"). Collins's meditation on growing up, then, gently satirizes poems like Dylan Thomas's "Fern Hill," which regrets what is lost*

---

1. A magic ritual, to protect the inspired poet from intrusion.

when we take on the knowledge of maturity. Collins is famous for these deceptively serious parodies. "Sonnet," for example, pokes fun at the formula of the Petrarchan sonnet. But by the end of the poem Collins turns the parody into a genuine love poem, and he comments on the idealized, Platonic love relations typical of sonnet cycles.

Picnic, Lightning

"My very photogenic mother died in a freak accident (picnic, lightning) when I was three." —Lolita

It is possible to be struck by a meteor
or a single-engine plane
while reading in a chair at home.
Safes drop from rooftops
and flatten the odd pedestrian   5
mostly within the panels of the comics,
but still, we know it is possible,
as well as the flash of summer lightning,
the thermos toppling over,
spilling out on the grass.   10

And we know the message
can be delivered from within.
The heart, no valentine,
decides to quit after lunch,
the power shut off like a switch,   15
or a tiny dark ship is unmoored
into the flow of the body's rivers,
the brain a monastery,
defenseless on the shore.

This is what I think about   20
when I shovel compost
into a wheelbarrow,

and when I fill the long flower boxes,
then press into rows
the limp roots of red impatiens—   25
the instant hand of Death
always ready to burst forth
from the sleeve of his voluminous cloak.

Then the soil is full of marvels,
bits of leaf like flakes off a fresco,   30
red-brown pine needles, a beetle quick
to burrow back under the loam.
Then the wheelbarrow is a wilder blue,
the clouds a brighter white,

and all I hear is the rasp of the steel edge   35
against a round stone,
the small plants singing
with lifted faces, and the click
of the sundial
as one hour sweeps into the next.   40

                                        1998

On Turning Ten

The whole idea of it makes me feel
like I'm coming down with something,
something worse than any stomach ache
or the headaches I get from reading in bad light—
a kind of measles of the spirit,   5
a mumps of the psyche,
a disfiguring chicken pox of the soul.

You tell me it is too early to be looking back,
but that is because you have forgotten
the perfect simplicity of being one   10
and the beautiful complexity introduced by two.
But I can lie on my bed and remember every digit.

At four I was an Arabian wizard.
I could make myself invisible
by drinking a glass of milk a certain way.   15
At seven I was a soldier, at nine a prince.

But now I am mostly at the window
watching the late afternoon light.
Back then it never fell so solemnly
against the side of my tree house,   20
and my bicycle never leaned against the garage
as it does today,
all the dark blue speed drained out of it.

This is the beginning of sadness, I say to myself,
as I walk through the universe in my sneakers.   25
It is time to say good-bye to my imaginary friends,
time to turn the first big number.
It seems only yesterday I used to believe
there was nothing under my skin but light.
If you cut me I would shine.   30
But now when I fall upon the sidewalks of life,
I skin my knees. I bleed.

                                        1998

Sonnet

All we need is fourteen lines, well, thirteen now,
and after this next one just a dozen
to launch a little ship on love's storm-tossed seas,
then only ten more left like rows of beans.
How easily it goes unless you get Elizabethan   5
and insist the iambic bongos must be played
and rhymes positioned at the ends of lines,
one for every station of the cross.
But hang on here while we make the turn
into the final six where all will be resolved,   10
where longing and heartache will find an end,

where Laura will tell Petrarch to put down his pen,
take off those crazy medieval tights,
blow out the lights, and come at last to bed.

1999

E. E. (Edward Estlin) Cummings
1894–1962

> "Buffalo Bill 's" and "in Just-" appeared in Cummings's first book,
> Tulips and Chimneys (1923). They are both among the "tulips,"
> or organic poems, in contrast to the sonnets that make up the
> "chimneys" section. "Buffalo Bill 's" appeared in a subsection called
> "Portraits," while "in Just-" was the first of three "Chansons Inno-
> centes," or songs of innocence. The title calls to mind Blake's Songs
> of Innocence and Experience. Immediately reviewers fixed on the
> unique typography of Cummings's poems, which garnered him con-
> siderable criticism and recognition.

Buffalo Bill 's

Buffalo Bill 's
defunct
     who used to
     ride a watersmooth-silver
                    stallion   5
and break onetwothreefourfive pigeonsjustlikethat
                        Jesus

he was a handsome man
                and what i want to know is
how do you like your blueeyed boy   10
Mister Death

1920, 1923

in Just-

                    in Just-
spring   when the world is mud-
luscious the little
lame balloonman

whistles   far   and wee   5

and eddieandbill come
running from marbles and
piracies and it's
spring

when the world is puddle-wonderful   10

the queer
old balloonman whistles
far   and   wee
and bettyandisbel come dancing

from hop-scotch and jump-rope and   15

it's
spring
and
      the

            goat-footed[1]   20

balloonMan   whistles
far
and
wee

                    1920, 1923

   1. An allusion to satyrs, the lewd forest gods of Greek mythology.

Emily Dickinson
1830–1886

> Only a handful of Dickinson's poems were published in her life-time. "Because I could not stop for Death—," "The Soul Selects Her Own Society—," and "I heard a Fly buzz—when I died—" were written during the Civil War, but they were not published until the 1890s. "After great pain" was first published in 1929. A rare exception is "A narrow Fellow in the Grass," written in 1865 and published in the Springfield Daily Republican in February 1866 under the title "The Snake," which links the poem to the biblical Garden of Eden. Four years after Dickinson died, an editor for the Atlantic Monthly smoothed and regularized some of her poems and published them in a book, which critics instantly praised. But editors did not restore her idiosyncratic punctuation and expressions until the twentieth century. Written in 1861, "Wild Nights—Wild Nights!" worried Dickinson's literary executor, who feared that readers would see in the poem more than the "virgin recluse" put there. Most readers today do not so easily dismiss the sexual sugges-tiveness of her poems. Similarly, the poems are ambiguous about religious beliefs, including the immortality of the soul. Dickinson is notoriously difficult to pin down: her poems often support entirely contradictory interpretations.

249

Wild Nights—Wild Nights!
Were I with thee
Wild Nights should be
Our luxury!

Futile—the Winds—   5
To a Heart in port—
Done with the Compass—
Done with the Chart!

Rowing in Eden—
Ah, the Sea!   10
Might I but moor—Tonight—
In Thee!

1891

303

The Soul selects her own Society—
Then—shuts the Door—
To her divine Majority—
Present no more—

Unmoved—she notes the Chariots—pausing—   5
At her low Gate—
Unmoved—an Emperor be kneeling
Upon her Mat—

I've known her—from an ample nation—
Choose One—   10
Then—close the Valves of her attention—
Like Stone—

1890

341

After great pain, a formal feeling comes—
The Nerves sit ceremonious, like Tombs—
The stiff Heart questions was it He, that bore,
And Yesterday, or Centuries before?

The Feet, mechanical, go round—   5
Of Ground, or Air, or Ought¹—
A Wooden way

---

1. Nothing, or anything.

Regardless grown,
A Quartz contentment, like a stone—

This is the Hour of Lead—   10
Remembered, if outlived,
As Freezing persons, recollect the Snow—
First—Chill—then Stupor—then the letting go—

1929

465

I heard a Fly buzz—when I died—
The Stillness in the Room
Was like the Stillness in the Air—
Between the Heaves of Storm—

The Eyes around—had wrung them dry—   5
And Breaths were gathering firm
For that last Onset—when the King
Be witnessed—in the Room—

I willed my Keepsakes—Signed away
What portion of me be   10
Assignable—and then it was
There interposed a Fly—

With Blue—uncertain stumbling Buzz—
Between the light—and me—
And then the Windows failed—and then   15
I could not see to see—

1896

712

Because I could not stop for Death—
He kindly stopped for me—

The Carriage held but just Ourselves—
And Immortality.

We slowly drove—He knew no haste   5
And I had put away
My labor and my leisure too,
For His Civility—

We passed the School, where Children strove
At Recess—in the Ring—   10
We passed the Fields of Gazing Grain—
We passed the Setting Sun—

Or rather—He passed Us—
The Dews drew quivering and chill—
For only Gossamer, my Gown—   15
My Tippet—only Tulle[1]—

We paused before a House that seemed
A Swelling of the Ground—
The Roof was scarcely visible—
The Cornice—in the Ground—   20

Since then—'tis Centuries—and yet
Feels shorter than the Day
I first surmised the Horses' Heads
Were toward Eternity—

1890

986

A narrow Fellow in the Grass
Occasionally rides—
You may have met Him—did you not
His notice sudden is—

1. Thin silk. "Tippet": a shawl.

The Grass divides as with a Comb—   5
A spotted shaft is seen—
And then it closes at your feet
And opens further on—

He likes a Boggy Acre
A Floor too cool for Corn—   10
Yet when a Boy, and Barefoot—
I more than once at Noon

Have passed, I thought, a Whip lash
Unbraiding in the Sun
When stooping to secure it   15
It wrinkled, and was gone—

Several of Nature's People
I know, and they know me—
I feel for them a transport
Of cordiality—   20

But never met this Fellow
Attended, or alone
Without a tighter breathing
And Zero at the Bone—

                              1866

John Donne
1572–1631

> *Donne wrote poems for a coterie of friends, an elite society, and cir-*
> *culated them only in manuscript. Those included here were not*
> *published until two years after his death. Donne's poems "The Sun*
> *Rising," "The Canonization," and "The Flea" all depict a love af-*
> *fair remarkable for the age, perhaps for any age, and their bawdy*
> *conceits are striking even today. "A Valediction Forbidding Mourn-*
> *ing" is less cheerful but equally suggestive and intricate. To under-*
> *stand these "metaphysical" poems, as Donne's style of startling,*
> *extended metaphors (or conceits) came to be called, you must pa-*

tiently unravel the intricate comparisons. His Holy Sonnets, including "Death be not proud" and "Batter my heart," express a piety belied by the love poems, though they were possibly written around the same time.

The Sun Rising

    Busy old fool, unruly sun,
      Why dost thou thus,
Through windows, and through curtains call on us?
Must to thy motions lovers' seasons run?
      Saucy pedantic wretch, go chide   5
      Late school boys and sour prentices,
   Go tell court huntsmen that the king will ride,
   Call country ants to harvest offices;
Love, all alike, no season knows nor clime,
Nor hours, days, months, which are the rags of time.   10

    Thy beams, so reverend and strong
      Why shouldst thou think?[1]
I could eclipse and cloud them with a wink,
But that I would not lose her sight so long;
      If her eyes have not blinded thine,   15
      Look, and tomorrow late, tell me,
   Whether both th' Indias of spice and mine
   Be where thou leftst them, or lie here with me.
Ask for those kings whom thou saw'st yesterday,
And thou shalt hear, All here in one bed lay.   20
      She's all states, and all princess, I,
      Nothing else is.
Princes do but play us; compared to this,
All honor's mimic, all wealth alchemy.
      Thou, sun, art half as happy as we,   25
      In that the world's contracted thus.
      Thine age asks ease, and since thy duties be

---

1. Reverse these two lines and they will make sense.

To warm the world, that's done in warming us.
Shine here to us, and thou art everywhere;
This bed thy center is, these walls, thy sphere.[2]   30

1633

The Canonization[3]

    For God's sake hold your tongue, and let me love,
    Or chide my palsy, or my gout,
My five gray hairs, or ruined fortune, flout,
    With wealth your state, your mind with arts improve,
      Take you a course, get you a place,[4]   5
      Observe his honor, or his grace,
Or the King's real, or his stampèd face
    Contemplate; what you will, approve,
    So you will let me love.

Alas, alas, who's injured by my love?   10
    What merchant's ships have my sighs drowned?
Who says my tears have overflowed his ground?
    When did my colds a forward spring remove?[5]
      When did the heats which my veins fill
      Add one more to the plaguy bill?[6]   15
Soldiers find wars, and lawyers find out still
    Litigious men, which quarrels move,
    Though she and I do love.

---

2. Though Donne was Galileo's contemporary, this conceit presumes that the sun revolves around the earth. The bed, like the earth, is the center of the sun's orbit; the walls are the region or "sphere" through which the sun passes.

3. Candidates for sainthood are canonized only after they have undergone a rigorous scrutiny in which a "devil's advocate" exposes all the defects that might undermine such a pronouncement.

4. A "place" is an appointment; "take you a course" means pursue a career.

5. The speaker's "colds" have not robbed the early spring of its warmth; "colds" might refer to the chill a rejected lover feels when given a "cold shoulder."

6. A public list of plague victims during an epidemic.

Call us what you will, we are made such by love;
   Call her one, me another fly,   20
We're tapers too, and at our own cost die,[7]
   And we in us find the eagle and the dove.
     The phoenix riddle hath more wit
     By us: we two being one, are it.
So, to one neutral thing both sexes fit.   25
   We die and rise the same, and prove
   Mysterious by this love.

We can die by it, if not live by love,
   And if unfit for tombs and hearse
Our legend be, it will be fit for verse;   30
   And if no piece of chronicle we prove,
     We'll build in sonnets pretty rooms;[8]
     As well a well-wrought urn becomes
The greatest ashes, as half-acre tombs;
   And by these hymns, all shall approve   35
   Us canonized for love.

And thus invoke us: You whom reverend love
   Made one another's hermitage;
You, to whom love was peace, that now is rage;[9]
   Who did the whole world's soul contract, and drove   40
     Into the glasses of your eyes
     (So made such mirrors, and such spies,
That they did all to you epitomize)[1]
   Countries, towns, courts: Beg from above
   A pattern of your love!   45

1633

---

7. "To die" was a conventional metaphor for orgasm, and superstition in Donne's day held that each ejaculation cost a man one day of life.

8. I.e., the pretty sonnets will contain their story, just as urns store ashes as well as giant mausoleums do.

9. I.e., lust.

1. Putting "epitomize" between "did" and "all" will help make sense of this line: a too-simple paraphrase of this and the preceding three lines might read, "whose eyes have seen it all."

The Flea[2]

Mark but this flea, and mark in this,
How little that which thou deniest me is;
It sucked me first, and now sucks thee,
And in this flea, our two bloods mingled be;
Thou know'st that this cannot be said   5
A sin, nor shame nor loss of maidenhead,
   Yet this enjoys before it woo,[3]
   And pampered swells with one blood made of two,[4]
   And this, alas, is more than we would do.

Oh stay, three lives in one flea spare,   10
Where we almost, yea more than married are.
This flea is you and I, and this
Our marriage bed, and marriage temple is;
Though parents grudge, and you, we are met,
And cloisered in these living walls of jet.[5]   15
   Though use make you apt to kill me,
   Let not to that, self murder added be,
   And sacrilege, three sins in killing three.

Cruel and sudden, hast thou since
Purpled thy nail, in blood of innocence?   20
Wherein could this flea guilty be,
Except in that drop which it sucked from thee?
Yet thou triumph'st, and say'st that thou
Find'st not thy self, nor me the weaker now;
   'Tis true, then learn how false, fears be;   25
   Just so much honor, when thou yield'st to me,
     Will waste, as this flea's death took life from thee.[6]

1633

2. Fleas were a conventional item in Renaissance love poetry. Typically, the speaker envies the flea for its ability to roam the beloved's body at will, a liberty denied the speaker.

3. I.e., the flea does not have to court the woman before he "enjoys" her.

4. In the Renaissance, doctors believed that pregnancy resulted from the man's blood mixing with the woman's during intercourse.

5. I.e., the black body of the flea.

6. I.e., having sex with the speaker will hurt the woman's honor about as much as the flea's death lessened her life.

A Valediction: Forbidding Mourning[7]

As virtuous men pass mildly away,
   And whisper to their souls to go,
Whilst some of their sad friends do say
   The breath goes now, and some say, no;

So let us melt, and make no noise,   5
   No tear-floods, nor sigh-tempests move,
'Twere profanation of our joys
   To tell the laity our love.

Moving of th' earth brings harms and fears,
   Men reckon what it did and meant;   10
But trepidation of the spheres,[8]
   Though greater far, is innocent.

Dull sublunary[9] lovers' love
   (Whose soul is sense) cannot admit
Absence, because it doth remove   15
   Those things which elemented[1] it.

But we by a love so much refined
   That our selves know not what it is,
Inter-assurèd of the mind,
   Care less, eyes, lips, and hands to miss.   20

Our two souls therefore, which are one,
   Though I must go, endure not yet
A breach, but an expansion,
   Like gold to airy thinness beat.

7. Some evidence suggests that Donne wrote this poem in 1611 when he had to leave his wife to take a trip to the Continent.

8. Geocentric astronomers trying to explain why the planets did not orbit the earth in perfect circles like the stars suggested that they periodically and suddenly stopped themselves and reversed their direction.

9. Beneath the moon's orbit, and thus earthly as opposed to heavenly; in other words, subject to decay and corruption.

1. I.e., composed.

If they be two, they are two so   25
  As stiff twin compasses² are two;
Thy soul, the fixed foot, makes no show
  To move, but doth, if th' other do.

And though it in the center sit,
  Yet when the other far doth roam,   30
It leans and hearkens after it,
  And grows erect, as that comes home.

Such wilt thou be to me, who must
  Like th' other foot, obliquely run.
Thy firmness makes my circle just,   35
  And makes me end where I begun.

                                    1633

Holy Sonnet

10

Death, be not proud, though some have callèd thee
Mighty and dreadful, for thou are not so;
For those whom thou think'st thou dost overthrow
Die not, poor Death, nor yet canst thou kill me.
From rest and sleep, which but thy pictures be,   5
Much pleasure; then from thee much more must flow,
And soonest our best men with thee do go,
Rest of their bones, and soul's delivery.
Thou art slave to fate, chance, kings, and desperate men,
And dost with poison, war, and sickness dwell,   10
And poppy or charms can make us sleep as well
And better than thy stroke; why swell'st thou then?
One short sleep past, we wake eternally,
And death shall be no more; Death, thou shalt die.

                                    1633

2. I.e., compasses used to draw circles, not to find magnetic north.

Holy Sonnet

14

Batter my heart, three-personed God;[3] for you
As yet but knock, breathe, shine, and seek to mend;
That I may rise and stand, o'erthrow me, and bend
Your force to break, blow, burn, and make me new.
I, like an unsurped town, to another due,   5
Labor to admit you, but O, to no end;
Reason, your viceroy in me, me should defend,
But is captived, and proves weak or untrue.
Yet dearly I love you, and would be loved fain,[4]
But am betrothed unto your enemy.   10
Divorce me, untie or break that knot again;
Take me to you, imprison me, for I,
Except you enthrall me, never shall be free,
Nor ever chaste, except you ravish me.

1633

Rita Dove

1952–

> *"The House Slave" explores the ambiguous position of plantation slaves who worked in the master's "big house" rather than the fields in the pre–Civil War South. The life of a house slave was often less difficult and dangerous than the field hand's, and sometimes allowed for a measure of education. House workers enjoyed a high status among slaves, but because their ascendency depended on their closeness to their aristocratic owners, it was often accompanied by feelings of guilt. Perhaps this poem suggests an analogue in the status of the economically successful, modern day African American. Dove based her poetry sequence* Thomas and Beulah *(1987), which won the Pulitzer Prize and the wide general audience that*

---

3. God the Father, Son, and Holy Spirit.   4. I.e., with pleasure.

*follows such recognition, on the lives of her grandparents. "Daystar"
is one of the* Beulah *poems in the collection.*

The House Slave

The first horn lifts its arm over the dew-lit grass
and in the slave quarters there is a rustling—
children are bundled into aprons, cornbread

and water gourds grabbed, a salt pork breakfast taken.
I watch them driven into the vague before-dawn   5
while their mistress sleeps like an ivory toothpick

and Massa dreams of asses, rum and slave-funk.
I cannot fall asleep again. At the second horn,
the whip curls across the backs of the laggards—

sometimes my sister's voice, unmistaken, among them.   10
"Oh! pray," she cries. "Oh! pray!" Those days
I lie on my cot, shivering in the early heat,

and as the fields unfold to whiteness,
and they spill like bees among the fat flowers,
I weep. It is not yet daylight.   15

                                        1987

Daystar

She wanted a little room for thinking:
but she saw diapers steaming on the line,
a doll slumped behind the door.

So she lugged a chair behind the garage
to sit out the children's naps.   5

Sometimes there were things to watch—
the pinched armor of a vanished cricket,
a floating maple leaf. Other days
she stared until she was assured
when she closed her eyes   10
she'd see only her own vivid blood.

She had an hour, at best, before Liza appeared
pouting from the top of the stairs.
And just *what* was mother doing
out back with the field mice? Why,   15

building a palace. Later
that night when Thomas rolled over and
lurched into her, she would open her eyes
and think of the place that was hers
for an hour—where   20
she was nothing,
pure nothing, in the middle of the day.

                                        1987

T. S. (Thomas Stearns) Eliot
1888–1965

> *Eliot was working on his Ph.D. in philosophy at Harvard when he
> began writing "The Love Song of J. Alfred Prufrock." When he
> traveled to London, he met Ezra Pound, who persuaded the
> Chicago Poetry magazine to publish "Prufrock" in 1915. The poem
> established Eliot as one of the new poets using a "modern" style that
> refused to make any concessions to what we might call the "common
> reader." "Prufrock," like most of Eliot's poetry, is characterized by
> striking conceits (like the simile in lines 2–3) and allusions to liter-
> ary tradition (such as Hamlet and the Bible). Eliot's poetry may be
> disconcerting on a first read: because he leaves out logical links and
> signposts between images, it can be hard to figure out the literal
> level of "Prufrock." Even so, the poem is easier to understand than*

it first appears. Gauging Prufrock's character will give you a fair es-
timate of the "modern" or "anti-hero" Eliot helped define: the sensi-
tive figure crippled by his insight into human character.

The Love Song of J. Alfred Prufrock

S'io credesse che mia risposta fosse
A persona che mai tornasse al mondo,
Questa fiamma staria senza piu scosse.
Ma perciocche giammai di questo fondo
Non torno vivo alcun, s'i'odo il vero,
Senza tema d'infamia ti rispondo.[1]

Let us go then, you and I,
When the evening is spread out against the sky
Like a patient etherised upon a table;
Let us go, through certain half-deserted streets,
The muttering retreats   5
Of restless nights in one-night cheap hotels
And sawdust restaurants with oyster-shells:
Streets that follow like a tedious argument
Of insidious intent
To lead you to an overwhelming question . . .   10
Oh, do not ask, "What is it?"
Let us go and make our visit.

In the room the women come and go
Talking of Michelangelo.

The yellow fog that rubs its back upon the window-panes,   15
The yellow smoke that rubs its muzzle on the window-panes
Licked its tongue into the corners of the evening,

1. Dante, *Inferno* 27.61–66; spoken by Guido da Montefeltro, whom Dante and Virgil find among the false counselors (each spirit is concealed within a flame): "If I thought my answer were given / to anyone who would ever return to the world, / this flame would stand still without moving any further. / But since never from this abyss / has anyone ever returned alive, if what I hear is true, / without fear of infamy I answer you."

Lingered upon the pools that stand in drains,
Let fall upon its back the soot that falls from chimneys,
Slipped by the terrace, made a sudden leap,   20
And seeing that it was a soft October night,
Curled once about the house, and fell asleep.

And indeed there will be time
For the yellow smoke that slides along the street,
Rubbing its back upon the window-panes;   25
There will be time, there will be time
To prepare a face to meet the faces that you meet;
There will be time to murder and create,
And time for all the works and days of hands
That lift and drop a question on your plate;   30
Time for you and time for me,
And time yet for a hundred indecisions,
And for a hundred visions and revisions,
Before the taking of a toast and tea.

In the room the women come and go   35
Talking of Michelangelo.

And indeed there will be time
To wonder, "Do I dare?" and, "Do I dare?"
Time to turn back and descend the stair,
With a bald spot in the middle of my hair—   40
(They will say: "How his hair is growing thin!")
My morning coat, my collar mounting firmly to the chin,
My necktie rich and modest, but asserted by a simple pin—
(They will say: "But how his arms and legs are thin!")
Do I dare   45
Disturb the universe?
In a minute there is time
For decisions and revisions which a minute will reverse.

For I have known them all already, known them all—
Have known the evenings, mornings, afternoons,   50

I have measured out my life with coffee spoons;
I know the voices dying with a dying fall[2]
Beneath the music from a farther room.
    So how should I presume?

And I have known the eyes already, known them all—   55
The eyes that fix you in a formulated phrase,
And when I am formulated, sprawling on a pin,
When I am pinned and wriggling on the wall,
Then how should I begin
To spit out all the butt-ends of my days and ways?   60
    And how should I presume?

And I have known the arms already, known them all—
Arms that are braceleted and white and bare
(But in the lamplight, downed with light brown hair!)
Is it perfume from a dress   65
That makes me so digress?
Arms that lie along a table, or wrap about a shawl.
    And should I then presume?
    And how should I begin?

        .   .   .   .   .   .

Shall I say, I have gone at dusk through narrow streets   70
And watched the smoke that rises from the pipes
Of lonely men in shirt-sleeves, leaning out of windows? . . .

I should have been a pair of ragged claws
Scuttling across the floors of silent seas.

        .   .   .   .   .   .

And the afternoon, the evening, sleeps so peacefully!   75
Smoothed by long fingers,
Asleep . . . tired . . . or it malingers,
Stretched on the floor, here beside you and me.
Should I, after tea and cakes and ices,
Have the strength to force the moment to its crisis?   80
But though I have wept and fasted, wept and prayed,

---

2. An echo of Shakespeare's *Twelfth Night* (1.1.1–4): "If music be the food of love, play on. . . . That strain again, it had a dying fall."

Though I have seen my head (grown slightly bald) brought in
    upon a platter,[3]
I am no prophet—and here's no great matter;
I have seen the moment of my greatness flicker,
And I have seen the eternal Footman hold my coat, and snicker,   85
And in short, I was afraid.

And would it have been worth it, after all,
After the cups, the marmalade, the tea,
Among the porcelain, among some talk of you and me,
Would it have been worth while,   90
To have bitten off the matter with a smile,
To have squeezed the universe into a ball
To roll it toward some overwhelming question,
To say: "I am Lazarus, come from the dead,
Come back to tell you all, I shall tell you all"—   95
If one, settling a pillow by her head,
    Should say: "That is not what I meant at all.
    That is not it, at all."

And would it have been worth it, after all,
Would it have been worth while,   100
After the sunsets and the dooryards and the sprinkled streets,
After the novels, after the teacups, after the skirts that trail
    along the floor—
And this, and so much more?—
It is impossible to say just what I mean!
But as if a magic lantern threw the nerves in patterns on a
    screen: 105
Would it have been worth while
If one, settling a pillow or throwing off a shawl,
And turning toward the window, should say:
    "That is not it at all,
    That is not what I meant, at all."   110

    . . . .

3. At her request, King Herod gave his daughter, Salome, the head of John the Baptist on
a serving plate (Matthew 14.1–12).

No! I am not Prince Hamlet, nor was meant to be;
Am an attendant lord, one that will do
To swell a progress,[4] start a scene or two,
Advise the prince; no doubt, an easy tool,
Deferential, glad to be of use,   115
Politic, cautious, and meticulous;
Full of high sentence, but a bit obtuse;
At times, indeed, almost ridiculous—
Almost, at times, the Fool.

I grow old . . . I grow old . . .   120
I shall wear the bottoms of my trousers rolled.

Shall I part my hair behind? Do I dare to eat a peach?
I shall wear white flannel trousers, and walk upon the beach.
I have heard the mermaids singing, each to each.

I do not think that they will sing to me.   125

I have seen them riding seaward on the waves
Combing the white hair of the waves blown back
When the wind blows the water white and black.

We have lingered in the chambers of the sea
By sea-girls wreathed with seaweed red and brown   130
Till human voices wake us, and we drown.

                                                              1917

Louise Erdrich

1954–

> *In an interview, Erdrich explained that the children speaking in "Indian Boarding School: The Runaways" have "been taken from their homes [and] their cultures by the Bureau of Indian Affairs."*

---

4. I.e., to enlarge the group accompanying a lord with one more body, as might be done with bit actors on the Elizabethan stage.

Earlier in this century, such schools attempted to acclimate Native American children to mainstream American life by obliterating their culture. The speaker in "Captivity" is a European woman captured by Native Americans. While you might think that her natural reaction to being rescued would be relief, the speaker's response is more complex. She is suspended between cultures, and her dream suggests some ambivalence. Erdrich herself has one foot in each culture: she has both German and Chippewa ancestors.

Indian Boarding School: The Runaways

Home's the place we head for in our sleep.
Boxcars stumbling north in dreams
don't wait for us. We catch them on the run.
The rails, old lacerations that we love,
shoot parallel across the face and break   5
just under Turtle Mountains. Riding scars
you can't get lost. Home is the place they cross.

The lame guard strikes a match and makes the dark
less tolerant. We watch through cracks in boards
as the land starts rolling, rolling till it hurts   10
to be here, cold in regulation clothes.
We know the sheriff's waiting at midrun
to take us back. His car is dumb and warm.
The highway doesn't rock, it only hums
like a wing of long insults. The worn-down welts   15
of ancient punishments lead back and forth.

All runaways wear dresses, long green ones,
the color you would think shame was. We scrub
the sidewalks down because it's shameful work.
Our brushes cut the stone in watered arcs   20
and in the soak frail outlines shiver clear
a moment, things us kids pressed on the dark

face before it hardened, pale, remembering
delicate old injuries, the spines of names and leaves.

1987

Captivity

> *He (my captor) gave me a bisquit, which I put in my pocket, and not dar-*
> *ing to eat it, buried it under a log, fearing he had put something in it to*
> *make me love him.*
>
> —from the narrative of the captivity of Mrs. Mary Rowlandson,
> who was taken prisoner by the Wampanoag when Lancaster,
> Massachusetts, was destroyed, in the year 1676

The stream was swift, and so cold
I thought I would be sliced in two.
But he dragged me from the flood
by the ends of my hair.
I had grown to recognize his face.   5
I could distinguish it from the others.
There were times I feared I understood
his language, which was not human,
and I knelt to pray for strength.

We were pursued! By God's agents   10
or pitch devils I did not know.
Only that we must march.
Their guns were loaded with swan shot.
I could not suckle and my child's wail
put them in danger.   15
He had a woman
with teeth black and glittering.
She fed the child milk of acorns.
The forest closed, the light deepened.

I told myself that I would starve   20
before I took food from his hands

but I did not starve.
One night
he killed a deer with a young one in her
and gave me to eat of the fawn.   25
It was so tender,
the bones like the stems of flowers,
that I followed where he took me.
The night was thick. He cut the cord
that bound me to the tree.   30

After that the birds mocked.
Shadows gaped and roared
and the trees flung down
their sharpened lashes.
He did not notice God's wrath.   35
God blasted fire from half-buried stumps.
I hid my face in my dress, fearing He would burn us all
but this, too, passed.

Rescued, I see no truth in things.
My husband drives a thick wedge   40
through the earth, still it shuts
to him year after year.
My child is fed of the first wheat.
I lay myself to sleep
on a Holland-laced pillowbeer.   45
I lay to sleep.
And in the dark I see myself
as I was outside their circle.

They knelt on deerskins, some with sticks,
and he led his company in the noise   50
until I could no longer bear
the thought of how I was.
I stripped a branch
and struck the earth,
in time, begging it to open   55

to admit me
as he was
and feed me honey from the rock.

1989

Carolyn Forché
1950—

> *In 1978, supported by a Guggenheim Fellowship, Forché traveled to El Salvador and produced her award-winning* The Country Between Us *(1981), which included "The Colonel." Beginning in 1960, El Salvador was ruled by a series of repressive military governments, and the country was in civil war by the late 1970s. Colonel Arturo Armando Molina ruled until 1977, when he was replaced by the extremely repressive General Carlos Humberto Romero, who, in turn, was ousted by a coup in 1979. When the colonel in this poem says, "As for the rights of anyone, tell your people to go fuck themselves," he is probably referring to the new emphasis on human rights in American foreign policy that President Jimmy Carter instituted. That policy was reversed in 1981 by Ronald Reagan, who spent millions of American dollars helping the newly elected Salvadorian government combat a coalition of leftist revolutionaries.*

The Colonel

What you have heard is true. I was in his house. His wife carried a tray of coffee and sugar. His daughter filed her nails, his son went out for the night. There were daily papers, pet dogs, a pistol on the cushion beside him. The moon swung bare on its black cord over the house. On the television was a cop show. It was in English. Broken bottles were embedded in the walls around the house to scoop the kneecaps from a man's legs or cut his hands to lace. On the windows there were gratings like those in liquor stores. We had dinner, rack of lamb, good wine, a gold bell was on the table for calling the maid. The maid brought green mangoes, salt, a type of bread. I was asked how I enjoyed the country. There was a brief commercial in Spanish. His wife took everything away. There was some talk of how difficult it had become to govern. The parrot said hello on the terrace. The colonel told it to shut up, and pushed himself from the table. My friend said to me with his eyes: say nothing. The colonel returned with a sack used to bring groceries home. He spilled many human ears on the table. They were like dried peach halves. There is no other way to say this. He took one of them in his hands, shook it in our faces, dropped it into a water glass. It came alive there. I am tired of fooling around he said. As for the rights of anyone, tell your people they can go fuck themselves. He swept the ears to the floor with his arm and held the last of his wine in the air.

Something for your poetry, no? he said. Some of the ears on the floor caught this scrap of his voice. Some of the ears on the floor were pressed to the ground.

1978

Robert Frost
1874–1963

Frost's formal style and rural subjects helped make his poetry particularly accessible to a popular reading audience. Even so, you must be careful to gauge the tone of these eight selections: Frost's poems are darker than his reputation might suggest. Many deal with the isolation and loneliness of the human condition. For instance, Frost's oldest child died in 1900, an event that probably inspired "Home Burial." And do not forget that the memorable line in "Mending Wall," "Good fences make good neighbors," is uttered by "an old-stone savage armed . . . [and moving] in darkness." Likewise, you may have seen the last three lines of "The Road Not Taken" quoted on a poster in high school, where it exhorted you to be an individual. But be careful to consider the context of those lines, and ask yourself, will the speaker, in "ages hence," be lying to himself? Though his rural subjects, as in "After Apple-Picking," "Out, Out—," and "Birches," often spark comparisons to those of

the Romantic poets a hundred years earlier, Frost was no worship-
per of Nature (it is interesting to think about his relationship to
Nature when reading the "city" poem "Acquainted with the
Night"). "Design," which Frost wrote when he was sixty-two, is a
Petrarchan sonnet that could only be written in the post-
Darwinian age since it takes seriously the possibility that the com-
plexity of the natural world is random.

Home Burial

He saw her from the bottom of the stairs
Before she saw him. She was starting down,
Looking back over her shoulder at some fear.
She took a doubtful step and then undid it
To raise herself and look again. He spoke   5
Advancing toward her: "What is it you see
From up there always?—for I want to know."
She turned and sank upon her skirts at that,
And her face changed from terrified to dull.
He said to gain time: "What is it you see?"   10
Mounting until she cowered under him.
"I will find out now—you must tell me, dear."
She, in her place, refused him any help,
With the least stiffening of her neck and silence.
She let him look, sure that he wouldn't see,   15
Blind creature; and awhile he didn't see.
But at last he murmured, "Oh," and again, "Oh."

"What is it—what?" she said.

                        "Just that I see."

"You don't," she challenged. "Tell me what it is."

"The wonder is I didn't see at once.   20
I never noticed it from here before.
I must be wonted to it—that's the reason.

The little graveyard where my people are!
So small the window frames the whole of it.
Not so much larger than a bedroom, is it?   25

There are three stones of slate and one of marble,
Broad-shouldered little slabs there in the sunlight
On the sidehill. We haven't to mind *those*.
But I understand: it is not the stones,
But the child's mound——"

                              "Don't, don't, don't,
        don't," she cried.   30

She withdrew, shrinking from beneath his arm
That rested on the banister, and slid downstairs;
And turned on him with such a daunting look,
He said twice over before he knew himself:
"Can't a man speak of his own child he's lost?"   35

"Not you!—Oh, where's my hat? Oh, I don't need it!
I must get out of here. I must get air.—
I don't know rightly whether any man can."

"Amy! Don't go to someone else this time.
Listen to me. I won't come down the stairs."   40
He sat and fixed his chin between his fists.
"There's something I should like to ask you, dear."

"You don't know how to ask it."

                              "Help me, then."

Her fingers moved the latch for all reply.

"My words are nearly always an offense.   45
I don't know how to speak of anything
So as to please you. But I might be taught,
I should suppose. I can't say I see how.

A man must partly give up being a man
With womenfolk. We could have some arrangement   50
By which I'd bind myself to keep hands off
Anything special you're a-mind to name.
Though I don't like such things, 'twixt those that love.
Two that don't love can't live together without them.
But two that do can't live together with them."   55
She moved the latch a little. "Don't—don't go.
Don't carry it to someone else this time.
Tell me about it if it's something human.
Let me into your grief. I'm not so much
Unlike other folks as your standing there   60
Apart would make me out. Give me my chance.
I do think, though, you overdo it a little.
What was it brought you up to think it the thing
To take your mother-loss of a first child
So inconsolably—in the face of love.   65
You'd think his memory might be satisfied——"

"There you go sneering now!"

                              "I'm not, I'm not!
You make me angry. I'll come down to you.
God, what a woman! And it's come to this,
A man can't speak of his own child that's dead."   70

"You can't because you don't know how to speak.
If you had any feelings, you that dug
With your own hand—how could you?—his little grave;
I saw you from that very window there,
Making the gravel leap and leap in air,   75
Leap up, like that, like that, and land so lightly
And roll back down the mound beside the hole.
I thought, Who is that man? I didn't know you.
And I crept down the stairs and up the stairs
To look again, and still your spade kept lifting.   80
Then you came in. I heard your rumbling voice

Out in the kitchen, and I don't know why,
But I went near to see with my own eyes.
You could sit there with the stains on your shoes
Of the fresh earth from your own baby's grave   85
And talk about your everyday concerns.
You had stood the spade up against the wall
Outside there in the entry, for I saw it."

"I shall laugh the worst laugh I ever laughed.
I'm cursed. God, if I don't believe I'm cursed."   90

"I can repeat the very words you were saying:
'Three foggy mornings and one rainy day
Will rot the best birch fence a man can build.'
Think of it, talk like that at such a time!
What had how long it takes a birch to rot   95
To do with what was in the darkened parlor?
You *couldn't* care! The nearest friends can go
With anyone to death, comes so far short
They might as well not try to go at all.
No, from the time when one is sick to death,   100
One is alone, and he dies more alone.
Friends make pretense of following to the grave,
But before one is in it, their minds are turned
And making the best of their way back to life
And living people, and things they understand.   105
But the world's evil. I won't have grief so
If I can change it. Oh, I won't, I won't!"

"There, you have said it all and you feel better.
You won't go now. You're crying. Close the door.
The heart's gone out of it: why keep it up?   110
Amy! There's someone coming down the road!"

"*You*—oh, you think the talk is all. I must go—
Somewhere out of this house. How can I make you——"

"If—you—do!" She was opening the door wider.
"Where do you mean to go? First tell me that.   115
I'll follow and bring you back by force. I *will!*—"

                                        1914

After Apple-Picking

My long two-pointed ladder's sticking through a tree
Toward heaven still,
And there's a barrel that I didn't fill
Beside it, and there may be two or three
Apples I didn't pick upon some bough.   5
But I am done with apple-picking now.
Essence of winter sleep is on the night,
The scent of apples: I am drowsing off.
I cannot rub the strangeness from my sight
I got from looking through a pane of glass   10
I skimmed this morning from the drinking trough
And held against the world of hoary grass.
It melted, and I let it fall and break.
But I was well
Upon my way to sleep before it fell,   15
And I could tell
What form my dreaming was about to take.
Magnified apples appear and disappear,
Stem end and blossom end,
And every fleck of russet showing clear.   20
My instep arch not only keeps the ache,
It keeps the pressure of a ladder-round.
I feel the ladder sway as the boughs bend.
And I keep hearing from the cellar bin
The rumbling sound   25
Of load on load of apples coming in.
For I have had too much
Of apple-picking: I am overtired
Of the great harvest I myself desired.
There were ten thousand thousand fruit to touch, 30

Cherish in hand, lift down, and not let fall.
For all
That struck the earth,
No matter if not bruised or spiked with stubble,
Went surely to the cider-apple heap   35
As of no worth.
One can see what will trouble
This sleep of mine, whatever sleep it is.
Were he not gone,
The woodchuck could say whether it's like his   40
Long sleep, as I describe its coming on,
Or just some human sleep.

1914

Mending Wall

Something there is that doesn't love a wall,
That sends the frozen-ground-swell under it,
And spills the upper boulders in the sun;
And makes gaps even two can pass abreast.
The work of hunters is another thing: 5
I have come after them and made repair
Where they have left not one stone on a stone,
But they would have the rabbit out of hiding,
To please the yelping dogs. The gaps I mean,
No one has seen them made or heard them made,   10
But at spring mending-time we find them there.
I let my neighbor know beyond the hill;
And on a day we meet to walk the line
And set the wall between us once again.
We keep the wall between us as we go.   15
To each the boulders that have fallen to each.
And some are loaves and some so nearly balls
We have to use a spell to make them balance:
'Stay where you are until our backs are turned!'
We wear our fingers rough with handling them.   20
Oh, just another kind of outdoor game,

One on a side. It comes to little more:
There where it is we do not need the wall:
He is all pine and I am apple orchard.
My apple trees will never get across   25
And eat the cones under his pines, I tell him.
He only says, 'Good fences make good neighbors.'
Spring is the mischief in me, and I wonder
If I could put a notion in his head:
'*Why* do they make good neighbors? Isn't it   30
Where there are cows? But here there are no cows.
Before I built a wall I'd ask to know
What I was walling in or walling out,
And to whom I was like to give offense.
Something there is that doesn't love a wall,   35
That wants it down.' I could say 'Elves' to him,
But it's not elves exactly, and I'd rather
He said it for himself. I see him there
Bringing a stone grasped firmly by the top
In each hand, like an old-stone savage armed.   40
He moves in darkness as it seems to me,
Not of woods only and the shade of trees.
He will not go behind his father's saying,
And he likes having thought of it so well
He says again, 'Good fences make good neighbors.'   45

1914

"Out, Out—"

The buzz saw snarled and rattled in the yard
And made dust and dropped stove-length sticks of wood,
Sweet-scented stuff when the breeze drew across it.
And from there those that lifted eyes could count
Five mountain ranges one behind the other   5
Under the sunset far into Vermont.
And the saw snarled and rattled, snarled and rattled,
As it ran light, or had to bear a load.
And nothing happened: day was all but done.

Call it a day, I wish they might have said   10
To please the boy by giving him the half hour
That a boy counts so much when saved from work.
His sister stood beside them in her apron
To tell them "Supper." At the word, the saw,
As if to prove saws knew what supper meant,   15
Leaped out at the boy's hand, or seemed to leap—
He must have given the hand. However it was,
Neither refused the meeting. But the hand!
The boy's first outcry was a rueful laugh,
As he swung toward them holding up the hand,   20
Half in appeal, but half as if to keep
The life from spilling. Then the boy saw all—
Since he was old enough to know, big boy
Doing a man's work, though a child at heart—
He saw all spoiled. "Don't let him cut my hand off—   25
The doctor, when he comes. Don't let him, sister!"
So. But the hand was gone already.
The doctor put him in the dark of ether.
He lay and puffed his lips out with his breath.
And then—the watcher at his pulse took fright.   30
No one believed. They listened at his heart.
Little—less—nothing!—and that ended it.
No more to build on there. And they, since they
Were not the one dead, turned to their affairs.

1916

The Road Not Taken

Two roads diverged in a yellow wood,
And sorry I could not travel both
And be one traveler, long I stood
And looked down one as far as I could
To where it bent in the undergrowth;   5

Then took the other, as just as fair,
And having perhaps the better claim,

Because it was grassy and wanted wear;
Though as for that the passing there
Had worn them really about the same,   10

And both that morning equally lay
In leaves no step had trodden black.
Oh, I kept the first for another day!
Yet knowing how way leads on to way,
I doubted if I should ever come back.   15

I shall be telling this with a sigh
Somewhere ages and ages hence:
Two roads diverged in a wood, and I—
I took the one less traveled by,
And that has made all the difference.   20

1916

Birches

When I see birches bend to left and right
Across the lines of straighter darker trees,
I like to think some boy's been swinging them.
But swinging doesn't bend them down to stay
As ice-storms do. Often you must have seen them   5
Loaded with ice a sunny winter morning
After a rain. They click upon themselves
As the breeze rises, and turn many-colored
As the stir cracks and crazes their enamel.
Soon the sun's warmth makes them shed crystal shells   10
Shattering and avalanching on the snow-crust—
Such heaps of broken glass to sweep away
You'd think the inner dome of heaven had fallen.
They are dragged to the withered bracken by the load,
And they seem not to break; though once they are bowed   15
So low for long, they never right themselves:
You may see their trunks arching in the woods
Years afterwards, trailing their leaves on the ground

Like girls on hands and knees that throw their hair
Before them over their heads to dry in the sun.　　　　　　20
But I was going to say when Truth broke in
With all her matter-of-fact about the ice-storm
I should prefer to have some boy bend them
As he went out and in to fetch the cows—
Some boy too far from town to learn baseball,　　　　　25
Whose only play was what he found himself,
Summer or winter, and could play alone.
One by one he subdued his father's trees
By riding them down over and over again
Until he took the stiffness out of them,　　　　　　　　30
And not one but hung limp, not one was left
For him to conquer. He learned all there was
To learn about not launching out too soon
And so not carrying the tree away
Clear to the ground. He always kept his poise　　　　　35
To the top branches, climbing carefully
With the same pains you use to fill a cup
Up to the brim, and even above the brim.
Then he flung outward, feet first, with a swish,
Kicking his way down through the air to the ground.　　40
So was I once myself a swinger of birches.
And so I dream of going back to be.
It's when I'm weary of considerations,
And life is too much like a pathless wood
Where your face burns and tickles with the cobwebs　　45
Broken across it, and one eye is weeping
From a twig's having lashed across it open.
I'd like to get away from earth awhile
And then come back to it and begin over.
May no fate willfully misunderstand me　　　　　　　50
And half grant what I wish and snatch me away
Not to return. Earth's the right place for love:
I don't know where it's likely to go better.
I'd like to go by climbing a birch tree,
And climb black branches up a snow-white trunk　　55
Toward heaven, till the tree could bear no more,

But dipped its top and set me down again.
That would be good both going and coming back.
One could do worse than be a swinger of birches.

1916

Stopping by Woods on a Snowy Evening

Whose woods these are I think I know.
His house is in the village though;
He will not see me stopping here
To watch his woods fill up with snow.

My little horse must think it queer   5
To stop without a farmhouse near
Between the woods and frozen lake
The darkest evening of the year.

He gives his harness bells a shake
To ask if there is some mistake.   10
The only other sound's the sweep
Of easy wind and downy flake.

The woods are lovely, dark and deep,
But I have promises to keep,
And miles to go before I sleep,   15
And miles to go before I sleep.

1923

Acquainted with the Night

I have been one acquainted with the night.
I have walked out in rain—and back in rain.
I have outwalked the furthest city light.

I have looked down the saddest city lane.
I have passed by the watchman on his beat   5
And dropped my eyes, unwilling to explain.

I have stood still and stopped the sound of feet
When far away an interrupted cry
Came over houses from another street,

But not to call me back or say good-by;   10
And further still at an unearthly height,
One luminary clock against the sky

Proclaimed the time was neither wrong nor right.
I have been one acquainted with the night.

1928

Design

I found a dimpled spider, fat and white,
On a white heal-all,[1] holding up a moth
Like a white piece of rigid satin cloth—
Assorted characters of death and blight
Mixed ready to begin the morning right,   5
Like the ingredients of a witches' broth—
A snow-drop spider, a flower like a froth,
And dead wings carried like a paper kite.

What had that flower to do with being white,
The wayside blue and innocent heal-all?   10
What brought the kindred spider to that height,
Then steered the white moth thither in the night?
What but design of darkness to appall?—
If design govern in a thing so small.

1936

---

1. One of a variety of plants in the mint family; the flowers are usually violet-blue.

Allen Ginsberg
1926–1998

> *"A Supermarket in California" appeared in Ginsberg's provocative* Howl and Other Poems *(1956), a volume that made Ginsberg famous at least partly because its publisher was tried for obscenity and acquitted. That book put him in the company of Jack Kerouac and the other Beat writers centered in San Francisco. In the 1960s he became a well-known figure among hippies and one of the voices of the counterculture generation: Ginsberg coined the term "flower power." As this poem makes clear, Ginsberg consciously echoes Walt Whitman and assumed for himself the long beard and sandals of the prophet. Here he questions whether the consumer society of modern America is the same country Whitman celebrated a hundred years earlier.*

A Supermarket in California

What thoughts I have of you tonight, Walt Whitman, for I walked down the sidestreets under the trees with a headache self-conscious looking at the full moon.

In my hungry fatigue, and shopping for images, I went into the neon fruit supermarket, dreaming of your enumerations!

What peaches and what penumbras! Whole families shopping at night! Aisles full of husbands! Wives in the avocados, babies in the tomatoes!—and you, García Lorca, what were you doing down by the watermelons?

I saw you, Walt Whitman, childless, lonely old grubber, poking among the meats in the refrigerator and eyeing the grocery boys.

I heard you asking questions of each: Who killed the pork chops? What price bananas? Are you my Angel?   5

I wandered in and out of the brilliant stacks of cans following you, and followed in my imagination by the store detective.

We strode down the open corridors together in our solitary
fancy tasting artichokes, possessing every frozen delicacy, and
never passing the cashier.

Where are we going, Walt Whitman? The doors close in an
hour. Which way does your beard point tonight?
    (I touch your book and dream of our odyssey in the
supermarket and feel absurd.)
    Will we walk all night through solitary streets? The trees add
shade to shade, lights out in the houses, we'll both be lonely.   10
    Will we stroll dreaming of the lost America of love past blue
automobiles in driveways, home to our silent cottage?
    Ah, dear father, graybeard, lonely old courage-teacher, what
America did you have when Charon quit poling his ferry and
you got out on a smoking bank and stood watching the boat
disappear on the black waters of Lethe?

1956

Thomas Gray
1716–1771

> *"Elegy Written in a Country Churchyard," Gray's best-known poem,
> was written to mourn the death of Gray's close friend, Richard West,
> who died of tuberculosis in 1742. Though "Elegy" represents one of
> Gray's earliest efforts at writing poetry, it was revised for five years
> before publication. When the public finally read "Elegy," Gray be-
> came an immediate celebrity. This elegy is unusual in that it consid-
> ers not the death of an individual nor human mortality in general,
> but the deaths of a particular group of people: commoners.*

Elegy Written in a Country Churchyard

The curfew tolls the knell of parting day,
    The lowing herd wind slowly o'er the lea,
The plowman homeward plods his weary way,
    And leaves the world to darkness and to me.

Now fades the glimmering landscape on the sight,   5
   And all the air a solemn stillness holds,
Save where the beetle wheels his droning flight,
   And drowsy tinklings lull the distant folds;

Save that from yonder ivy-mantled tower
   The moping owl does to the moon complain   10
Of such, as wandering near her secret bower,
   Molest her ancient solitary reign.

Beneath those rugged elms, that yew tree's shade,
   Where heaves the turf in many a moldering heap,
Each in his narrow cell forever laid,   15
   The rude forefathers of the hamlet sleep.

The breezy call of incense-breathing morn,
   The swallow twittering from the straw-built shed,
The cock's shrill clarion, or the echoing horn,
   No more shall rouse them from their lowly bed.   20

For them no more the blazing hearth shall burn,
   Or busy housewife ply her evening care;
No children run to lisp their sire's return,
   Or climb his knees the envied kiss to share.

Oft did the harvest to their sickle yield,   25
   Their furrow oft the stubborn glebe has broke;
How jocund did they drive their team afield!
   How bowed the woods beneath their sturdy stroke!

Let not Ambition mock their useful toil,
   Their homely joys, and destiny obscure;   30
Nor Grandeur hear with a disdainful smile
   The short and simple annals of the poor.

The boast of heraldry, the pomp of power,
　And all that beauty, all that wealth e'er gave,
Awaits alike the inevitable hour.   35
　The paths of glory lead but to the grave.

Nor you, ye proud, impute to these the fault,
　If Memory o'er their tomb no trophies raise,
Where through the long-drawn aisle and fretted vault
　The pealing anthem swells the note of praise.   40

Can storied urn or animated bust
　Back to its mansion call the fleeting breath?
Can Honor's voice provoke the silent dust,
　Or Flattery soothe the dull cold ear of Death?

Perhaps in this neglected spot is laid   45
　Some heart once pregnant with celestial fire;
Hands that the rod of empire might have swayed,
　Or waked to ecstasy the living lyre.

But Knowledge to their eyes her ample page
　Rich with the spoils of time did ne'er unroll;   50
Chill Penury repressed their noble rage,
　And froze the genial current of the soul.

Full many a gem of purest ray serene,
　The dark unfathomed caves of ocean bear:
Full many a flower is born to blush unseen,   55
　And waste its sweetness on the desert air.

Some village Hampden[1] that with dauntless breast
　The little tyrant of his fields withstood;
Some mute inglorious Milton here may rest,
　Some Cromwell guiltless of his country's blood.   60

---

1. Leader of the opposition to Charles I in the controversy over ship money; killed in battle in the civil wars.

The applause of listening senates to command,
　　The threats of pain and ruin to despise,
To scatter plenty o'er a smiling land,
　　And read their history in a nation's eyes,

Their lot forbade; nor circumscribed alone　　　　　　　　65
　　Their growing virtues, but their crimes confined;
Forbade to wade through slaughter to a throne,
　　And shut the gates of mercy on mankind,

The struggling pangs of conscious truth to hide,
　　To quench the blushes of ingenuous shame,　　　　　70
Or heap the shrine of Luxury and Pride
　　With incense kindled at the Muse's flame.

Far from the madding crowd's ignoble strife,
　　Their sober wishes never learned to stray;
Along the cool sequestered vale of life　　　　　　　　75
　　They kept the noiseless tenor of their way.

Yet even these bones from insult to protect
　　Some frail memorial still erected nigh,
With uncouth rhymes and shapeless sculpture decked,
　　Implores the passing tribute of a sigh.　　　　　　　80

Their name, their years, spelt by the unlettered Muse,
　　The place of fame and elegy supply:
And many a holy text around she strews,
　　That teach the rustic moralist to die.

For who to dumb Forgetfulness a prey,　　　　　　　　85
　　This pleasing anxious being e'er resigned,
Left the warm precincts of the cheerful day,
　　Nor cast one longing lingering look behind?

On some fond breast the parting soul relies,
    Some pious drops the closing eye requires;   90
Even from the tomb the voice of Nature cries,
    Even in our ashes live their wonted fires.

For thee, who mindful of the unhonored dead
    Dost in these lines their artless tale relate;
If chance, by lonely contemplation led,   95
    Some kindred spirit shall inquire thy fate,

Haply some hoary-headed swain may say,
    "Oft have we seen him at the peep of dawn
Brushing with hasty steps the dews away
    To meet the sun upon the upland lawn.   100

"There at the foot of yonder nodding beech
    That wreathes its old fantastic roots so high,
His listless length at noontide would he stretch,
    And pore upon the brook that babbles by.

"Hard by yon wood, now smiling as in scorn,   105
    Muttering his wayward fancies he would rove,
Now drooping, woeful wan, like one forlorn,
    Or crazed with care, or crossed in hopeless love.

"One morn I missed him on the customed hill,
    Along the heath and near his favorite tree;
Another came; nor yet beside the rill,   110
    Nor up the lawn, nor at the wood was he;

"The next with dirges due in sad array
    Slow through the churchway path we saw him borne.
Approach and read (for thou canst read) the lay,   115
    Graved on the stone beneath yon aged thorn."

THE EPITAPH

Here rests his head upon the lap of Earth
 A youth to Fortune and to Fame unknown.
Fair Science frowned not on his humble birth,
 And Melancholy marked him for her own.   120

Large was his bounty, and his soul sincere,
 Heaven did a recompense as largely send:
He gave to Misery all he had, a tear,
 He gained from Heaven ('twas all he wished) a friend.

No farther seek his merits to disclose,   125
 Or draw his frailties from their dread abode
(There they alike in trembling hope repose),
 The bosom of his Father and his God.

                                                    1751

Thomas Hardy
1840–1928

> *Hardy wrote "Hap" in 1866, just seven years after Darwin's* Origin
> of Species, *though the poem was not published until 1898. Clearly,
> this Petrarchan sonnet is inspired by Darwin's theory that human
> beings are the result of random, natural forces rather than a divine
> plan. "Hap" is short for "happenstance," or chance. "Convergence of
> the Twain" and "Channel Firing" are both occasional poems, or po-
> ems triggered by historical events. The sinking of the* Titanic *in
> 1912 gave Western society reason to reflect on its place in the uni-
> verse and relation to God. "Channel Firing" comments on the Eng-
> lish Navy's gunnery practice in April 1914, just four months before
> the war everyone expected, World War I, finally erupted.*

Hap

If but some vengeful god would call to me
From up the sky, and laugh: "Thou suffering thing,
Know that thy sorrow is my ecstasy,
That thy love's loss is my hate's profiting!"

Then would I bear it, clench myself, and die,   5
Steeled by the sense of ire unmerited;
Half-eased in that a Powerfuller than I
Had willed and meted me the tears I shed.

But not so. How arrives it joy lies slain,
And why unblooms the best hope ever sown?   10
—Crass Casualty obstructs the sun and rain,
And dicing Time for gladness casts a moan. . . .
These purblind Doomsters had as readily strown
Blisses about my pilgrimage as pain.

1898

The Convergence of the Twain
Lines on the Loss of the Titanic[1]

I

In a solitude of the sea
Deep from human vanity,
And the Pride of Life that planned her, stilly couches she.

---

1. On April 15, 1912, the R.M.S. *Titanic* sank on its maiden voyage from Southampton to New York. The ship was thought to be unsinkable because it was constructed with many water-tight sections. It struck an iceberg, which tore a long gash in its side, and quickly sank.

2

Steel chambers, late the pyres
Of her salamandrine fires,[2]   5
Cold currents thrid,[3] and turn to rhythmic tidal lyres.

3

Over the mirrors meant
To glass the opulent
The sea-worm crawls—grotesque, slimed, dumb, indifferent.

4

Jewels in joy designed   10
To ravish the sensuous mind
Lie lightless, all their sparkles bleared and black and blind.

5

Dim moon-eyed fishes near
Gaze at the gilded gear
And query: "What does this vaingloriousness down here?"   15

6

Well: while was fashioning
This creature of cleaving wing,
The Immanent Will that stirs and urges everything

7

Prepared a sinister mate
For her—so gaily great—   20
A Shape of Ice, for the time far and dissociate.

---

2. According to legend, salamanders can live in fire. The boilers of the *Titanic* were similarly remarkable for burning though they were under water, so to speak.
3. I.e., thread.

8

And as the smart ship grew
In stature, grace, and hue,
In shadowy silent distance grew the Iceberg too.

9

Alien they seemed to be: 25
No mortal eye could see
The intimate welding of their later history.

10

Or sign that they were bent
By paths coincident
On being anon twin halves of one august event,   30

11

'Till the Spinner of the Years
Said "Now!" And each one hears,
And consummation comes, and jars two hemispheres.

1912

Channel Firing

That night your great guns, unawares,
Shook all our coffins as we lay,
And broke the chancel window-squares,
We thought it was the Judgment-day.

And sat upright. While drearisome   5
Arose the howl of wakened hounds:
The mouse let fall the altar-crumb,
The worms drew back into the mounds,

The glebe cow drooled. Till God called, "No;
It's gunnery practice out at sea   10
Just as before you went below;
The world is as it used to be:

"All nations striving strong to make
Red war yet redder. Mad as hatters
They do no more for Christés sake   15
Than you who are helpless in such matters.

"That this is not the judgment-hour
For some of them's a blessed thing,
For if it were they'd have to scour
Hell's floor for so much threatening. . . .   20

"Ha, ha. It will be warmer when
I blow the trumpet (if indeed
I ever do; for you are men,
And rest eternal sorely need)."

So down we lay again. "I wonder,   25
Will the world ever saner be,"
Said one, "than when He sent us under
In our indifferent century!"

And many a skeleton shook his head.
"Instead of preaching forty year,"   30
My neighbour Parson Thirdly said,
"I wish I had stuck to pipes and beer."

Again the guns disturbed the hour,
Roaring their readiness to avenge,
As far inland as Stourton Tower,   35
And Camelot, and starlit Stonehenge.

1914

Robert Hayden
1913–1980

> *Hayden's birth parents gave him up for adoption when he was two years old, and "Those Winter Sundays" recounts his youth growing up in the working-class, Detroit home of his adoptive family. Much of Hayden's work deals with racial injustice in America, but, as he declared, he wanted to be a black poet "the way [W. B.] Yeats was an Irish poet." That is, he wanted his sensibility to be suffused with a racial awareness, and his work to be political in a broad sense of that word, but he allows neither to narrow the scope of his work. No reader of the 1962 book in which Hayden published "Those Winter Sundays" could ignore the racial injustices that kept this family poor. But at the same time Hayden does not reserve "love's austere and lonely offices" for the working-class, black American.*

Those Winter Sundays

Sundays too my father got up early
and put his clothes on in the blueblack cold,
then with cracked hands that ached
from labor in the weekday weather made
banked fires blaze. No one ever thanked him.   5

I'd wake and hear the cold splintering, breaking.
When the rooms were warm, he'd call,
and slowly I would rise and dress,
fearing the chronic angers of that house,

Speaking indifferently to him,   10
who had driven out the cold
and polished my good shoes as well.
What did I know, what did I know
of love's austere and lonely offices?

1962

Seamus Heaney
1939–

> Heaney put "Digging" on the first page of his first book in 1966, suggesting he meant it to inaugurate and justify his vocation. For Ireland's Catholics, potatoes are rich symbols: they represent both the sustenance of the earth and the terrible famines in the 1840s under England's colonial rule. The Irish cut "turf" from peat bogs to burn in their stoves and fireplaces like coal. By the mid-1970s, the public recognized Heaney as Ireland's chief poet, but he was criticized for not taking a stand against England's oppression of Irish Catholics. Heaney responded with North in 1975, but it hardly endorsed militant nationalism. In North, the bogs figure as the racial memory bank of Celts: the bog woman in "Punishment" is an ancient Celt unearthed in modern times. The archeological evidence suggests that she was ritually executed for adultery. The women chained to the rails are contemporary Catholics who were tarred, shaved, and stripped naked by soldiers in the Irish Republican Army for the crime of dating British soldiers.

Digging

Between my finger and my thumb
The squat pen rests; snug as a gun.

Under my window, a clean rasping sound
When the spade sinks into gravelly ground:
My father, digging. I look down   5

Till his straining rump among the flowerbeds
Bends low, comes up twenty years away
Stooping in rhythm through potato drills[1]
Where he was digging.

The coarse boot nestled on the lug, the shaft   10
Against the inside knee was levered firmly.

---

1. Small furrows in which seeds are sown.

He rooted out tall tops, buried the bright edge deep
To scatter new potatoes that we picked
Loving their cool hardness in our hands.

By god, the old man could handle a spade.   15
Just like his old man.

My grandfather cut more turf in a day
Than any other man on Toner's bog.
Once I carried him milk in a bottle
Corked sloppily with paper. He straightened up   20
To drink it, then fell to right away
Nicking and slicing neatly, heaving sods
Over his shoulder, going down and down
For the good turf. Digging.

The cold smell of potato mould, the squelch and slap   25
Of soggy peat, the curt cuts of an edge
Through living roots awaken in my head.
But I've no spade to follow men like them.

Between my finger and my thumb
The squat pen rests.   30
I'll dig with it.

1966

Punishment

I can feel the tug
of the halter at the nape
of her neck, the wind
on her naked front.

It blows her nipples   5
to amber beads,
it shakes the frail rigging
of her ribs.

I can see her drowned
body in the bog,   10
the weighing stone,
the floating rods and boughs.

Under which at first
she was a barked sapling
that is dug up   15
oak-bone, brain-firkin:[1]

her shaved head
like a stubble of black corn,
her blindfold a soiled bandage,
her noose a ring   20

to store
the memories of love.
Little adulteress,
before they punished you

you were flaxen-haired,   25
undernourished, and your
tar-black face was beautiful.
My poor scapegoat,

I almost love you
but would have cast, I know,   30
the stones of silence.
I am the artful voyeur

of your brain's exposed
and darkened combs,
your muscles' webbing   35
and all your numbered bones:

1. A small wooden cask or vessel.

I who have stood dumb
when your betraying sisters,
cauled in tar,
wept by the railings,   40

who would connive
in civilized outrage
yet understand the exact
and tribal, intimate revenge.

1975

Robert Herrick

1591–1674

> *Herrick carried on a slow life as a country minister until the Puritans took over England in the 1640s. Then he was deprived of his parish and forced to return to London, where he prepared his verse for publication. More than fourteen hundred poems—including the three here—came out at once in 1648. Public opinion during the Puritan regime was not likely to praise his poems "of youth, of love, and . . . of cleanly wantonness," as Herrick described his own work. Actually, no one noticed his poems, not even to condemn their salaciousness. He was ignored until the nineteenth century. "To the Virgins to Make Much of Time" is a seduction poem using the conventional* carpe diem *strategy, just as "Upon Julia's Clothes" is a typical poem in praise of the speaker's beloved. But "Delight in Disorder" suggests that underlying these conventions is a distinct philosophy of life. In the mind of a seventeenth-century reader, the word "precise" in the last line would have called up images of Puritans and their ethic.*

Delight in Disorder

A sweet disorder in the dress
Kindles in clothes a wantonness.
A lawn about the shoulders thrown

Into a fine distractiòn;
An erring lace, which here and there   5
Enthralls the crimson stomacher;
A cuff neglectful, and thereby
Ribbons to flow confusedly;
A winning wave, deserving note,
In the tempestuous petticoat;   10
A careless shoestring, in whose tie
I see a wild civility;
Do more bewitch me than when art
Is too precise in every part.

                    1648

To the Virgins, to Make Much of Time

Gather ye rosebuds while ye may,
    Old time is still a-flying;
And this same flower that smiles today
    Tomorrow will be dying.

The glorious lamp of heaven, the sun,   5
    The higher he's a-getting,
The sooner will his race be run,
    And nearer he's to setting.

That age is best which is the first,
    When youth and blood are warmer;   10
But being spent, the worse, and worst
    Times still succeed the former.

Then be not coy, but use your time,
    And, while ye may, go marry;
For, having lost but once your prime,   15
    You may forever tarry.

                    1648

Upon Julia's Clothes

Whenas in silks my Julia goes,
Then, then, methinks, how sweetly flows
That liquefaction of her clothes.

Next, when I cast mine eyes, and see
That brave vibration, each way free,   5
O, how that glittering taketh me!

1648

Gerard Manley Hopkins
1844–1889

> *At twenty-two years old, against his parents' will, Hopkins con-*
> *verted to Catholicism, and a few years later he joined the Jesuit or-*
> *der and burned all his poems. With his rector's blessing he composed*
> *ten sonnets on nature in 1877, including "God's Grandeur" and*
> *"The Windhover," each remarkable for its striking rhythms. Hop-*
> *kins called it "sprung rhythm," which he developed from ancient*
> *Welsh verse that combines in each line any number of lightly*
> *stressed syllables with a set number of stressed syllables. Yet more*
> *striking are Hopkins's conceits, which were like nothing anyone else*
> *was writing in Victorian England. In fact, the poems were not pub-*
> *lished until 1918, when they found proper companions with modern*
> *poems, like Eliot's and Pound's. "Margaret" in "Spring and Fall" is*
> *not based on a real girl; Hopkins invented her when he wrote the*
> *poem on September 7, 1880. "God's Grandeur," "The Windhover,"*
> *and "Spring and Fall" all come to us from letters Hopkins sent to*
> *Robert Bridges, a fellow poet, who saved them for posterity.*

God's Grandeur

The world is charged with the grandeur of God.
  It will flame out, like shining from shook foil;[1]
  It gathers to a greatness, like the ooze of oil
Crushed. Why do men then now not reck his rod?
Generations have trod, have trod, have trod;   5
  And all is seared with trade; bleared, smeared with toil;
  And wears man's smudge and shares man's smell: the soil
Is bare now, nor can foot feel, being shod.

And for all this, nature is never spent;
  There lives the dearest freshness deep down things;   10
And though the last lights off the black West went
  Oh, morning, at the brown brink eastward, springs—
Because the Holy Ghost over the bent
  World broods with warm breast and with ah! bright wings.
1877   *1918*

The Windhover[2]

To Christ Our Lord

I caught this morning morning's minion, king-
  dom of daylight's dauphin, dapple-dawn-drawn Falcon, in
    his riding
Of the rolling level underneath him steady air, and striding
High there, how he rung upon the rein of a wimpling wing
In his ecstasy! then off, off forth on swing,   5
  As a skate's heel sweeps smooth on a bow-bend: the hurl
    and gliding

---

1. In a letter to Robert Bridges (January 4, 1883), Hopkins says: "I mean foil in its sense of leaf or tinsel, and no other word whatever will give the effect I want. Shaken goldfoil gives off broad glares like sheet lightning and also, and this is true of nothing else, owing to its zigzag dints and crossings and network of small many cornered facets, a sort of fork lightning too."

2. "A name for the kestrel [a species of small hawk], from its habit of hovering or hanging with its head to the wind" [O.E.D.].

Rebuffed the big wind. My heart in hiding
Stirred for a bird,—the achieve of, the mastery of the thing!

Brute beauty and valour and act, oh, air, pride, plume, here
    Buckle!³ AND the fire that breaks from thee then, a billion   10
Times told lovelier, more dangerous, O my chevalier!

    No wonder of it; shéer plód makes plough down sillion
Shine, and blue-bleak embers, ah my dear,
    Fall, gall themselves, and gash gold-vermilion.
1877   *1918*

Spring and Fall

To a Young Child

Márgarét, áre you gríeving
Over Goldengrove unleaving?
Leáves, líke the things of man, you
With your fresh thoughts care for, can you?
Áh! ás the heart grows older   5
It will come to such sights colder
By and by, nor spare a sigh
Though worlds of wanwood leafmeal lie;
And yet you *will* weep and know why.
Now no matter, child, the name: 10
Sórrow's spríngs áre the same.
Nor mouth had, no nor mind, expressed
What heart heard of, ghost guessed:
It ís the blight man was born for,
It is Margaret you mourn for.   15
1880   *1918*

---

3. "Buckle" can be understood two ways: either the elements in line 9 are fastened together as if by a buckle, or they crumble as a support might buckle. The verb also can be read as an indicative or an imperative, as if the speaker were either describing an action or commanding it.

A. E. (Alfred Edward) Housman
1859–1936

Housman was tormented for years by his love for his college room-
mate and close friend, Moses Jackson. When Jackson went to India
to make his fortune and marry, Housman transferred his affections
to Jackson's brother, who died unexpectedly. This event might have
triggered Housman's burst of creative energy in the mid-1890s,
which produced all of these poems. The speaker in these poems is
Terence Hearsay, a youth from Shropshire, a county that figures in
the English imagination the way the states Iowa or Nebraska might
in the American. "1887" commemorates the fiftieth anniversary of
Queen Victoria's reign, and its apparent endorsement of Empire
made Housman's book popular when England went to war against
the Boers in South Africa. English soldiers dead in the foreign fields
had these poems buttoned in their pockets. Housman was an athe-
ist, as "The Immortal Part" suggests, which calls into question the
advice Terence gives in "To An Athlete Dying Young" and "Shot? So
Quick, So Clean an Ending?" (Housman wrote these about the
same time that Oscar Wilde was convicted of homosexuality in a
sensational trial and sentenced to two years of hard labor, which
makes Terence's approval of the suicide more understandable.) These
celebrations of the dead should be read in the context of "Terence,
This Is Stupid Stuff . . . ," which suggests that the speaker might
not be entirely sincere.

1887

From Clee to heaven the beacon burns,
   The shires have seen it plain,
From north and south the sign returns
   And beacons burn again.

Look left, look right, the hills are bright,   5
   The dales are light between,
Because 'tis fifty years to-night
   That God has saved the Queen.

Now, when the flame they watch not towers
    About the soil they trod,   10
Lads, we'll remember friends of ours
    Who shared the work with God.

To skies that knit their heartstrings right,
    To fields that bred them brave,
The saviours come not home to-night: 15
    Themselves they could not save.

It dawns in Asia, tombstones show
    And Shropshire names are read;
And the Nile spills his overflow
    Beside the Severn's[1] dead.   20

We pledge in peace by farm and town
    The Queen they served in war,
And fire the beacons up and down
    The land they perished for.

"God save the Queen" we living sing,   25
    From height to height 'tis heard;
And with the rest your voices ring,
    Lads of the Fifty-third.

Oh, God will save her, fear you not:
    Be you the men you've been,   30
Get you the sons your fathers got,
    And God will save the Queen.

1896

1. The Severn River divides England from Wales.

To an Athlete Dying Young

The time you won your town the race
We chaired you through the market-place;
Man and boy stood cheering by,
And home we brought you shoulder-high.

Today, the road all runners come,   5
Shoulder-high we bring you home,
And set you at your threshold down,
Townsman of a stiller town.

Smart lad, to slip betimes away
From fields where glory does not stay   10
And early though the laurel grows
It withers quicker than the rose.

Eyes the shady night has shut
Cannot see the record cut,
And silence sounds no worse than cheers   15
After earth has stopped the ears:

Now you will not swell the rout
Of lads that wore their honours out,
Runners whom renown outran
And the name died before the man.   20

So set, before its echoes fade,
The fleet foot on the sill of shade,
And hold to the low lintel up
The still-defended challenge-cup.

And round that early-laurelled head   25
Will flock to gaze the strengthless dead,
And find unwithered on its curls
The garland briefer than a girl's.

1896

The Immortal Part

When I meet the morning beam,
Or lay me down at night to dream,
I hear my bones within me say,
"Another night, another day.

"When shall this slough of sense be cast,   5
This dust of thoughts be laid at last,
The man of flesh and soul be slain
And the man of bone remain?

"This tongue that talks, these lungs that shout,
These thews that hustle us about,   10
This brain that fills the skull with schemes,
And its humming hive of dreams,—

"These to-day are proud in power
And lord it in their little hour:
The immortal bones obey control   15
Of dying flesh and dying soul.

" 'Tis long till eve and morn are gone:
Slow the endless night comes on,
And late to fulness grows the birth
That shall last as long as earth.   20

"Wanderers eastward, wanderers west,
Know you why you cannot rest?
'Tis that every mother's son
Travails with a skeleton.

"Lie down in the bed of dust;   25
Bear the fruit that bear you must;
Bring the eternal seed to light,
And morn is all the same as night.

"Rest you so from trouble sore,
Fear the heat o' the sun no more,   30
Nor the snowing winter wild,
Now you labor not with child.

"Empty vessel, garment cast,
We that wore you long shall last.
—Another night, another day."   35
So my bones within me say.

Therefore they shall do my will
To-day while I am master still,
And flesh and soul, now both are strong,
Shall hale the sullen slaves along,   40

Before this fire of sense decay,
This smoke of thought blow clean away,
And leave with ancient night alone
The stedfast and enduring bone.

1896

Shot? So quick, so clean an ending?

Shot? so quick, so clean an ending?
   Oh that was right, lad, that was brave:
Yours was not an ill for mending,
   'Twas best to take it to the grave.

Oh you had forethought, you could reason,   5
   And saw your road and where it led,
And early wise and brave in season
   Put the pistol to your head.

Oh soon, and better so than later
   After long disgrace and scorn,   10
You shot dead the household traitor,
   The soul that should not have been born.

Right you guessed the rising morrow
  And scorned to tread the mire you must:
Dust's your wages, son of sorrow,   15
  But men may come to worse than dust.

Souls undone, undoing others,—
  Long time since the tale began.
You would not live to wrong your brothers:
  Oh lad, you died as fits a man.   20

Now to your grave shall friend and stranger
  With ruth and some with envy come:
Undishonoured, clear of danger,
  Clean of guilt, pass hence and home.

Turn safe to rest, no dreams, no waking;   25
  And here, man, here's the wreath I've made.
'Tis not a gift that's worth the taking,
  But wear it and it will not fade.

                                          1896

"Terence, this is stupid stuff . . ."

  "Terence, this is stupid stuff:
You eat your victuals fast enough;
There can't be much amiss, 'tis clear,
To see the rate you drink your beer.
But oh, good Lord, the verse you make,   5
It gives a chap the belly-ache.
The cow, the old cow, she is dead;
It sleeps well, the hornéd head:
We poor lads, 'tis our turn now
To hear such tunes as killed the cow.   10
Pretty friendship 'tis to rhyme
Your friends to death before their time
Moping melancholy mad:
Come, pipe a tune to dance to, lad."

Why, if 'tis dancing you would be,   15
There's brisker pipes than poetry.
Say, for what were hop-yards meant,
Or why was Burton built on Trent?
Oh many a peer of England brews
Livelier liquor than the Muse,   20
And malt does more than Milton can
To justify God's ways to man.
Ale, man, ale's the stuff to drink
For fellows whom it hurts to think:
Look into the pewter pot   25
To see the world as the world's not.
And faith, 'tis pleasant till 'tis past:
The mischief is that 'twill not last.
Oh I have been to Ludlow fair
And left my necktie God knows where,   30
And carried halfway home, or near,
Pints and quarts of Ludlow beer:
Then the world seemed none so bad,
And I myself a sterling lad;
And down in lovely muck I've lain,   35
Happy till I woke again.
Then I saw the morning sky:
Heigho, the tale was all a lie;
The world, it was the old world yet,
I was I, my things were wet,   40
And nothing now remained to do
But begin the game anew.

Therefore, since the world has still
Much good, but much less good than ill,
And while the sun and moon endure   45
Luck's a chance, but trouble's sure,
I'd face it as a wise man would,
And train for ill and not for good.
'Tis true, the stuff I bring for sale
Is not so brisk a brew as ale: 50
Out of a stem that scored the hand

I wrung it in a weary land.
But take it: if the smack is sour,
The better for the embittered hour;
It should do good to heart and head   55
When your soul is in my soul's stead;
And I will friend you, if I may,
In the dark and cloudy day.

    There was a king reigned in the East:
There, when kings will sit to feast,   60
They get their fill before they think
With poisoned meat and poisoned drink.
He gathered all that springs to birth
From the many-venomed earth;
First a little, thence to more,   65
He sampled all her killing store;
And easy, smiling, seasoned sound,
Sate the king when healths went round.
They put arsenic in his meat
And stared aghast to watch him eat;   70
They poured strychnine in his cup
And shook to see him drink it up:
They shook, they stared as white's their shirt:
Them it was their poison hurt.
—I tell the tale that I heard told.   75
Mithridates, he died old.[1]

                                        1896

---

1. In the first century B.C.E., King Mithridates VI took small doses of poison until he de-
veloped an immunity to it.

Langston Hughes
1902–1967

> *Not long after he graduated from high school, Hughes published "The Negro Speaks of Rivers" in the political magazine* The Crisis. *The poem counters white views of blacks as a primitive race without history by linking African Americans to ancient black civilizations. Hughes went to Columbia University, where he began meeting the leaders of the Harlem Renaissance, a movement among African American artists in literature, music, painting, dance, and the like. In 1926, at just twenty-four years old, Hughes published an essay in the widely circulated, leftist paper* The Nation, *which argued that African Americans should create a "racial art." That concept was controversial in the 1920s because many intellectuals, black and white, thought that subcultures should dissolve themselves in the American mainstream. "Harlem" and "Theme for English B" came much later in Hughes's career, after he had established himself as one of America's most successful poets, but both illustrate what he called for in 1926. Hughes wanted these and the other poems in* Montage of a Dream Deferred *(1951) to express contemporary Harlem by borrowing from the "current of Afro-American popular music . . . jazz, ragtime, swing, blues, boogie-woogie, and bebop."*

The Negro Speaks of Rivers

(To W. E. B. Du Bois)[1]

I've known rivers:
I've known rivers ancient as the world and older than the
    flow of human blood in human veins.
My soul has grown deep like the rivers.

---

1. (1868–1963); American historian, educator, and activist; one of the founders of the NAACP.

I bathed in the Euphrates when dawns were young.
I built my hut near the Congo and it lulled me to sleep.   5
I looked upon the Nile and raised the pyramids above it.
I heard the singing of the Mississippi when Abe Lincoln
      went down to New Orleans, and I've seen its muddy
      bosom turn all golden in the sunset.

I've known rivers:
Ancient, dusky rivers.

My soul has grown deep like the rivers.   10

1926

Harlem

What happens to a dream deferred?

Does it dry up
like a raisin in the sun?
Or fester like a sore—
And then run?   5
Does it stink like rotten meat?
Or crust and sugar over—
like a syrupy sweet?

Maybe it just sags
like a heavy load.   10

Or does it explode?

1951

Theme for English B

The instructor said,

> *Go home and write*
> *a page tonight.*
> *And let that page come out of you—*
> *Then, it will be true.*   5

I wonder if it's that simple?
I am twenty-two, colored, born in Winston-Salem.
I went to school there, then Durham, then here
to this college on the hill above Harlem.
I am the only colored student in my class.   10
The steps from the hill lead down into Harlem,
through a park, then I cross St. Nicholas,
Eighth Avenue, Seventh, and I come to the Y,
the Harlem Branch Y, where I take the elevator
up to my room, sit down, and write this page: 15

It's not easy to know what is true for you or me
at twenty-two, my age. But I guess I'm what
I feel and see and hear, Harlem, I hear you:
hear you, hear me—we two—you, me, talk on this page.
(I hear New York, too.) Me—who?   20
Well, I like to eat, sleep, drink, and be in love.
I like to work, read, learn, and understand life.
I like a pipe for a Christmas present,
or records—Bessie,[2] bop, or Bach.
I guess being colored doesn't make me *not* like   25
the same things other folks like who are other races.
So will my page be colored that I write?
Being me, it will not be white.
But it will be
a part of you, instructor.   30

2. Bessie Smith (1894?–1937), American blues singer.

You are white—
yet a part of me, as I am a part of you.
That's American.
Sometimes perhaps you don't want to be a part of me.
Nor do I often want to be a part of you.   35
But we are, that's true!
I guess you learn from me—
although you're older—and white—
and somewhat more free.

This is my page for English B.   40

1951

Randall Jarrell
1914–1965

> In 1942 Jarrell joined the Army Air Force and spent World War II
> teaching celestial navigation to flyers in Arizona. During these
> years, he wrote "The Death of the Ball Turret Gunner," which he
> published in 1945. Jarrell explained that the machine gunner in
> the plexiglass sphere attached to the underside of a World War II
> bomber reminded him of a fetus still in its mother's womb. The
> hose in the last line, Jarrell noted, would have been a steam hose.

The Death of the Ball Turret Gunner

From my mother's sleep I fell into the State,
And I hunched in its belly till my wet fur froze.
Six miles from earth, loosed from its dream of life,
I woke to black flak and the nightmare fighters.
When I died they washed me out of the turret with a hose.   5

1945

Ben Jonson

1572–1637

> Jonson, a colleague of Shakespeare, gathered around himself England's first "school" of literature, the Cavaliers, characterized by their classical learning and frank, playful treatment of sexual themes, a direct challenge to the Puritan ethic of seventeenth-century England. "Song: To Celia" is a translation stitched together from various parts of the Epistles of Philostratus, an ancient Greek philosopher. The key to the poem is how the speaker (and you) interpret the symbolic action in lines 9–16. "On My First Daughter" and "On My First Son" are epitaphs: poems that might have been carved on tombstones. We do not know if Jonson really had a daughter, but his son, Benjamin ("child of the right hand" is what the name means in Hebrew), died in 1603 on his seventh birthday.

Song: To Celia

Drink to me only with thine eyes,
And I will pledge with mine;
Or leave a kiss but in the cup,
And I'll not look for wine.
The thirst that from the soul doth rise,   5
Doth ask a drink divine:
But might I of Jove's nectar sup,
I would not change for thine.
I sent thee late a rosy wreath,
Not so much honoring thee,   10
As giving it a hope, that there
It could not withered be.
But thou thereon did'st only breathe,
And sent'st it back to me;
Since when it grows and smells, I swear,   15
Not of itself, but thee.

1616

On My First Daughter

Here lies, to each her parents' ruth,
Mary, the daughter of their youth;
Yet all heaven's gifts being heaven's due,
It makes the father less to rue.
At six months' end she parted hence   5
With safety of her innocence;
Whose soul heaven's queen, whose name she bears,
In comfort of her mother's tears,
Hath placed amongst her virgin-train:
Where, while that severed doth remain,[1]   10
This grave partakes the fleshly birth;
Which cover lightly, gentle earth!

1616

On My First Son

Farewell, thou child of my right hand, and joy;
My sin was too much hope of thee, loved boy:
Seven years thou wert lent to me, and I thee pay,
Exacted by thy fate, on the just day.
O could I lose all father now! for why   5
Will man lament the state he should envỳ,
To have so soon 'scaped world's and flesh's rage,
And, if no other misery, yet age?
Rest in soft peace, and asked, say, "Here doth lie
Ben Jonson his best piece of poetry."   10
For whose sake henceforth all his vows be such
As what he loves may never like too much.

1616

---

1. The severing of the soul from the body is only temporary, according to orthodoxy. They will reunite at the end of time.

John Keats

1795–1821

> *One evening in October 1816, the twenty-one-year-old Keats stayed*
> *up late with his former teacher reading George Chapman's trans-*
> *lation of Homer. The vigor of the Elizabethan poetry astonished*
> *Keats, who had known Homer only through Alexander Pope's for-*
> *mal, abstract translations. After walking home at dawn, Keats*
> *wrote "On First Looking into Chapman's Homer" in about an hour*
> *and sent it to his teacher, who found the Petrarchan sonnet waiting*
> *for him at breakfast. Sir William Herschel's discovery of Uranus in*
> *1781 probably inspired the first simile in the sestet. In the second*
> *simile, Keats confused Cortez with Balboa, who was the first Euro-*
> *pean to see the Pacific Ocean. The foreboding of his own death ex-*
> *pressed in "When I Have Fears," written in January 1818, intensified*
> *later that year, when Keats nursed his younger brother through the*
> *final stages of tuberculosis. Then came the great burst of writing that*
> *produced the other poems here. In them you can trace Keats's evolv-*
> *ing attitude toward death: first "La Belle Dame sans Merci"; then*
> *"Ode to a Nightingale" and "Ode on a Grecian Urn," written*
> *about the same time; finally "To Autumn." "La Belle Dame sans*
> *Merci," a pseudo-medieval poem, means "The beautiful woman*
> *without pity." The nightingale is a conventional symbol of immor-*
> *tality. Inside the Grecian urn, perhaps, are the cremated remains of*
> *a person; on its outside are the scenes described in the first four stan-*
> *zas of the poem. Autumn, of course, is a conventional symbol for the*
> *end of life; in this poem Keats may be reconciling himself to death.*

On First Looking into Chapman's Homer

Much have I traveled in the realms of gold,
  And many goodly states and kingdoms seen;
  Round many western islands have I been
Which bards in fealty to Apollo[1] hold.
Oft of one wide expanse had I been told   5
  That deep-browed Homer ruled as his demesne;[2]

---

1. God of poetic inspiration.

Yet did I never breathe its pure serene
Till I heard Chapman speak out loud and bold:
Then felt I like some watcher of the skies
    When a new planet swims into his ken;   10
Or like stout Cortez when with eagle eyes
    He stared at the Pacific—and all his men
Looked at each other with a wild surmise—
    Silent, upon a peak in Darien.

1816

When I Have Fears

When I have fears that I may cease to be
    Before my pen has gleaned my teeming brain,
Before high-piléd books, in charact'ry,
    Hold like rich garners the full-ripened grain;
When I behold, upon the night's starred face,   5
    Huge cloudy symbols of a high romance,
And think that I may never live to trace
    Their shadows, with the magic hand of chance;
And when I feel, fair creature of an hour,
    That I shall never look upon thee more,   10
Never have relish in the faery power
    Of unreflecting love!—then on the shore
Of the wide world I stand alone, and think
Till Love and Fame to nothingness do sink.
1818   *1848*

La Belle Dame sans Merci

O what can ail thee, Knight at arms,
    Alone and palely loitering?
The sedge has withered from the Lake
    And no birds sing!

2. I.e., domain.

O what can ail thee, Knight at arms,   5
    So haggard, and so woebegone?
The squirrel's granary is full
    And the harvest's done.

I see a lily on thy brow
    With anguish moist and fever dew,   10
And on thy cheeks a fading rose
    Fast withereth too.

"I met a Lady in the Meads,
    Full beautiful, a faery's child,
Her hair was long, her foot was light   15
    And her eyes were wild.

"I made a Garland for her head,
    And bracelets too, and fragrant Zone;[3]
She looked at me as she did love
    And made sweet moan.   20

"I set her on my pacing steed
    And nothing else saw all day long,
For sidelong would she bend and sing
    A faery's song.

"She found me roots of relish sweet,   25
    And honey wild, and manna dew,
And sure in language strange she said
    'I love thee true.'

"She took me to her elfin grot
    And there she wept and sighed full sore,   30
And there I shut her wild wild eyes
    With kisses four.

---

3. I.e., girdle.

"And there she lulléd me asleep,
 And there I dreamed, Ah Woe betide!
The latest dream I ever dreamt   35
 On the cold hill side.

"I saw pale Kings, and Princes too,
 Pale warriors, death-pale were they all;
They cried, 'La belle dame sans merci
 Hath thee in thrall!'   40

"I saw their starved lips in the gloam
 With horrid warning gapéd wide,
And I awoke, and found me here
 On the cold hill's side.

"And this is why I sojourn here,   45
 Alone and palely loitering;
Though the sedge is withered from the Lake
 And no birds sing."

          1820

Ode to a Nightingale

I

My heart aches, and a drowsy numbness pains
 My sense, as though of hemlock I had drunk,
Or emptied some dull opiate to the drains
 One minute past, and Lethe-wards[4] had sunk:
'Tis not through envy of thy happy lot,   5
 But being too happy in thine happiness—
  That thou, light-wingéd Dryad of the trees,
   In some melodious plot
 Of beechen green, and shadows numberless,
  Singest of summer in full-throated ease. 10

---

4. Toward the river Lethe, whose waters in Hades bring the dead forgetfulness.

2

O, for a draught of vintage! that hath been
  Cooled a long age in the deep-delvéd earth,
Tasting of Flora and the country green,
  Dance, and Provençal song, and sunburnt mirth!
O for a beaker full of the warm South,   15
  Full of the true, the blushful Hippocrene,[5]
    With beaded bubbles winking at the brim,
      And purple-stainéd mouth;
  That I might drink, and leave the world unseen,
    And with thee fade away into the forest dim: 20

3

Fade far away, dissolve, and quite forget
  What thou among the leaves hast never known,
The weariness, the fever, and the fret
  Here, where men sit and hear each other groan;
Where palsy shakes a few, sad, last gray hairs,   25
  Where youth grows pale, and specter-thin, and dies,
    Where but to think is to be full of sorrow
      And leaden-eyed despairs,
  Where Beauty cannot keep her lustrous eyes,
    Or new Love pine at them beyond tomorrow.   30

4

Away! away! for I will fly to thee,
  Not charioted by Bacchus and his pards,[6]
But on the viewless wings of Poesy,
  Though the dull brain perplexes and retards:
Already with thee! tender is the night,   35
  And haply the Queen-Moon is on her throne,

5. The fountain of the Muses (goddesses of poetry and the arts) on Mt. Helicon in Greece; its waters inspire poets.

6. "Bacchus": god of wine, often depicted in a chariot drawn by leopards ("pards").

Clustered around by all her starry Fays;
   But here there is no light,
Save what from heaven is with the breezes blown
   Through verdurous glooms and winding mossy ways.   40

5

I cannot see what flowers are at my feet,
   Nor what soft incense hangs upon the boughs,
But, in embalméd darkness, guess each sweet
   Wherewith the seasonable month endows
The grass, the thicket, and the fruit tree wild;   45
   White hawthorn, and the pastoral eglantine;
     Fast fading violets covered up in leaves;
      And mid-May's eldest child,
The coming musk-rose, full of dewy wine,
   The murmurous haunt of flies on summer eves.   50

6

Darkling I listen; and for many a time
   I have been half in love with easeful Death,
Called him soft names in many a muséd rhyme,
   To take into the air my quiet breath;
Now more than ever seems it rich to die,   55
   To cease upon the midnight with no pain,
     While thou art pouring forth thy soul abroad
      In such an ecstasy!
Still wouldst thou sing, and I have ears in vain—
   To thy high requiem become a sod.   60

7

Thou wast not born for death, immortal Bird!
   No hungry generations tread thee down;
The voice I hear this passing night was heard
   In ancient days by emperor and clown:

Perhaps the selfsame song that found a path   65
   Through the sad heart of Ruth,[7] when, sick for home,
     She stood in tears amid the alien corn;
       The same that ofttimes hath
Charmed magic casements, opening on the foam
   Of perilous seas, in faery lands forlorn.   70

8

Forlorn! the very word is like a bell
   To toll me back from thee to my sole self!
Adieu! the fancy cannot cheat so well
   As she is famed to do, deceiving elf.
Adieu! adieu! thy plaintive anthem fades   75
   Past the near meadows, over the still stream,
     Up the hill side; and now 'tis buried deep
       In the next valley-glades:
   Was it a vision, or a waking dream?
     Fled is that music:—Do I wake or sleep?   80

1820

Ode on a Grecian Urn

I

Thou still unravished bride of quietness,
   Thou foster child of silence and slow time,
Sylvan historian, who canst thus express
   A flowery tale more sweetly than our rhyme:
What leaf-fringed legend haunts about thy shape   5
   Of deities or mortals, or of both,
     In Tempe or the dales of Arcady?[8]
   What men or gods are these? What maidens loath?

---

7. In the Old Testament, a woman of great loyalty and modesty who, as a stranger in Judah, won a husband while gleaning in the barley fields ("the alien corn," line 67).

8. The Greeks considered Tempe and Arcadia to be perfect examples of rural landscapes.

What mad pursuit? What struggle to escape?
　　What pipes and timbrels? What wild ecstasy?　　　　10

2

Heard melodies are sweet, but those unheard
　　Are sweeter; therefore, ye soft pipes, play on;
Not to the sensual ear, but, more endeared,
　　Pipe to the spirit ditties of no tone:
Fair youth, beneath the trees, thou canst not leave　　　15
　　Thy song, nor ever can those trees be bare;
　　　Bold Lover, never, never canst thou kiss,
Though winning near the goal—yet, do not grieve;
　　She cannot fade, though thou hast not thy bliss,
　　Forever wilt thou love, and she be fair!　　　　20

3

Ah, happy, happy boughs! that cannot shed
　　Your leaves, nor ever bid the Spring adieu;
And, happy melodist, unweariéd,
　　Forever piping songs forever new;
More happy love! more happy, happy love!　　　　25
　　Forever warm and still to be enjoyed,
　　　Forever panting, and forever young;
All breathing human passion far above,
　　That leaves a heart high-sorrowful and cloyed,
　　　A burning forehead, and a parching tongue.　　　30

4

Who are these coming to the sacrifice?
　　To what green altar, O mysterious priest,
Lead'st thou that heifer lowing at the skies,
　　And all her silken flanks with garlands dressed?
What little town by river or sea shore,　　　　35
　　Or mountain-built with peaceful citadel,
　　　Is emptied of this folk, this pious morn?

And, little town, thy streets forevermore
    Will silent be; and not a soul to tell
        Why thou art desolate, can e'er return.   40

5

O Attic[9] shape! Fair attitude! with brede[1]
    Of marble men and maidens overwrought,
With forest branches and the trodden weed;
    Thou, silent form, dost tease us out of thought
As doth eternity: Cold Pastoral!   45
    When old age shall this generation waste,
        Thou shalt remain, in midst of other woe
    Than ours, a friend to man, to whom thou say'st,
"Beauty is truth, truth beauty,"—that is all
    Ye know on earth, and all ye need to know.   50

                                                              1820

To Autumn

1

Season of mists and mellow fruitfulness,
    Close bosom-friend of the maturing sun;
Conspiring with him how to load and bless
    With fruit the vines that round the thatch-eaves run;
To bend with apples the mossed cottage-trees,   5
    And fill all fruit with ripeness to the core;
        To swell the gourd, and plump the hazel shells
    With a sweet kernel; to set budding more,
And still more, later flowers for the bees,
Until they think warm days will never cease,   10
        For Summer has o'er-brimmed their clammy cells.

---

9. Greek, especially Athenian.   1. I.e., woven pattern.

2

Who hath not seen thee oft amid thy store?
    Sometimes whoever seeks abroad may find
Thee sitting careless on a granary floor,
    Thy hair soft-lifted by the winnowing wind;   15
Or on a half-reaped furrow sound asleep,
    Drowsed with the fume of poppies, while thy hook
        Spares the next swath and all its twinéd flowers:
And sometimes like a gleaner thou dost keep
    Steady thy laden head across a brook;   20
    Or by a cider-press, with patient look,
        Thou watchest the last oozings hours by hours.

3

Where are the songs of Spring? Aye, where are they?
    Think not of them, thou hast thy music too—
While barréd clouds bloom the soft-dying day,   25
    And touch the stubble-plains with rosy hue;
Then in a wailful choir the small gnats mourn
    Among the river sallows, borne aloft
        Or sinking as the light wind lives or dies;
And full-grown lambs loud bleat from hilly bourn;   30
    Hedge crickets sing; and now with treble soft
    The redbreast whistles from a garden-croft;
        And gathering swallows twitter in the skies.

                                                    1820

Galway Kinnell
1927–

> *Kinnell is known for both his political poetry, which addresses the*
> *destructive capacity of technology, and for poems that explore the*
> *natural world on a number of levels. The selection here, "Black-*
> *berry Eating," literally describes eating blackberries right off the*
> *vine. But lines 9–13 compare the blackberries to "certain peculiar*

words" and, presumably, eating the blackberries is like writing a
poem with these words. Carrying out the logic of this analogy leads
to some interesting questions: Why would writing poems with
words like "strengths" and "squinched" be a "black art"? And why
are these long, monosyllabic words "black language"? What's the
meaning of the thorns? Is this poem itself an example of "black art"?

Blackberry Eating

I love to go out in late September
among the fat, overripe, icy, black blackberries
to eat blackberries for breakfast,
the stalks very prickly, a penalty
they earn for knowing the black art   5
of blackberry making; and as I stand among them
lifting the stalks to my mouth, the ripest berries
fall almost unbidden to my tongue,
as words sometimes do, certain peculiar words
like *strengths* or *squinched* or *broughamed*,   10
many-lettered, one-syllabled lumps,
which I squeeze, squinch open, and splurge well
in the silent, startled, icy, black language
of blackberry eating in late September.

                                                        1980

Yusef Komunyakaa
1947–

Komunyakaa was an army correspondent during the Vietnam War.
The speaker in "Facing It" is visiting the Vietnam Veterans Memo-
rial in Washington, D.C., two long, low arms of polished black gran-
ite on which are engraved the names of the American dead. Compare
the African American speaker's reflection in the granite to the white
veteran's image, which floats toward the speaker. "We Never Know"
describes in disturbingly sexual terms the experience of killing some-
one. The speaker is an American soldier; the dead man is either

North Vietnamese or a Viet Cong soldier. To make sense of this poem,
you might determine how this experience has affected the American.

Facing It

My black face fades,
hiding inside the black granite.
I said I wouldn't,
dammit: No tears.
I'm stone. I'm flesh.   5
My clouded reflection eyes me
like a bird of prey, the profile of night
slanted against morning. I turn
this way—the stone lets me go.
I turn that way—I'm inside   10
the Vietnam Veterans Memorial
again, depending on the light
to make a difference.
I go down the 58,022 names,
half-expecting to find   15
my own in letters like smoke.
I touch the name Andrew Johnson;
I see the booby trap's white flash.
Names shimmer on a woman's blouse
but when she walks away   20
the names stay on the wall.
Brushstrokes flash, a red bird's
wings cutting across my stare.
The sky. A plane in the sky.
A white vet's image floats   25
closer to me, then his pale eyes
look through mine. I'm a window.
He's lost his right arm
inside the stone. In the black mirror
a woman's trying to erase names: 30
No, she's brushing a boy's hair.

                            1988

We Never Know

He danced with tall grass
for a moment, like he was swaying
with a woman. Our gun barrels
glowed white-hot.
When I got to him,   5
a blue halo
of flies had already claimed him.
I pulled the crumbled photograph
from his fingers.
There's no other way   10
to say this: I fell in love.
The morning cleared again,
except for a distant mortar
& somewhere choppers taking off.
I slid the wallet into his pocket   15
& turned him over, so he wouldn't be
kissing the ground.

1988

Maxine Kumin

1925–

> *Kumin won the Pulitzer Prize in 1973 for* Up Country: Poems of
> New England, *her fourth book of poems, which included "Wood-
> chucks." The first group of poems in the book was inspired by her
> property in rural New Hampshire. She creates the persona of the
> hermit, the person fleeing human society and, like Henry David
> Thoreau, taking up residence among the plants and animals of a
> country place. The speaker in "Woodchucks" is all the more surpris-
> ing given the cluster of nature-loving poems within which it dwells.*

Woodchucks — Caddy Shack

Gassing the woodchucks didn't turn out right.
The knockout bomb from the Feed and Grain Exchange
was featured as merciful, quick at the bone
and the case we had against them was airtight,
both exits shoehorned shut with puddingstone,   5
but they had a sub-sub-basement out of range.

1) Varmitt
2) menace to society

Next morning they turned up again, no worse
for the cyanide than we for our cigarettes
and state-store Scotch, all of us up to scratch.
They brought down the marigolds as a matter of course
and then took over the vegetable patch   10
nipping the broccoli shoots, beheading the carrots.

3) Hairry member of the RAT Family

The food from our mouths, I said, righteously thrilling
to the feel of the .22, the bullets' neat noses.
I, a lapsed pacifist fallen from grace   15
puffed with Darwinian pieties for killing,
now drew a bead on the littlest woodchuck's face.
He died down in the everbearing roses.

Ten minutes later I dropped the mother. She
flipflopped in the air and fell, her needle teeth   20
still hooked in a leaf of early Swiss chard.
Another baby next. O one-two-three
the murderer inside me rose up hard,
the hawkeye killer came on stage forthwith.

There's one chuck left. Old wily fellow, he keeps   25
me cocked and ready day after day after day.
All night I hunt his humped-up form. I dream
I sight along the barrel in my sleep.
If only they'd all consented to die unseen
gassed underground the quiet Nazi way.   30

1973

Philip Larkin
1922–1985

Larkin was part of a wave of English writers who, in the 1950s and after, reacted against modernists like T. S. Eliot and Ezra Pound and strove to write in an easier, less academic style. An "aubade" celebrates the coming of dawn, but clearly Larkin uses the term ironically, since the coming of another sunrise terrifies the speaker. You might consider why this fear leads to indecision, as the speaker declares in the fourth stanza. The theme of this poem is the particular concern of existentialist philosophers who were burdened by the terrible experience of World War II. But ever since Darwin first suggested we shared an ancestor with apes, many men and women have had to confront and somehow resolve the dilemma explored here.

Aubade

I work all day, and get half-drunk at night.
Waking at four to soundless dark, I stare.
In time the curtain-edges will grow light.
Till then I see what's really always there:
Unresting death, a whole day nearer now,   5
Making all thought impossible but how
And where and when I shall myself die.
Arid interrogation: yet the dread
Of dying, and being dead,
Flashes afresh to hold and horrify.   10

The mind blanks at the glare. Not in remorse
—The good not done, the love not given, time
Torn off unused—nor wretchedly because
An only life can take so long to climb
Clear of its wrong beginnings, and may never;   15
But at the total emptiness for ever,
The sure extinction that we travel to
And shall be lost in always. Not to be here,

Not to be anywhere,
And soon; nothing more terrible, nothing more true.   20

This is a special way of being afraid
No trick dispels. Religion used to try,
That vast moth-eaten musical brocade
Created to pretend we never die,
And specious stuff that says *No rational being*   25
Can fear a thing it will not feel, not seeing
That this is what we fear—no sight, no sound,
No touch or taste or smell, nothing to think with,
Nothing to love or link with,
The anaesthetic from which none come round.   30

And so it stays just on the edge of vision,
A small unfocused blur, a standing chill
That slows each impulse down to indecision.
Most things may never happen: this one will,   — death
And realisation of it rages out   35
In furnace-fear when we are caught without
People or drink. Courage is no good:
It means not scaring others. Being brave
Lets no one off the grave.
Death is no different whined at than withstood.   40

Slowly light strengthens, and the room takes shape.
It stands plain as a wardrobe, what we know,
Have always known, know that we can't escape,
Yet can't accept. One side will have to go.
Meanwhile telephones crouch, getting ready to ring   45
In locked-up offices, and all the uncaring
Intricate rented world begins to rouse.
The sky is white as clay, with no sun.
Work has to be done.
Postmen like doctors go from house to house.   50

1977

Li-Young Lee
1957–

>   Lee combines a variety of traditions, from Chinese poetry to Walt
>   Whitman, to whom he is often compared. For the Chinese influ-
>   ence, you might compare the concluding stanzas of "Visions and
>   Interpretations" to Pound's translation of the Chinese poem "The
>   River-Merchant's Wife." Despite this affinity with old forms, "Vi-
>   sions and Interpretations" is one of the few examples of postmodern
>   poetry in this volume. One of the poem's main concerns is the na-
>   ture of poetry and its relation to real experience. This poem is,
>   among other things, about writing poems. "The Gift" is an excel-
>   lent example of the emotive power of simple diction and mundane
>   incident. Among the poem's striking features is the juxtaposition of
>   a son's love for his father with a husband's love for his wife.

Visions and Interpretations

Because this graveyard is a hill,
I must climb up to see my dead,
stopping once midway to rest
beside this tree.

It was here, between the anticipation   5
of exhaustion, and exhaustion,
between vale and peak,
my father came down to me

and we climbed arm in arm to the top.
He cradled the bouquet I'd brought,   10
and I, a good son, never mentioned his grave,
erect like a door behind him.

And it was here, one summer day, I sat down
to read an old book. When I looked up
from the noon-lit page, I saw a vision   15
of a world about to come, and a world about to go.

Truth is, I've not seen my father
since he died, and, no, the dead
do not walk arm in arm with me.

If I carry flowers to them, I do so without their help,   20
the blossoms not always bright, torch-like,
but often heavy as sodden newspaper.

Truth is, I came here with my son one day,
and we rested against this tree,
and I fell asleep, and dreamed   25

a dream which, upon my boy waking me, I told.
Neither of us understood.
Then we went up.

Even this is not accurate.
Let me begin again: 30

Between two griefs, a tree.
Between my hands, white chrysanthemums, yellow
    chrysanthemums.

The old book I finished reading
I've since read again and again.

And what was far grows near,   35
and what is near grows more dear,

and all of my visions and interpretations
depend on what I see,

and between my eyes is always
the rain, the migrant rain.   40

1986

The Gift

To pull the metal splinter from my palm
my father recited a story in a low voice.
I watched his lovely face and not the blade.
Before the story ended, he'd removed
the iron sliver I thought I'd die from.   5

I can't remember the tale,
but hear his voice still, a well
of dark water, a prayer.
And I recall his hands,
two measures of tenderness   10
he laid against my face,
the flames of discipline
he raised above my head.

Had you entered that afternoon
you would have thought you saw a man   15
planting something in a boy's palm,
a silver tear, a tiny flame.
Had you followed that boy
you would have arrived here,
where I bend over my wife's right hand.   20

Look how I shave her thumbnail down
so carefully she feels no pain.
Watch as I lift the splinter out.
I was seven when my father
took my hand like this,   25
and I did not hold that shard
between my fingers and think,
Metal that will bury me,
christen it Little Assassin,
Ore Going Deep for My Heart.   30
And I did not lift up my wound and cry,

Death visited here!
I did what a child does
when he's given something to keep.
I kissed my father.   35
                              1986

Robert Lowell
1917–1977

> *"Skunk Hour" contrasts the human and natural worlds in Castine,*
> *Maine, where Lowell had a summer residence. He composed it in*
> *the summer of 1957, after Elizabeth Bishop encouraged him to write*
> *in a looser, less formal style. The poem breaks with the impersonal*
> *style instituted by T. S. Eliot, a style that was still popular among*
> *many prominent American poets in the 1950s. In fact, Lowell's*
> *poem could in some sense be considered confessional: Lowell had*
> *bipolar disorder, also known as manic depression, and in the fall of*
> *1957, extremely manic, he checked himself into a psychiatric hospi-*
> *tal in Boston.*

Skunk Hour

(*For Elizabeth Bishop*)

Nautilus Island's hermit
heiress still lives through winter in her Spartan cottage;
her sheep still graze above the sea.
Her son's a bishop. Her farmer
is first selectman in our village;   5
she's in her dotage.

Thirsting for
the hierarchic privacy
of Queen Victoria's century,
she buys up all   10

the eyesores facing her shore,
and lets them fall.

The season's ill—
we've lost our summer millionaire,
who seemed to leap from an L. L. Bean   15
catalogue. His nine-knot yawl
was auctioned off to lobstermen.
A red fox stain covers Blue Hill.

And now our fairy
decorator brightens his shop for fall;   20
his fishnet's filled with orange cork,
orange, his cobbler's bench and awl;
there is no money in his work,
he'd rather marry.

One dark night,   25
my Tudor Ford climbed the hill's skull;
I watched for love-cars. Lights turned down,
they lay together, hull to hull,
where the graveyard shelves on the town. . . .
My mind's not right.   30

A car radio bleats,
"Love, O careless Love. . . ." I hear
my ill-spirit sob in each blood cell,
as if my hand were at its throat. . . .
I myself am hell;   35
nobody's here—

only skunks, that search
in the moonlight for a bite to eat.
They march on their soles up Main Street:
white stripes, moonstruck eyes' red fire   40
under the chalk-dry and spar spire
of the Trinitarian Church.

I stand on top
of our back steps and breathe the rich air—
a mother skunk with her column of kittens swills the garbage
    pail.   45
She jabs her wedge-head in a cup
of sour cream, drops her ostrich tail,
and will not scare.

              1959

Susan Ludvigson

1942–

> *Ludvigson says that the images in her poetry come from her child-*
> *hood and her dreams and credits "learning to listen to one's inner*
> *ear and trusting to the unconscious." "After Love" was published in*
> Everything Winged Must Be Dreaming *(1993). Winged creatures*
> *appear in many of the poems, either on the literal level or, as here,*
> *in a metaphor. That context emphasizes Ludvigson's decision to*
> *compare reason to a* moth *rather than some other animal. You*
> *might ask yourself: Why not a pheasant or a peacock or a swallow*
> *or an angel, which appear in her other poems?*

After Love

She remembers how reason
escaped from the body,
flew out with a sigh,
went winging up
to a corner of the ceiling   5
and fluttered there,
a moth, a translucence,
waiting.

She did not hear it
return, did not see   10
but felt its brush

against her breasts
quieter, quieter,
until it slipped
back in, powdered   15
wings intact.

      1993

Archibald MacLeish
1892–1982

> *When MacLeish published "Ars Poetica" (the art of poetry), it be-*
> *came a sort of manifesto for the American, mid-century poets asso-*
> *ciated with New Criticism (represented in this volume by Williams,*
> *Moore, Lowell, Bishop, Ransom, Stevens, and Jarrell). "Ars Poetica"*
> *erects the pillars of New Critical aesthetics: that poetry, because it is*
> *experienced rather than interpreted, is something completely differ-*
> *ent from ordinary language (and therefore does not convey a mean-*
> *ing the way we think of, for example, a political speech meaning*
> *something); that the proper subject matter of poetry is the univer-*
> *sal, timeless truths of the human heart, like grief and love; and that*
> *these truths are conveyed through images (an "empty doorway" for*
> *"grief "). Reforming society, then, according to MacLeish and the*
> *New Critics, is not the business of poetry. For this reason, some of*
> *the more political poets in this volume would dispute the philosophy*
> *presented in "Ars Poetica."*

Ars Poetica

A poem should be palpable and mute
As a globed fruit,

Dumb
As old medallions to the thumb,

Silent as the sleeve-worn stone   5
Of casement ledges where the moss has grown—

A poem should be wordless
As the flight of birds.

*

A poem should be motionless in time
As the moon climbs,   10

Leaving, as the moon releases
Twig by twig the night-entangled trees,

Leaving, as the moon behind the winter leaves,
Memory by memory the mind—

A poem should be motionless in time   15
As the moon climbs.

*

A poem should be equal to:
Not true.

For all the history of grief
An empty doorway and a maple leaf.   20

For love
The leaning grasses and two lights above the sea—

A poem should not mean
But be.

1926

Christopher Marlowe
1564–1593

> *Marlowe was Shakespeare's contemporary and his chief rival as playwright. "The Passionate Shepherd to His Love" circulated in manuscript throughout London's literary circles, as was the case with many poems in the Elizabethan era (it was not published until eight years after Marlowe's untimely death in a bar fight). Its original audience, then, was aristocrats (both men and women)*

and well-educated men of letters, and it was widely read by these groups. "The Passionate Shepherd" is the best example in this volume of the pastoral lyric—a popular form in the Elizabethan age. No one would mistake the shepherds for real people.

The Passionate Shepherd to His Love

Come live with me and be my love,
And we will all the pleasures prove
That valleys, groves, hills, and fields,
Woods, or steepy mountain yields.

And we will sit upon the rocks,   5
Seeing the shepherds feed their flocks,
By shallow rivers to whose falls
Melodious birds sing madrigals.

And I will make thee beds of roses
And a thousand fragrant posies,   10
A cap of flowers, and a kirtle
Embroidered all with leaves of myrtle;

A gown made of the finest wool
Which from our pretty lambs we pull;
Fair lined slippers for the cold,   15
With buckles of the purest gold;

A belt of straw and ivy buds,
With coral clasps and amber studs:
And if these pleasures may thee move,
Come live with me, and be my love.   20

The shepherds' swains shall dance and sing
For thy delight each May morning:
If these delights thy mind may move,
Then live with me and be my love.

1599, 1600

Andrew Marvell
1621–1678

> *Marvell, a friend of John Milton, published little during his lifetime: his housekeeper, who represented herself as his widow, brought out a collection of his poems after his death. The speaker in "To His Coy Mistress" is the persona speaking in a conventional* carpe diem *poem: the artful seducer. In fact, this poem is probably the most famous example of its kind in the English language. Note how the poem breaks down into a logical, three-point argument: "If," "but," "therefore."*

To His Coy Mistress

Had we but world enough, and time,
This coyness, lady, were no crime.
We would sit down, and think which way
To walk, and pass our long love's day.
Thou by the Indian Ganges' side   5
Shouldst rubies[1] find; I by the tide
Of Humber would complain. I would
Love you ten years before the flood,
And you should, if you please, refuse
Till the conversion of the Jews.   10
My vegetable[2] love should grow
Vaster than empires and more slow;
An hundred years should go to praise
Thine eyes, and on thy forehead gaze;
Two hundred to adore each breast,   15
But thirty thousand to the rest;
An age at least to every part,
And the last age should show your heart.
For, lady, you deserve this state,
Nor would I love at lower rate.   20

---

1. Rubies were thought to help preserve virginity. "Ganges": the Ganges River.

2. I.e., characterized by plantlike growth.

But at my back I always hear
Time's wingèd chariot hurrying near;
And yonder all before us lie
Deserts of vast eternity.
Thy beauty shall no more be found;   25
Nor, in thy marble vault, shall sound
My echoing song; then worms shall try
That long-preserved virginity,
And your quaint[3] honor turn to dust,
And into ashes all my lust: 30
The grave's a fine and private place,
But none, I think, do there embrace.
    Now therefore, while the youthful hue
Sits on thy skin like morning dew,
And while thy willing soul transpires   35
At every pore with instant fires,
Now let us sport us while we may,
And now, like amorous birds of prey,
Rather at once our time devour
Than languish in his slow-chapped power.   40
Let us roll all our strength and all
Our sweetness up into one ball,
And tear our pleasures with rough strife
Through the iron gates of life:
Thus, though we cannot make our sun   45
Stand still, yet we will make him run.

                                    1681

Edna St. Vincent Millay
1892–1950
   *Millay exemplified the rakish free spirit of Greenwich Village in
   the years during and after World War I. She took many lovers and
   wrote frankly about them in her verse. "What Lips My Lips Have*

---

3. Has several meanings, including: fine, elegant, fastidious, and oversubtle; also with a pun on the Middle English noun "queynte," meaning a woman's genitals.

Kissed" was the fifth of a sequence of eight sonnets that helped win her the Pulitzer Prize in 1922. The season motif appears throughout the sequence: the third sonnet begins with these lines: "I know I am but summer to your heart, / And not the full four seasons of the year[.]" "Love Is Not All" was part of a 1931 sequence, Fatal Interview. *Though its rhyme scheme indicates it is a Shakespearean sonnet, the poem seems to divide like a Petrarchan sonnet. Part of the poem's subtlety derives from the last line: is the speaker unsure or confident?*

What Lips My Lips Have Kissed

What lips my lips have kissed, and where, and why,
I have forgotten, and what arms have lain
Under my head till morning; but the rain
Is full of ghosts tonight, that tap and sigh
Upon the glass and listen for reply,   5
And in my heart there stirs a quiet pain
For unremembered lads that not again
Will turn to me at midnight with a cry.
Thus in the winter stands the lonely tree,
Nor knows what birds have vanished one by one,   10
Yet knows its boughs more silent than before:
I cannot say what loves have come and gone,
I only know that summer sang in me
A little while, that in me sings no more.

1922

Love Is Not All: It Is Not Meat Nor Drink

Love is not all: it is not meat nor drink
Nor slumber nor a roof against the rain;
Nor yet a floating spar to men that sink
And rise and sink and rise and sink again;
Love can not fill the thickened lung with breath,   5
Nor clean the blood, nor set the fractured bone;

Yet many a man is making friends with death
Even as I speak, for lack of love alone.
It well may be that in a difficult hour,
Pinned down by pain and moaning for release,   10
Or nagged by want past resolution's power,
I might be driven to sell your love for peace,
Or trade the memory of this night for food.
It well may be. I do not think I would.

1931

John Milton
1608–1674

*Milton wrote "When I Consider How My Light Is Spent" after go-
ing blind around 1651. His eyesight deteriorated while he was writ-
ing political pamphlets defending Parliament's 1649 execution of
King Charles I, though it would be fair to say he considered the
king's downfall to be God's work, since Charles was overthrown by
a Puritan revolution that was as much religious and cultural as it
was political. For example, the Puritan government closed down
England's theaters. Milton's fortunes fell when the monarchy was
restored in 1660. Blind and poor, he wrote his greatest work, the
epic* Paradise Lost, *which was instantly recognized by English au-
diences as a work worthy of Homer or Virgil when it was published
in 1667. When his short lyrics—including this one—were first pub-
lished in 1673, readers would have known Milton as England's fa-
mous, blind epic poet.*

When I Consider How My Light Is Spent

When I consider how my light is spent
　Ere half my days, in this dark world and wide,
　And that one talent which is death to hide
　Lodged with me useless, though my soul more bent
To serve therewith my Maker, and present   5

My true account, lest he returning chide;
"Doth God exact day-labor, light denied?"
I fondly ask; but Patience to prevent
That murmur, soon replies, "God doth not need
  Either man's work or his own gifts; who best   10
  Bear his mild yoke, they serve him best. His state
Is kingly. Thousands at his bidding speed
  And post o'er land and ocean without rest:
  They also serve who only stand and wait."

1673

Marianne Moore
1887–1972

> *Moore's career paralleled Pound's and Eliot's, and as editor of the influential* Dial *magazine, she mentored many of America's mid-century poets—people like Elizabeth Bishop. The way she frames her question about poetry's importance is, then, somewhat surprising, especially when you consider "Poetry" alongside a work like MacLeish's "Ars Poetica." It is difficult to gauge her attitude toward those things "that we do not admire" because we can't understand them: the "immovable critic" of course is a figure of some contempt, but Moore's famous love of the Dodgers suggests that the frivolity and inutility of the baseball fan is something the speaker admires.*

Poetry

I, too, dislike it: there are things that are important beyond all
    this fiddle.
  Reading it, however, with a perfect contempt for it, one
    discovers in
it after all, a place for the genuine.
    Hands that can grasp, eyes
      that can dilate, hair that can rise   5
        if it must, these things are important not because a

high-sounding interpretation can be put upon them but
      because they are
useful. When they become so derivative as to become
      unintelligible,
the same thing may be said for all of us, that we
      do not admire what   10
      we cannot understand: the bat
         holding on upside down or in quest of something to

eat, elephants pushing, a wild horse taking a roll, a tireless wolf under
   a tree, the immovable critic twitching his skin like a horse
         that feels a flea, the base-
ball fan, the statistician—   15
      nor is it valid
         to discriminate against "business documents and

school-books"; all these phenomena are important. One must
      make a distinction
however: when dragged into prominence by half poets, the
      result is not poetry,
nor till the poets among us can be   20
      "literalists of
      the imagination"—above
         insolence and triviality and can present

for inspection, "imaginary gardens with real toads in them,"
      shall we have
it. In the meantime, if you demand on the one hand,   25
the raw material of poetry in
      all its rawness and
      that which is on the other hand
         genuine, then you are interested in poetry.

                                             1921, 1935

Sharon Olds

1942–

> *Both of these poems appeared in Olds's second volume,* The Dead
> and the Living. *The book is a sort of biography of its speaker, who
> seems to be Olds herself. We learn of the speaker's alcoholic, abusive
> father, her suffering mother and sister, her miscarriage and abor-
> tion. Both selections here are among the "Poems for the Living."
> "Sex Without Love," in a sequence called "The Men," is sand-
> wiched between two poems describing sexual ecstasy between the
> speaker and her husband—that is, sex with love—which should
> help you determine the speaker's tone. "The One Girl at the Boys'
> Party" is one of twenty poems about "The Children": Consider here
> the relationship between mathematics and female sexuality, mathe-
> matics and female power.*

Sex Without Love

How do they do it, the ones who make love
without love? Beautiful as dancers,
gliding over each other like ice-skaters
over the ice, fingers hooked
inside each other's bodies, faces   5
red as steak, wine, wet as the
children at birth whose mothers are going to
give them away. How do they come to the
come to the come to the God come to the
still waters, and not love   10
the one who came there with them, light
rising slowly as steam off their joined
skin? These are the true religious,
the purists, the pros, the ones who will not
accept a false Messiah, love the   15
priest instead of the God. They do not
mistake the lover for their own pleasure,
they are like great runners: they know they are alone
with the road surface, the cold, the wind,

the fit of their shoes, their over-all cardio-   20
vascular health—just factors, like the partner
in the bed, and not the truth, which is the
single body alone in the universe
against its own best time.

1984

The One Girl at the Boys' Party

When I take our girl to the swimming party
I set her down among the boys. They tower and
bristle, she stands there smooth and sleek,
her math scores unfolding in the air around her.
They will strip to their suits, her body hard and   5
indivisible as a prime number,
they'll plunge in the deep end, she'll subtract
her height from ten feet, divide it into
hundreds of gallons of water, the numbers
bouncing in her mind like molecules of chlorine   10
in the bright blue pool. When they climb out,
her ponytail will hand its pencil lead
down her back, her narrow silk suit
with hamburgers and french fries printed on it
will glisten in the brilliant air, and they will   15
see her sweet face, solemn and
sealed, a factor of one, and she will
see their eyes, two each,
their legs, two each, and the curves of their sexes,
one each, and in her head she'll be doing her   20
wild multiplying, as the drops
sparkle and fall to the power of a thousand from her body.

1984

Wilfred Owen
1893–1918

> *Owen enlisted in the British Army to fight the Germans in World War I, was dispatched to the front, sickened, and was sent to Scotland to recuperate, where he wrote "Dulce Et Decorum Est" in October 1917. Originally he dedicated it to Jessie Pope, an author of children's books and editor of patriotic war poems; Pope is probably the "friend" in line 25. Owen translated the title, a popular motto, thus: "It is sweet and meet to die for one's country. Sweet! and decorous!" He was returned to the front and killed a week before the cease-fire. This poem was not published until 1920, when it came to be heard as, essentially, the plea of a dead soldier.*

Dulce Et Decorum Est

Bent double, like old beggars under sacks,
Knock-kneed, coughing like hags, we cursed through sludge,
Till on the haunting flares we turned our backs
And towards our distant rest began to trudge.
Men marched asleep. Many had lost their boots   5
But limped on, blood-shod. All went lame; all blind;
Drunk with fatigue; deaf even to the hoots
Of tired, outstripped Five-Nines[1] that dropped behind.

Gas! GAS! Quick, boys!—An ecstasy of fumbling,
Fitting the clumsy helmets just in time;   10
But someone still was yelling out and stumbling,
And flound'ring like a man in fire or lime . . .
Dim, through the misty panes[2] and thick green light,
As under a green sea, I saw him drowning.

In all my dreams, before my helpless sight,   15
He plunges at me, guttering, choking, drowning.

---

1. I.e., 5.9-inch caliber shells.   2. Of the gas mask's celluloid window.

If in smothering dreams you too could pace
Behind the wagon that we flung him in,
And watch the white eyes writhing in his face,
His hanging face, like a devil's sick of sin;   20
If you could hear, at every jolt, the blood
Come gargling from the froth-corrupted lungs,
Obscene as cancer, bitter as the cud
Of vile, incurable sores on innocent tongues,—
My friend, you would not tell with such high zest   25
Pope To children ardent for some desperate glory,
The old Lie: Dulce et decorum est
Pro patria mori.

1920

Marge Piercy
1936–

> In her poetry and prose, Piercy engages with social myths that she
> believes inform the behavior of women and men. She has rewritten
> traditional stories and, in "Barbie doll," offers a critical look at a
> female icon. "Barbie doll" eschews subtlety in favor of shock, but
> this poem is more complex than you might at first think. For exam-
> ple, it seems obvious that we are meant to read the last two lines
> ironically. But why does Piercy use the word "consummation"
> rather than "ending"? The third stanza compares the woman's good
> nature to a fan belt—a striking metaphor. How are the two simi-
> lar? What does a fan belt do? How does it wear out?

Barbie doll

This girlchild was born as usual
and presented dolls that did pee-pee
and miniature GE stoves and irons
and wee lipsticks the color of cherry candy.
Then in the magic of puberty, a classmate said: 5
You have a great big nose and fat legs.

She was healthy, tested intelligent,
possessed strong arms and back,
abundant sexual drive and manual dexterity.
She went to and fro apologizing.   10
Everyone saw a fat nose on thick legs.

She was advised to play coy,
exhorted to come on hearty,
exercise, diet, smile and wheedle.
Her good nature wore out   15
like a fan belt.
So she cut off her nose and her legs
and offered them up.

In the casket displayed on satin she lay
with the undertaker's cosmetics painted on,   20
a turned-up putty nose,
dressed in a pink and white nightie.
Doesn't she look pretty? everyone said.
Consummation at last.
To every woman a happy ending.   25

                                         1973

Sylvia Plath
1932–1963

> *In England on a Fulbright scholarship, at twenty-four years old, Plath
> married the British poet Ted Hughes. She finished writing "Metaphors"
> on March 20, 1959, just after she discovered to her disappointment that
> she wasn't pregnant. "Daddy" was written on October 12, 1962, shortly
> after she decided to divorce Hughes. Though it is* emotionally *autobi-
> ographical it is not* factual, *at least not the parts about her father. Otto
> Plath was not a Nazi and was not abusive. Nevertheless, when she fin-
> ished the poem, Plath declared, "It is over. . . . My life can begin." But
> before "Daddy" appeared in print, Plath, who was living in London
> with her two young children, committed suicide. She was thirty. She
> died on the verge of the feminist movement, and women have turned
> to her life and poems to voice their own struggles since the 1960s.*

Metaphors

I'm a riddle in nine syllables,
An elephant, a ponderous house,
A melon strolling on two tendrils.
O red fruit, ivory, fine timbers!
This loaf's big with its yeasty rising.   5
Money's new-minted in this fat purse.
I'm a means, a stage, a cow in calf.
I've eaten a bag of green apples,
Boarded the train there's no getting off.

1961

Daddy

You do not do, you do not do
Any more, black shoe
In which I have lived like a foot
For thirty years, poor and white,
Barely daring to breathe or Achoo.   5

Daddy, I have had to kill you.
You died before I had time——
Marble-heavy, a bag full of God,
Ghastly statue with one gray toe[1]
Big as a Frisco seal   10

And a head in the freakish Atlantic
Where it pours bean green over blue
In the waters off beautiful Nauset.
I used to pray to recover you.
Ach, du.[2]   15

---

1. Plath's father's toe turned black from gangrene.

2. "Ah, you" (German).

In the German tongue, in the Polish town
Scraped flat by the roller
Of wars, wars, wars.
But the name of the town is common.
My Polack friend   20

Says there are a dozen or two.
So I never could tell where you
Put your foot, your root,
I never could talk to you.
The tongue stuck in my jaw.   25

It stuck in a barb wire snare.
Ich, ich, ich, ich,[3]
I could hardly speak.
I thought every German was you.
And the language obscene   30

An engine, an engine
Chuffing me off like a Jew.
A Jew to Dachau, Auschwitz, Belsen.[4]
I began to talk like a Jew.
I think I may well be a Jew.   35

The snows of the Tyrol, the clear beer of Vienna
Are not very pure or true.
With my gypsy ancestress and my weird luck
And my Taroc pack and my Taroc pack[5]
I may be a bit of a Jew.   40

I have always been scared of *you*,
With your Luftwaffe,[6] your gobbledygoo.
And your neat moustache

---

3. "I, I, I, I" (German).
4. German concentration camps where millions of Jews were murdered during World War II.

5. Tarot cards, used for fortune-telling.
6. The German air force.

And your Aryan eye, bright blue.
Panzer[7]-man, panzer-man, O You—   45

Not God but a swastika
So black no sky could squeak through.
Every woman adores a Fascist,
The boot in the face, the brute
Brute heart of a brute like you.   50

You stand at the blackboard, daddy,
In the picture I have of you,
A cleft in your chin instead of your foot
But no less a devil for that, no not
Any less the black man who   55

Bit my pretty red heart in two.
I was ten when they buried you.
At twenty I tried to die   — *tried to kill herself*
And get back, back, back to you.
I thought even the bones would do.   60

But they pulled me out of the sack,
And they stuck me together with glue,
And then I knew what to do.
I made a model of you,
A man in black with a Meinkampf[8] look   65

And a love of the rack and the screw.
And I said I do, I do.
So daddy, I'm finally through.
The black telephone's off at the root,
The voices just can't worm through.   70

If I've killed one man, I've killed two—
The vampire who said he was you

7. "Armor" (German), especially, during World War II, referring to the German armored tank corps.

8. *Mein Kampf* ("My Struggle") is the title of Hitler's political autobiography and Nazi polemic, written before his rise to power.

And drank my blood for a year,
Seven years, if you want to know.
Daddy, you can lie back now.   75

There's a stake in your fat black heart
And the villagers never liked you.
They are dancing and stamping on you.
They always *knew* it was you.
Daddy, daddy, you bastard, I'm through.   80

                    1965

Edgar Allan Poe
1809–1849

> Poe wrote "The Raven" in a deliberate attempt to become famous.
> He didn't want the poem to be too high for popular or too low for
> critical taste, so it is not surprising that between January and
> March 1845, it was published both in a New York newspaper and
> in two literary journals. "The Raven" earned him little money, but
> it did establish Poe as a celebrity. Though ravens are conventionally
> associated with evil, Poe's symbolism, like Coleridge's, is psychologi-
> cal. Poe attempts to convey in the sound of the words the melan-
> choly and foreboding felt by the speaker.

The Raven

Once upon a midnight dreary, while I pondered, weak and weary,
Over many a quaint and curious volume of forgotten lore—
While I nodded, nearly napping, suddenly there came a tapping,
As of some one gently rapping, rapping at my chamber door.
" 'Tis some visiter," I muttered, "tapping at my chamber door—   5
                    Only this and nothing more."

Ah, distinctly I remember it was in the bleak December;
And each separate dying ember wrought its ghost upon the floor.
Eagerly I wished the morrow;—vainly I had sought to borrow
From my books surcease of sorrow—sorrow for the lost
    Lenore—   10
For the rare and radiant maiden whom the angels name
    Lenore—
                       Nameless *here* for evermore.

And the silken, sad, uncertain rustling of each purple curtain
Thrilled me—filled me with fantastic terrors never felt before;
So that now, to still the beating of my heart, I stood repeating   15
" 'Tis some visiter entreating entrance at my chamber door—
Some late visiter entreating entrance at my chamber door;—
                  This it is and nothing more."

Presently my soul grew stronger; hesitating then no longer,
"Sir," said I, "or Madam, truly your forgiveness I implore;   20
But the fact is I was napping, and so gently you came rapping,
And so faintly you came tapping, tapping at my chamber door,
That I scarce was sure I heard you"—here I opened wide the
    door;—
                Darkness there and nothing more.

Deep into that darkness peering, long I stood there wondering,
    fearing,   25
Doubting, dreaming dreams no mortal ever dared to dream
    before;
But the silence was unbroken, and the stillness gave no token,
And the only word there spoken was the whispered word,
    "Lenore?"
This I whispered, and an echo murmured back the word,
    "Lenore!"
                Merely this and nothing more.   30

Back into the chamber turning, all my soul within me burning,
Soon again I heard a tapping somewhat louder than before.
"Surely," said I, "surely that is something at my window lattice;

Let me see, then, what thereat is, and this mystery explore—
Let my heart be still a moment and this mystery explore;—   35
    'Tis the wind and nothing more!"

Open here I flung the shutter, when, with many a flirt and
  flutter,
In there stepped a stately Raven of the saintly days of yore;
Not the least obeisance made he; not a minute stopped or
  stayed he;
But, with mien of lord or lady, perched above my chamber
  door—   40
Perched upon a bust of Pallas[1] just above my chamber door—
    Perched, and sat, and nothing more.

Then this ebony bird beguiling my sad fancy into smiling,
By the grave and stern decorum of the countenance it wore,
"Though thy crest be shorn and shaven, thou," I said, "art sure
  no craven,   45
Ghastly grim and ancient Raven wandering from the Nightly
  shore—
Tell me what thy lordly name is on the Night's Plutonian[2]
  shore!"
    Quoth the Raven "Nevermore."

Much I marvelled this ungainly fowl to hear discourse so plainly,
Though its answer little meaning—little relevancy bore;   50
For we cannot help agreeing that no living human being
Ever yet was blessed with seeing bird above his chamber door—
Bird or beast upon the sculptured bust above his chamber door,
    With such name as "Nevermore."

But the Raven, sitting lonely on the placid bust, spoke only   55
That one word, as if his soul in that one word he did outpour.
Nothing farther then he uttered—not a feather then he
  fluttered—

---

1. Athena, Greek goddess of wisdom and the arts.

2. Black; Pluto was the Greek god of the underworld.

Till I scarcely more than muttered "Other friends have flown
    before—
On the morrow *he* will leave me, as my Hopes have flown
    before."
               Then the bird said "Nevermore."   60

Startled at the stillness broken by reply so aptly spoken,
"Doubtless," said I, "what it utters is its only stock and store
Caught from some unhappy master whom unmerciful Disaster
Followed fast and followed faster till his songs one burden bore—
Till the dirges of his Hope that melancholy burden bore   65
               Of 'Never—nevermore.' "

But the Raven still beguiling my sad fancy into smiling,
Straight I wheeled a cushioned seat in front of bird, and bust
    and door;
Then, upon the velvet sinking, I betook myself to linking
Fancy unto fancy, thinking what this ominous bird of yore—   70
What this grim, ungainly, ghastly, gaunt, and ominous bird of
    yore
               Meant in croaking "Nevermore."

This I sat engaged in guessing, but no syllable expressing
To the fowl whose fiery eyes now burned into my bosom's core;
This and more I sat divining, with my head at ease reclining   75
On the cushion's velvet lining that the lamp-light gloated o'er,
But whose velvet-violet lining with the lamp-light gloating o'er,
               She shall press, ah, nevermore!

Then, methought, the air grew denser, perfumed from an
    unseen censer
Swung by seraphim whose foot-falls tinkled on the tufted
    floor.   80
"Wretch," I cried, "thy God hath lent thee—by these angels he
    hath sent thee
Respite—respite and nepenthe[3] from thy memories of Lenore;

---

3. Oblivion-inducing drug.

Quaff, oh quaff this kind nepenthe and forget this lost Lenore!"
        Quoth the Raven "Nevermore."

"Prophet!"said I, "thing of evil!—prophet still, if bird or
    devil!—   85
Whether Tempter sent, or whether tempest tossed thee here
    ashore,
Desolate yet all undaunted, on this desert land enchanted—
On this home by Horror haunted—tell me truly, I implore—
Is there—*is* there balm in Gilead?—tell me—tell me, I
    implore!"
        Quoth the Raven "Nevermore."   90

[handwritten: Is there happiness after death?]
[handwritten: NO]

"Prophet!" said I, "thing of evil!—prophet still, if bird or devil!
By that Heaven that bends above us—by that God we both
    adore—
Tell this soul with sorrow laden if, within the distant Aidenn,
[handwritten: (eating)]
It shall clasp a sainted maiden whom the angels name
    Lenore—
Clasp a rare and radiant maiden whom the angels name
    Lenore."   95
        Quoth the Raven "Nevermore."

"Be that word our sign of parting, bird or fiend!" I shrieked,
    upstarting—
"Get thee back into the tempest and the Night's Plutonian
    shore!
Leave no black plume as a token of that lie thy soul hath
    spoken!
Leave my loneliness unbroken!—quit the bust above my door! 100
Take thy beak from out my heart, and take thy form from off
    my door!"
        Quoth the Raven "Nevermore."

And the Raven, never flitting, still is sitting, *still* is sitting
On the pallid bust of Pallas just above my chamber door;
And his eyes have all the seeming of a demon's that is
    dreaming,   105

[handwritten: —making it worse for himself (raven keeps saying no)]

And the lamp-light o'er him streaming throws his shadow on
    the floor;
And my soul from out that shadow that lies floating on the
    floor
                    Shall be lifted—nevermore!

1845

Ezra Pound
1885–1972

> *In 1915, Pound translated a number of poems from Chinese ideo-*
> *graphs, and with these poems—which deposit all meaning in con-*
> *crete images—he meant to release himself from what he considered*
> *the tyranny of iambic pentameter. The rhythm of "The River-*
> *Merchant's Wife: A Letter," which is a translation of an eighth-*
> *century poem by Li Po, is based on syntax, not meter. The rhythmic*
> *unit is the sentence, not the foot, and it typically comprises a single*
> *line. For "In a Station of the Metro," Pound borrowed the tech-*
> *nique of juxtaposed images from Japanese* haiku *(a three-line poem*
> *of five, seven, and five syllables). He attempted to express through*
> *the image of the petals what he felt watching beautiful faces, one*
> *after another, emerge from the La Concorde station of the Paris*
> *subway. The image of the petals is meant to be equivalent to the*
> *emotion he wanted to express.*

The River-Merchant's Wife: A Letter

While my hair was still cut straight across my forehead
I played about the front gate, pulling flowers.
You came by on bamboo stilts, playing horse,
You walked about my seat, playing with blue plums.
And we went on living in the village of Chokan: 5
Two small people, without dislike or suspicion.
At fourteen I married My Lord you.
I never laughed, being bashful.
Lowering my head, I looked at the wall.
Called to, a thousand times, I never looked back.   10

At fifteen I stopped scowling,
I desired my dust to be mingled with yours
Forever and forever and forever.
Why should I climb the look out?

At sixteen you departed,   15
You went into far Ku-to-yen, by the river of swirling eddies,
And you have been gone five months.
The monkeys make sorrowful noise overhead.

You dragged your feet when you went out.
By the gate now, the moss is grown, the different mosses,   20
Too deep to clear them away!
The leaves fall early this autumn, in wind.
The paired butterflies are already yellow with August
Over the grass in the West garden;
They hurt me. I grow older.   25
If you are coming down through the narrows of the river
        Kiang,
Please let me know beforehand,
And I will come out to meet you
                As far as Cho-fu-Sa.

                                        By *Rihaku*
                                            1915

In a Station of the Metro

The apparition of these faces in the crowd;
Petals on a wet, black bough.

                        1916

John Crowe Ransom
1888–1974
> *As a college professor, Ransom trained a generation of southern writers who formed the core of the New Critical movement in literature. Aristocratic and traditional in politics and culture, the New Critics*

instituted the methods of close reading still taught in most English departments, though their insistence on a poem's autonomy from its poet and from its cultural context is largely rejected today. Ransom wrote "Bells for John Whiteside's Daughter" in the spring of 1924 after he watched a neighbor's daughter playing outside and imagined the aftermath of her death. You will probably find yourself perplexed by the repeated phrase "brown study." There is no clear meaning to the phrase: by interpreting it, you will interpret the poem.

Bells for John Whiteside's Daughter

There was such speed in her little body,
And such lightness in her footfall,
It is no wonder her brown study
Astonishes us all.

Her wars were bruited[1] in our high window.   5
We looked among orchard trees and beyond
Where she took arms against her shadow,
Or harried unto the pond

The lazy geese, like a snow cloud
Dripping their snow on the green grass,   10
Tricking and stopping, sleepy and proud,
Who cried in goose, Alas,

For the tireless heart within the little
Lady with rod that made them rise
From their noon apple-dreams and scuttle   15
Goose-fashion under the skies!

But now go the bells, and we are ready,
In one house we are sternly stopped
To say we are vexed at her brown study,
Lying so primly propped.   20

1924

1. I.e., loudly voiced.

Edwin Arlington Robinson
1869–1935

> *In 1897 Robinson published at his own expense* The Children of
> the Night, *which included "Richard Cory." The book was largely
> ignored until President Theodore Roosevelt happened across a copy
> and, attracted by what he considered a masculine style and progres-
> sive sentiments, started promoting Robinson—to the chagrin of
> some members of the literary community, who thought Robinson
> was second-rate. Many poets in the twentieth century, following the
> lead of Eliot and Pound, thought that if a poem was straightfor-
> ward and appealed to the mass market, it must be bad. Thus
> "Richard Cory" provides a good opportunity to reflect on poetry's
> purpose and definition.*

Richard Cory

Whenever Richard Cory went down town,
We people on the pavement looked at him:
He was a gentleman from sole to crown,
Clean favored, and imperially slim.

And he was always quietly arrayed,   5
And he was always human when he talked;
But still he fluttered pulses when he said,
"Good-morning," and he glittered when he walked.

And he was rich—yes, richer than a king—
And admirably schooled in every grace: 10
In fine, we thought that he was everything
To make us wish that we were in his place.

So on we worked, and waited for the light,
And went without the meat, and cursed the bread;
And Richard Cory, one calm summer night,   15
Went home and put a bullet through his head.

1869

Theodore Roethke

1908–1963

> Roethke's "Greenhouse Poems," which include "Root Cellar," reflect
> his childhood observations in Saginaw, Michigan, where his father
> owned a greenhouse. The bulbs and shoots are some of those "mini-
> mal creatures" in which Roethke delighted and which characterize
> most of his poetry. What raises this poem above mere (though vivid)
> description is that it joins "evil" to these things that would not "give
> up life." "My Papa's Waltz" initiated a group of seven autobio-
> graphical poems that express the poet's dissatisfaction with human
> society. Even so, it is very difficult to determine the speaker's atti-
> tude toward his father. In 1958 Roethke won the National Book
> Award for Words for the Wind, which reprinted his best work
> and added new poems, like "I Knew A Woman." That poem is in a
> section titled "Love Poems." Perhaps the most difficult part of this
> poem is to figure out the speaker's relation to this woman. Is he a
> child, she a mother? Is she a teacher? Is he a young man and she the
> older lover? "Turn, and Counter-turn, and Stand" are the stanzas
> in a Pindaric ode, which were sung and danced by the chorus in a
> Greek play, so this line suggests the woman taught the speaker po-
> etry and dance.

Root Cellar

Nothing would sleep in that cellar, dank as a ditch,
Bulbs broke out of boxes hunting for chinks in the dark,
Shoots dangled and drooped,
Lolling obscenely from mildewed crates,
Hung down long yellow evil necks, like tropical snakes.   5
And what a congress of stinks!
Roots ripe as old bait,
Pulpy stems, rank, silo-rich,
Leaf-mold, manure, lime, piled against slippery planks.
Nothing would give up life: 10
Even the dirt kept breathing a small breath.

1948

My Papa's Waltz

The whiskey on your breath
Could make a small boy dizzy;
But I hung on like death:
Such waltzing was not easy.

We romped until the pans   5
Slid from the kitchen shelf;
My mother's countenance
Could not unfrown itself.

The hand that held my wrist
Was battered on one knuckle;   10
At every step you missed
My right ear scraped a buckle.

You beat time on my head
With a palm caked hard by dirt,
Then waltzed me off to bed   15
Still clinging to your shirt.

1948

I Knew a Woman

I knew a woman, lovely in her bones,
When small birds sighed, she would sigh back at them;
Ah, when she moved, she moved more ways than one:
The shapes a bright container can contain!
Of her choice virtues only gods should speak,   5
Or English poets who grew up on Greek
(I'd have them sing in chorus, cheek to cheek).

How well her wishes went! She stroked my chin,
She taught me Turn, and Counter-turn, and Stand;
She taught me Touch, that undulant white skin;   10

I nibbled meekly from her proffered hand;
She was the sickle; I, poor I, the rake,
Coming behind her for her pretty sake
(But what prodigious mowing we did make).

Love likes a gander, and adores a goose: 15
Her full lips pursed, the errant note to seize;
She played it quick, she played it light and loose,
My eyes, they dazzled at her flowing knees;
Her several parts could keep a pure repose,
Or one hip quiver with a mobile nose   20
(She moved in circles, and those circles moved).

Let seed be grass, and grass turn into hay:
I'm martyr to a motion not my own;
What's freedom for? To know eternity.
I swear she cast a shadow white as stone.   25
But who would count eternity in days?
These old bones live to learn her wanton ways:
(I measure time by how a body sways).

                                        1958

William Shakespeare
1564–1616

> *Readers have long argued the identities of the speaker and listener
> in these sonnets, but with so little evidence of Shakespeare's life no
> one can prove or disprove that the poems are autobiographical. The
> 1609 edition is dedicated "TO THE ONLIE BEGETTER OF THESE
> INSUING SONNETS MR W. H.," whose identity has eluded the
> most careful scholars. Many candidates have been suggested, but
> none have been proven. It is clear that in the first 126 sonnets
> an older man addresses a younger man and urges him to marry.
> The relationship between these two men is intimate—some readers
> think they are sexually intimate, others do not. Sonnet 18 gives us
> Shakespeare's version of a conventional poetic boast: that the poet
> bestows immortality on his subject. In Sonnet 29 Shakespeare con-*

*tinues lauding the young man. Here, his friendship refreshes the
poet. Sonnet 73 is a fine example of how a Shakespearean sonnet
can develop an idea in successive, related images, each expressed in
a quatrain. Sonnet 116 speaks to the enduring quality of love. In
Sonnets 127–152, the speaker addresses a female persona who has
come to be called "the dark lady" on account of her complexion and
bawdy habits. Sonnet 130 satirizes the conventions of love poetry
that exaggerate the beloved's beauty. The mistress is not necessarily
ugly; these terms seem so negative merely because they are realistic.
You might consider whether this poem is more flattering than, say,
the first two quatrains of Sonnet 18.*

18

Shall I compare thee to a summer's day?
Thou art more lovely and more temperate:
Rough winds do shake the darling buds of May,
And summer's lease hath all too short a date;
Sometimes too hot the eye of heaven shines,   5
And often is his gold complexion dimmed;
And every fair from fair sometimes declines,
By chance or nature's changing course untrimmed;[1]
But thy eternal summer shall not fade,
Nor lose possession of that fair thou ow'st;   10
Nor shall death brag thou wand'rest in his shade,
When in eternal lines to Time thou grow'st:[2]
   So long as men can breathe, or eyes can see,
   So long lives this, and this gives life to thee.

1609

1. Divested of its beauty.
2. I.e., when you are grafted to Time in this immortal poetry.

29

When, in disgrace with fortune and men's eyes,
I all alone beweep my outcast state,
And trouble deaf heaven with my bootless³ cries,
And look upon myself, and curse my fate,
Wishing me like to one more rich in hope,   5
Featured like him, like him with friends possessed,
Desiring this man's art and that man's scope,
With what I most enjoy contented least;
Yet in these thoughts myself almost despising,
Haply I think on thee—and then my state,   10
Like to the lark at break of day arising
From sullen earth, sings hymns at heaven's gate;
    For thy sweet love rememb'red such wealth brings
    That then I scorn to change my state with kings.
                                                                1609

73

That time of year thou mayst in me behold
When yellow leaves, or none, or few, do hang
Upon those boughs which shake against the cold,
Bare ruined choirs, where late the sweet birds sang.
In me thou see'st the twilight of such day   5
As after sunset fadeth in the west;
Which by and by black night doth take away,
Death's second self, that seals up all in rest.
In me thou see'st the glowing of such fire,
That on the ashes of his youth doth lie,   10
As the deathbed whereon it must expire,
Consumed with that which it was nourished by.
    This thou perceiv'st, which makes thy love more strong,
    To love that well which thou must leave ere long.
                                                                1609

3. I.e., futile.

116

Let me not to the marriage of true minds
Admit impediments. Love is not love
Which alters when it alteration finds,
Or bends with the remover to remove:
Oh, no! it is an ever-fixèd mark,   5
That looks on tempests and is never shaken;
It is the star to every wandering bark,
Whose worth's unknown, although his height be taken.
Love's not Time's fool, though rosy lips and cheeks
Within his bending sickle's compass come;   10
Love alters not with his brief hours and weeks,
But bears it out even to the edge of doom.
    If this be error and upon me proved,
    I never writ, nor no man ever loved.

1609

130

My mistress' eyes are nothing like the sun;
Coral is far more red than her lips' red;
If snow be white, why then her breasts are dun;[4]
If hairs be wires, black wires grow on her head.
I have seen roses damasked, red and white,   5
But no such roses see I in her cheeks;
And in some perfumes is there more delight
Than in the breath that from my mistress reeks.
I love to hear her speak, yet well I know
That music hath a far more pleasing sound;   10
I grant I never saw a goddess go;
My mistress, when she walks, treads on the ground.
    And yet, by heaven, I think my love as rare
    As any she belied with false compare.

1609

4. I.e., dull grayish brown.

Percy Bysshe Shelley
1792–1822

> In late 1817, Shelley and another poet, Horace Smith, challenged
> each other to write a poem about a statue of Ramses II, the Egyp-
> tian pharoah whom Moses and the Jews escaped in Exodus
> ("Ozymandias" is his Greek name). Shelley's poem, with obvious
> implications for contemporary politics (England had recently de-
> feated Napoleon and so dominated Europe), was published in
> Leigh Hunt's radical newspaper The Examiner in February 1818.
> "Ode to the West Wind" was inspired by an autumn storm Shelley
> witnessed on the edge of a wood near Florence. The last lines might
> refer to Shelley's labors on behalf of the working classes; though an
> aristocrat himself, he hoped for the overthrow of the privileged
> classes. He concluded his "Defense of Poetry" with these lines: "Poets
> are . . . the trumpets which sing to battle, and feel not what they
> inspire: the influence which is moved not, but moves. Poets are the
> unacknowledged legislators of the World."

Ozymandias

I met a traveler from an antique land
Who said: Two vast and trunkless legs of stone
Stand in the desert . . . Near them, on the sand,
Half sunk, a shattered visage lies, whose frown,
And wrinkled lip, and sneer of cold command,   5
Tell that its sculptor well those passions read
Which yet survive, stamped on these lifeless things,
The hand that mocked them, and the heart that fed:
And on the pedestal these words appear:
"My name is Ozymandias, king of kings: 10
Look on my works, ye Mighty, and despair!"
Nothing beside remains. Round the decay
Of that colossal wreck, boundless and bare
The lone and level sands stretch far away.

1818

Ode to the West Wind

1

O wild West Wind, thou breath of Autumn's being,
Thou, from whose unseen presence the leaves dead
Are driven, like ghosts from an enchanter fleeing,

Yellow, and black, and pale, and hectic red,
Pestilence-stricken multitudes: O thou,   5
Who chariotest to their dark wintry bed

The wingéd seeds, where they lie cold and low,
Each like a corpse within its grave, until
Thine azure sister of the Spring shall blow

Her clarion[1] o'er the dreaming earth, and fill   10
(Driving sweet buds like flocks to feed in air)
With living hues and odors plain and hill:

Wild Spirit, which art moving everywhere;
Destroyer and preserver; hear, oh, hear!

2

Thou on whose stream, mid the steep sky's commotion,   15
Loose clouds like earth's decaying leaves are shed,
Shook from the tangled boughs of Heaven and Ocean,

Angels of rain and lightning: there are spread
On the blue surface of thine aëry surge,
Like the bright hair uplifted from the head   20

---

1. Melodious trumpet-call.

Of some fierce Maenad,[2] even from the dim verge
Of the horizon to the zenith's height,
The locks of the approaching storm. Thou dirge

Of the dying year, to which this closing night
Will be the dome of a vast sepulcher,   25
Vaulted with all thy congregated might

Of vapors, from whose solid atmosphere
Black rain, and fire, and hail will burst: oh, hear!

3

Thou who didst waken from his summer dreams
The blue Mediterranean, where he lay,   30
Lulled by the coil of his crystálline streams,

Beside a pumice isle in Baiae's bay,
And saw in sleep old palaces and towers
Quivering within the wave's intenser day,

All overgrown with azure moss and flowers   35
So sweet, the sense faints picturing them! Thou
For whose path the Atlantic's level powers

Cleave themselves into chasms, while far below
The sea-blooms and the oozy woods which wear
The sapless foliage of the ocean, know   40

Thy voice, and suddenly grow gray with fear,
And tremble and despoil themselves: oh, hear!

2. Frenzied dancer, worshiper of Dionysus (Greek god of wine and fertility).

4

If I were a dead leaf thou mightest bear;
If I were a swift cloud to fly with thee;
A wave to pant beneath thy power, and share   45

The impulse of thy strength, only less free
Than thou, O uncontrollable! If even
I were as in my boyhood, and could be

The comrade of thy wanderings over Heaven,
As then, when to outstrip thy skyey speed   50
Scarce seemed a vision; I would ne'er have striven

As thus with thee in prayer in my sore need.
Oh, lift me as a wave, a leaf, a cloud!
I fall upon the thorns of life! I bleed!

A heavy weight of hours has chained and bowed   55
One too like thee: tameless, and swift, and proud.

5

Make me thy lyre,[3] even as the forest is:
What if my leaves are falling like its own!
The tumult of thy mighty harmonies

Will take from both a deep, autumnal tone,   60
Sweet though in sadness. Be thou, Spirit fierce,
My spirit! Be thou me, impetuous one!

Drive my dead thoughts over the universe
Like withered leaves to quicken a new birth!
And, by the incantation of this verse,   65

---

3. Small harp traditionally used to accompany songs and recited poems.

Scatter, as from an unextinguished hearth
Ashes and sparks, my words among mankind!
Be through my lips to unawakened earth

The trumpet of a prophecy! O Wind,
If Winter comes, can Spring be far behind?   70

1820

Bruce Springsteen
1949–

> *Springsteen's songs celebrate the outcast, the working-class dreamer. "The River," the title song to Springsteen's acclaimed 1980 album, is an excellent example of a contemporary ballad, and, like "Sir Patrick Spens," it tells a story with terse details. But each detail suggests so much that you can flesh out the picture with little effort. For example, the fields of green to which the speaker and Mary, flush with their young love and lust, escape, represent a way of life. And by contrast, though the speaker doesn't tell us, we can imagine that the valley is smothered in the gray, industrial dinginess that gave the Rust Belt its name. Likewise, the Johnstown Company alludes to Johnstown, Pennsylvania, the site of a terrible flood caused by a breaking dam. In the valley below the dam was the working-class, factory town; above was a picturesque lake and the yachting resorts of the factory owners.*

The River

I come from down in the valley
Where mister, when you're young
They bring you up to do
Like your daddy done

Me and Mary we met in high school   5
When she was just seventeen
We'd drive out of this valley
Down to where the fields were green

We'd go down to the river
And into the river we'd dive   10
Oh down to the river we'd ride

Then I got Mary pregnant
And, man, that was all she wrote
And for my 19th birthday
I got a union card and a wedding coat   15

We went down to the courthouse
And the judge put it all to rest
No wedding day smiles, no walk down the aisle
No flowers, no wedding dress

That night we went down to the river   20
And into the river we'd dive
Oh down to the river we did ride

I got a job working construction
For the Johnstown Company
But lately there ain't been much work   25
On account of the economy

Now all them things that seemed so important
Well, mister they vanished right into the air
Now I just act like I don't remember
Mary acts like she don't care   30

But I remember us riding in my brother's car
Her body tan and wet down at the reservoir
At night on them banks I'd lie awake
And pull her close just to feel each breath she'd take

Now those memories come back to haunt me   35
They haunt me like a curse
Is a dream a lie if it don't come true
Or is it something worse

That sends me down to the river
Though I know the river is dry   40
That sends me down to the river tonight
Down to the river
My baby and I
Oh down to the river we ride

1980

William Stafford
1914–1993

After Stafford published his first book at age forty-six, readers
quickly recognized and noted his extraordinary moral authority.
"Traveling through the Dark" tells the story of something that actu-
ally happened to Stafford while he was driving the seventy-mile
mountain road home from a Wednesday night class in Oregon.
Stafford said he wanted to "deliver for the reader something of
the loneliness and the minimum scope for action we all have in ex-
treme situations." Note the literal and metaphoric uses of "swerve"
in lines 4 and 17.

Traveling through the Dark

Traveling through the dark I found a deer
dead on the edge of the Wilson River road.
It is usually best to roll them into the canyon:
that road is narrow; to swerve might make more dead.

By glow of the tail-light I stumbled back of the car   5
and stood by the heap, a doe, a recent killing;
she had stiffened already, almost cold.
I dragged her off; she was large in the belly.

My fingers touching her side brought me the reason—
her side was warm; her fawn lay there waiting,   10
alive, still, never to be born.
Beside that mountain road I hesitated.

The car aimed ahead its lowered parking lights;
under the hood purred the steady engine.
I stood in the glare of the warm exhaust turning red;   15
around our group I could hear the wilderness listen. *pressure to make decision.*

I thought hard for us all—my only swerving—,
then pushed her over the edge into the river.

                                                    1962

Wallace Stevens

1879–1955
> *Stevens is famous for the beautiful sounds his lines produce: read*
> *these aloud without worrying about meaning, and you'll hear the*
> *fine rhythms. "Anecdote of the Jar" displays the kind of contrast be-*
> *tween the human and natural worlds that is typical of Romantic*
> *poetry, like Wordsworth's "Nutting." A good way into this poem is*
> *to decide whether or not the speaker, like a Romantic, regrets what*
> *the "gray and bare" jar does to the "slovenly wilderness." In a letter,*
> *Stevens explained that "Sunday Morning" is "simply an expression*
> *of paganism, although, of course, I did not think that I was ex-*
> *pressing paganism when I wrote it." Likewise, "The Emperor of*
> *Ice-Cream" seems to deny the orthodox, Christian view of life and*
> *death. While it is difficult to determine what the ice-cream man*
> *symbolizes in line 8, the last line seems to be unambiguous: there is*
> *no God.*

Anecdote of the Jar

I placed a jar in Tennessee,
And round it was, upon a hill.
It made the slovenly wilderness
Surround that hill.

The wilderness rose up to it,   5
And sprawled around, no longer wild.
The jar was round upon the ground
And tall and of a port in air.

It took dominion everywhere.
The jar was gray and bare.   10
It did not give of bird or bush,
Like nothing else in Tennessee.

                              1923

Sunday Morning

                    I

Complacencies of the peignoir, and late
Coffee and oranges in a sunny chair,
And the green freedom of a cockatoo
Upon a rug mingle to dissipate
The holy hush of ancient sacrifice.   5
She dreams a little, and she feels the dark
Encroachment of that old catastrophe,
As a calm darkens among water-lights.
The pungent oranges and bright, green wings
Seem things in some procession of the dead,   10
Winding across wide water, without sound.
The day is like wide water, without sound,
Stilled for the passing of her dreaming feet

Over the seas, to silent Palestine,
Dominion of the blood and sepulchre.[1]   15

2

Why should she give her bounty to the dead?
What is divinity if it can come
Only in silent shadows and in dreams?
Shall she not find in comforts of the sun,
In pungent fruit and bright, green wings, or else   20
In any balm or beauty of the earth,
Things to be cherished like the thought of heaven?
Divinity must live within herself:
Passions of rain, or moods in falling snow;
Grievings in loneliness, or unsubdued   25
Elations when the forest blooms; gusty
Emotions on wet roads on autumn nights;
All pleasures and all pains, remembering
The bough of summer and the winter branch.
These are the measures destined for her soul.   30

3

Jove in the clouds had his inhuman birth.
No mother suckled him, no sweet land gave
Large-mannered motions to his mythy mind
He moved among us, as a muttering king,
Magnificent, would move among his hinds,   35
Until our blood, commingling, virginal,
With heaven, brought such requital to desire
The very hinds discerned it, in a star.
Shall our blood fail? Or shall it come to be
The blood of paradise? And shall the earth   40
Seem all of paradise that we shall know?

---

1. I.e., the holy sepulcher, the cave in Jerusalem where Jesus was entombed; much blood
was shed during the Crusades (eleventh–thirteenth centuries) as Christians attempted to gain
control of Palestine.

The sky will be much friendlier then than now,
A part of labor and a part of pain,
And next in glory to enduring love,
Not this dividing and indifferent blue.   45

                                4

She says, "I am content when wakened birds,
Before they fly, test the reality
Of misty fields, by their sweet questionings;
But when the birds are gone, and their warm fields
Return no more, where, then, is paradise?"   50
There is not any haunt of prophecy,
Nor any old chimera[2] of the grave,
Neither the golden underground, nor isle
Melodious, where spirits gat them home,
Nor visionary south, nor cloudy palm   55
Remote on heaven's hill, that has endured
As April's green endures; or will endure
Like her remembrance of awakened birds,
Or her desire for June and evening, tipped
By the consummation of the swallow's wings.   60

                                5

She says, "But in contentment I still feel
The need of some imperishable bliss."
Death is the mother of beauty; hence from her,
Alone, shall come fulfilment to our dreams
And our desires. Although she strews the leaves   65
Of sure obliteration on our paths,
The path sick sorrow took, the many paths
Where triumph rang its brassy phrase, or love
Whispered a little out of tenderness,
She makes the willow shiver in the sun   70

---

2. In Greek mythology, a monster with a lion's head, goat's body, and serpent's tail. Also, an illusion or fabrication of the mind.

For maidens who were wont to sit and gaze
Upon the grass, relinquished to their feet.
She causes boys to pile new plums and pears
On disregarded plate. The maidens taste
And stray impassioned in the littering leaves.   75

6

Is there no change of death in paradise?
Does ripe fruit never fall? Or do the boughs
Hang always heavy in that perfect sky,
Unchanging, yet so like our perishing earth,
With rivers like our own that seek for seas   80
They never find, the same receding shores
That never touch with inarticulate pang?
Why set the pear upon those river-banks
Or spice the shores with odors of the plum?
Alas, that they should wear our colors there,   85
The silken weavings of our afternoons,
And pick the strings of our insipid lutes!
Death is the mother of beauty, mystical,
Within whose burning bosom we devise
Our earthly mothers waiting, sleeplessly.   90

7

Supple and turbulent, a ring of men
Shall chant in orgy on a summer morn
Their boisterous devotion to the sun,
Not as a god, but as a god might be,
Naked among them, like a savage source.   95
Their chant shall be a chant of paradise,
Out of their blood, returning to the sky;
And in their chant shall enter, voice by voice,
The windy lake wherein their lord delights,
The trees, like serafin, and echoing hills,   100
That choir among themselves long afterward.
They shall know well the heavenly fellowship

Of men that perish and of summer morn.
And whence they came and whither they shall go
The dew upon their feet shall manifest.   105

8

She hears, upon that water without sound,
A voice that cries, "The tomb in Palestine
Is not the porch of spirits lingering.
It is the grave of Jesus, where he lay."
We live in an old chaos of the sun,   110
Or old dependency of day and night,
Or island solitude, unsponsored, free,
Of that wide water, inescapable.
Deer walk upon our mountains, and the quail
Whistle about us their spontaneous cries;   115
Sweet berries ripen in the wilderness;
And, in the isolation of the sky,
At evening, casual flocks of pigeons make
Ambiguous undulations as they sink,
Downward to darkness, on extended wings.   120

1923

The Emperor of Ice-Cream

Call the roller of big cigars,
The muscular one, and bid him whip
In kitchen cups concupiscent curds.
Let the wenches dawdle in such dress
As they are used to wear, and let the boys   5
Bring flowers in last month's newspapers.
Let be be finale of seem
The only emperor is the emperor of ice-cream.

Take from the dresser of deal[3]
Lacking the three glass knobs, that sheet   10

3. I.e., pine or firwood.

On which she embroidered fantails once
And spread it so as to cover her face.
If her horny feet protrude, they come
To show how cold she is, and dumb.
Let the lamp affix its beam.   15
The only emperor is the emperor of ice-cream.

                                    1923

Leon Stokesbury
1945–

> *This meditation on death and dying comes from a book called* The
> Drifting Away *(1986), which is prefaced by a passage from* Huckle-
> berry Finn*: "I heard an owl, away off, who-whooing about
> somebody that was dead, and a whippowill and a dog crying about
> somebody that was going to die, and the wind was trying to whis-
> per something to me and I couldn't make out what it was . . ." This
> passage suggests that the speaker in "Unsent Message to My Brother
> in His Pain" is, like Huck, the sensible, good-hearted, innocent be-
> wildered by the mysteries of this world. The metaphor in the last
> two lines derives from this innocence.*

Unsent Message to My Brother in His Pain

Please do not die now. Listen.
Yesterday, storm clouds rolled
out of the west like thick muscles.
Lightning bloomed. Such a sideshow
of colors. You should have seen it.   5
A woman watched with me, then we slept.
Then, when I woke first, I saw
in her face that rest is possible.
The sky, it suddenly seems
important to tell you, the sky   10
was pink as a shell. Listen

to me. People orbit the moon now.
They must look like flies around
Fatty Arbuckle's head, that new
and that strange. My fellow American,   15
I bought a French cookbook. In it
are hundreds and hundreds of recipes.
If you come to see me, I shit you not,
we will cook with wine. Listen
to me. Listen to me, my brother,   20
please don't go. Take a later flight,
a later train. Another look around.

1986

Alfred, Lord Tennyson
1809–1892

>*"Ulysses" broke with the Romantic practice of autobiographical po-
>etry—the speaker is a character and the poem is a dramatic mono-
>logue. What Ulysses thinks is not necessarily what Tennyson thinks.
>Nevertheless, many critics think Tennyson's friend, Arthur Hallam,
>who died in 1833, inspired the lines about Achilles, and the rousing
>conclusion to the poem was taken at face value by Tennyson's Victo-
>rian readers. The poem alludes to Dante's version of Ulysses' final
>journey: he sailed across the Atlantic toward Purgatory, and God sank
>his ship to punish him for the impudence of the act. In the 1830s, sci-
>entific advancements and engineering feats like the railroad did in-
>deed make some think that humanity "strove with gods." "Crossing
>the Bar" was written in 1889, near the end of Tennyson's life, and he
>left instructions that it should conclude all posthumous collections of
>his poetry. The "bar" is the sandbar that forms naturally at the mouth
>of a harbor; it can be crossed safely only at high tide.*

Ulysses

It little profits that an idle king,
By this still hearth, among these barren crags,
Matched with an aged wife, I mete and dole

Unequal laws unto a savage race,
That hoard, and sleep, and feed, and know not me.   5

　　I cannot rest from travel: I will drink
Life to the lees: all times I have enjoyed
Greatly, have suffered greatly, both with those
That loved me, and alone; on shore, and when
Through scudding drifts the rainy Hyades[1]   10
Vext the dim sea: I am become a name;
For always roaming with a hungry heart
Much have I seen and known; cities of men
And manners, climates, councils, governments,
Myself not least, but honored of them all;   15
And drunk delight of battle with my peers,
Far on the ringing plains of windy Troy.
I am a part of all that I have met;
Yet all experience is an arch wherethrough
Gleams that untravelled world whose margin fades   20
For ever and for ever when I move.
How dull it is to pause, to make an end,
To rust unburnished, not to shine in use!
As though to breathe were life! Life piled on life
Were all too little, and of one to me   25
Little remains: but every hour is saved
From that eternal silence, something more,
A bringer of new things; and vile it were
For some three suns to store and hoard myself,
And this gray spirit yearning in desire   30
To follow knowledge like a sinking star,
Beyond the utmost bound of human thought.

　　This is my son, mine own Telemachus,
To whom I leave the scepter and the isle—
Well-loved of me, discerning to fulfill   35
This labor, by slow prudence to make mild

---

1. A group of stars in the constellation Taurus, believed to foretell the coming of rain when they rose with the sun.

A rugged people, and through soft degrees
Subdue them to the useful and the good.
Most blameless is he, centered in the sphere
Of common duties, decent not to fail   40
In offices of tenderness, and pay
Meet adoration to my household gods,
When I am gone. He works his work, I mine.

   There lies the port; the vessel puffs her sail:
There gloom the dark, broad seas. My mariners,   45
Souls that have toiled, and wrought, and thought with me—
That ever with a frolic welcome took
The thunder and the sunshine, and opposed
Free hearts, free foreheads—you and I are old;
Old age hath yet his honor and his toil;   50
Death closes all: but something ere the end,
Some work of noble note, may yet be done,
Not unbecoming men that strove with Gods.
The lights begin to twinkle from the rocks:
The long day wanes: the slow moon climbs: the deep   55
Moans round with many voices. Come, my friends,
'Tis not too late to seek a newer world.
Push off, and sitting well in order smite
The sounding furrows; for my purpose holds
To sail beyond the sunset, and the baths   60
Of all the western stars, until I die.
It may be that the gulfs will wash us down:
It may be we shall touch the Happy Isles,[2]
And see the great Achilles, whom we knew.
Though much is taken, much abides; and though   65
We are not now that strength which in old days
Moved earth and heaven; that which we are, we are,
One equal temper of heroic hearts,
Made weak by time and fate, but strong in will
To strive, to seek, to find, and not to yield.   70

1842

2. The Islands of the Blessed, the abode after death of those favored by the gods, especially heroes and patriots.

Crossing the Bar

Sunset and evening star,
    And one clear call for me!
And may there be no moaning of the bar,
    When I put out to sea,

But such a tide as moving seems asleep,   5
    Too full for sound and foam,
When that which drew from out the boundless deep
    Turns again home.

Twilight and evening bell,
    And after that the dark!   10
And may there be no sadness of farewell,
    When I embark;

For though from out our bourne of Time and Place
    The flood may bear me far,
I hope to see my Pilot face to face   15
    When I have crossed the bar.

                                        1889

Dylan Thomas
1914–1953

> *Fern Hill was a country farm, a largish, peasant plot with a damp,
> dark, creaky house on the side of a hill, rented by an aunt and un-
> cle. Thomas spent summers there in childhood, and remembered it
> as an Edenic farm in "Fern Hill." Thomas personifies "Time" in
> the first stanza and carries the metaphor through to the last: one
> way to enter the poem is to trace "Time's" character. Thomas wrote
> "Do Not Go Gentle into That Good Night" while watching his
> father, the once proud and fiery schoolteacher "who had a violent
> and quite personal dislike for God," wither, grow powerless, then
> die. "Do Not Go Gentle" is a villanelle; you might hypothesize*

why Thomas chose to write this poem in such a tightly structured form.

Fern Hill

Now as I was young and easy under the apple boughs
About the lilting house and happy as the grass was green,
    The night above the dingle[1] starry,
      Time let me hail and climb
        Golden in the heydays of his eyes,   5
And honoured among wagons I was prince of the apple towns
And once below a time I lordly had the trees and leaves
      Trail with daisies and barley
    Down the rivers of the windfall light.

And as I was green and carefree, famous among the barns   10
About the happy yard and singing as the farm was home,
    In the sun that is young once only,
      Time let me play and be
        Golden in the mercy of his means,
And green and golden I was huntsman and herdsman, the calves   15
Sang to my horn, the foxes on the hills barked clear and cold,
      And the sabbath rang slowly
    In the pebbles of the holy streams.

All the sun long it was running, it was lovely, the hay
Fields high as the house, the tunes from the chimneys, it was air   20
    And playing, lovely and watery
      And fire green as grass.
    And nightly under the simple stars
As I rode to sleep the owls were bearing the farm away,
All the moon long I heard, blessed among stables, the night-jars[2]   25

---

1. Small wooded valley.   2. Nocturnal birds.

Flying with the ricks,[3] and the horses
    Flashing into the dark.

And then to awake, and the farm, like a wanderer white
With the dew, come back, the cock on his shoulder: it was all
    Shining, it was Adam and maiden,   *—apples* 30
        The sky gathered again   *Adam &*
      And the sun grew round that very day.   *Eve?*
So it must have been after the birth of the simple light
In the first, spinning place, the spellbound horses walking warm
      Out of the whinnying green stable *—usually* 35
        On to the fields of praise.   *red*

And honoured among foxes and pheasants by the gay house
Under the new made clouds and happy as the heart was long,
    In the sun born over and over,
        I ran my heedless ways,   40
      My wishes raced through the house high hay
And nothing I cared, at my sky blue trades, that time allows
In all his tuneful turning so few and such morning songs
    Before the children green and golden
        Follow him out of grace,   45

Nothing I cared, in the lamb white days, that time would take me
Up to the swallow thronged loft by the shadow of my hand,
    In the moon that is always rising,
        Nor that riding to sleep
      I should hear him fly with the high fields   50
And wake to the farm forever fled from the childless land.
Oh as I was young and easy in the mercy of his means,
      Time held me green and dying
    Though I sang in my chains like the sea.

                          1946

Is he a slave working in

3. Haystacks.

Villanelle

Do Not Go Gentle into That Good Night

Do not go gentle into that good night,
Old age should burn and rave at close of day;
Rage, rage against the dying of the light.

Though wise men at their end know dark is right,
Because their words had forked no lightning they   5
Do not go gentle into that good night.

Good men, the last wave by, crying how bright
Their frail deeds might have danced in a green bay,
Rage, rage against the dying of the light.

rhymes

Wild men who caught and sang the sun in flight,   10
And learn, too late, they grieved it on its way,
Do not go gentle into that good night.

Grave men, near death, who see with blinding sight
Blind eyes could blaze like meteors and be gay,
Rage, rage against the dying of the light.   15

And you, my father, there on the sad height,
Curse, bless, me now with your fierce tears, I pray.
Do not go gentle into that good night.
Rage, rage against the dying of the light.

1952

Walt Whitman

1819–1892

> *Whitman popularized free verse in American and British poetry,
> but "A Noiseless Patient Spider" demonstrates that "free" does not
> mean "random." For example, note the similar syntax in lines 4
> and 8, which connects the action of the spider to that of the
> speaker's soul. This poem is an apostrophe: the speaker is talking to*

his soul. Its meaning depends on the comparison of the soul to the spider. You should ask yourself why Whitman chose a spider and not, say, a bird building a nest or a lion stalking its prey. "When I Heard the Learn'd Astronomer" is a latter-day Romantic poem, very similar in theme to Wordsworth's "The Tables Turned" and its pronouncement on science: "We murder to dissect."

A Noiseless Patient Spider

A noiseless patient spider,
I mark'd where on a little promontory it stood isolated,
Mark'd how to explore the vacant vast surrounding,
It launch'd forth filament, filament, filament, out of itself,
Ever unreeling them, ever tirelessly speeding them.   5

And you O my soul where you stand,
Surrounded, detached, in measureless oceans of space,
Ceaselessly musing, venturing, throwing, seeking the spheres
    to connect them,
Till the bridge you will need be form'd, till the ductile anchor
    hold,
Till the gossamer thread you fling catch somewhere, O my
    soul.   10

1881

When I Heard the Learn'd Astronomer

When I heard the learn'd astronomer,
When the proofs, the figures, were ranged in columns before
    me,
When I was shown the charts and diagrams, to add, divide,
    and measure them,
When I sitting heard the astronomer where he lectured with
    much applause in the lecture-room,
How soon unaccountable I became tired and sick,   5
Till rising and gliding out I wander'd off by myself,

In the mystical moist night-air, and from time to time,
Look'd up in perfect silence at the stars.

1865

Richard Wilbur

1921–

> *Influenced by the seventeenth-century metaphysical poets and the ironic stances of his contemporaries, Wilbur composes poetry with precision, wit, and a keen attention to meter. Of "Love Calls Us to the Things of This World" Wilbur wrote, "You must imagine the poem as occurring at perhaps seven-thirty in the morning; the scene is a bedroom high up in a city apartment building; outside the bedroom window, the first laundry of the day is being yanked across the sky and one has been awakened by the squeaking pulleys of the laundry-line." Pay particular attention to the soul: where it is in the beginning of the poem, how the laundry on the line is like the soul, and why the soul finally "accepts the waking body."*

Love Calls Us to the Things of This World

  The eyes open to a cry of pulleys,
And spirited from sleep, the astounded soul
Hangs for a moment bodiless and simple
As false dawn.
     Outside the open window
The morning air is all awash with angels.   5

  Some are in bed-sheets, some are in blouses,
Some are in smocks: but truly there they are.
Now they are rising together in calm swells
Of halcyon feeling, filling whatever they wear
With the deep joy of their impersonal breathing;   10

Now they are flying in place, conveying
The terrible speed of their omnipresence, moving
And staying like white water; and now of a sudden
They swoon down into so rapt a quiet
That nobody seems to be there.
                              The soul shrinks   15

          From all that it is about to remember,
From the punctual rape of every blessèd day
And cries,
              "Oh, let there be nothing on earth but laundry,
Nothing but rosy hands in the rising steam
And clear dances done in the sight of heaven."   20

          Yet, as the sun acknowledges
With a warm look the world's hunks and colors,
The soul descends once more in bitter love
To accept the waking body, saying now
In a changed voice as the man yawns and rises,   25

          "Bring them down from their ruddy gallows;
Let there be clean linen for the backs of thieves;
Let lovers go fresh and sweet to be undone,
And the heaviest nuns walk in a pure floating
Of dark habits,
              keeping their difficult balance."   30

                                        1956

William Carlos Williams
1883–1963

In 1923 Williams broke with his fellow modern poets by publishing
Spring and All, *perhaps in response to what he considered T. S.
Eliot's great catastrophe,* The Waste Land. *"Spring and All," the
first poem in the volume, seems to comment on the opening of
Eliot's poem, "April is the cruelest month." But Williams explained
that he did not want his poems to communicate ideas. They were*

"[t]o refine, to clarify, to intensify that eternal moment in which we alone live" through contact with things."The Red Wheelbarrow," the twenty-second poem (none had titles in the original book), is, perhaps, his best attempt to achieve that intensity. What depends on our seeing the wheelbarrow (on our really experiencing the things around us) is life. In such moments of heightened perception, time stops, and we are immortal even if, paradoxically, only for a short interval. "This Is Just to Say" challenges our notions of what is and is not poetry. As you read it, you should ask yourself what a text must contain to be a poem.

Spring and All

By the road to the contagious hospital
under the surge of the blue
mottled clouds driven from the
northeast—a cold wind. Beyond, the
waste of broad, muddy fields   5
brown with dried weeds, standing and fallen

patches of standing water
the scattering of tall trees

All along the road the reddish
purplish, forked, upstanding, twiggy   10
stuff of bushes and small trees
with dead, brown leaves under them
leafless vines—

Lifeless in appearance, sluggish
dazed spring approaches—   15

They enter the new world naked,
cold, uncertain of all

save that they enter. All about them
the cold, familiar wind—

Now the grass, tomorrow   20
the stiff curl of wildcarrot leaf
One by one objects are defined—
It quickens: clarity, outline of leaf

But now the stark dignity of
entrance—Still, the profound change   25
has come upon them: rooted, they
grip down and begin to awaken

                                          1923

The Red Wheelbarrow

so much depends
upon

a red wheel
barrow

glazed with rain   5
water

beside the white
chickens.
                1923

This Is Just to Say

I have eaten
the plums
that were in
the icebox

and which   5
you were probably
saving
for breakfast

Forgive me
they were delicious   10
so sweet
and so cold

　　　　1934

William Wordsworth

1770–1850

Wordsworth's 1798 Lyrical Ballads *revolutionized English poetry by lowering poetic diction to simple, ordinary language and by widening poetic subjects to include farmers, flowers, children, and the poet's spontaneous thoughts as they interact with the world. "The Tables Turned" celebrates the effect of this interaction. Wordsworth deplored how the Industrial Revolution was moving whole populations from the country to the cities, removing us from the rhythms of the natural world and leaving us in an increasingly artificial and inhumane environment. Likewise, he hated the modern attitude that the natural world is raw material waiting to be exploited. Much of our current love and respect for wilderness was first articulated by Wordsworth. "Nutting" compares the harvesting of nuts to a rape. Keeping the final lines of "Nutting" in mind helps explain Wordsworth's high regard for nature. "The World Is Too Much With Us" compares the modern, urbane, civilized, sensible unbelief of an Englishman in 1807 to paganism, which was popularly thought of as the superstitious, unlearned myths of half-savage country folk. Underlying the poem is Wordsworth's belief that civilization corrupts our natural nobility and our capacity to perceive the divine.*

The Tables Turned

Up! up! my Friend, and quit your books;
Or surely you'll grow double:
Up! up! my Friend, and clear your looks;
Why all this toil and trouble?

The sun, above the mountain's head,   5
A freshening lustre mellow
Through all the long green fields has spread,
His first sweet evening yellow.

Books! 'tis a dull and endless strife:
Come, hear the woodland linnet,   10
How sweet his music! on my life,
There's more of wisdom in it.

And hark! how blithe the throstle sings!
He, too, is no mean preacher:
Come forth into the light of things,   15
Let Nature be your Teacher.

She has a world of ready wealth,
Our minds and hearts to bless—
Spontaneous wisdom breathed by health,
Truth breathed by cheerfulness.   20

One impulse from a vernal wood
May teach you more of man,
Of moral evil and of good,
Than all the sages can.

Sweet is the lore which Nature brings;   25
Our meddling intellect
Mis-shapes the beauteous forms of things:—
We murder to dissect.

Enough of Science and of Art;
Close up those barren leaves;   30
Come forth, and bring with you a heart
That watches and receives.

1798

Nutting

————————It seems a day
(I speak of one from many singled out)
One of those heavenly days that cannot die;
When, in the eagerness of boyish hope,
I left our cottage-threshold, sallying forth   5
With a huge wallet o'er my shoulder slung,
A nutting-crook in hand; and turned my steps
Tow'rd some far-distant wood, a Figure quaint,
Tricked out in proud disguise of cast-off weeds[1]
Which for that service had been husbanded,   10
By exhortation of my frugal Dame[2]—
Motley accoutrement, of power to smile
At thorns, and brakes, and brambles,—and, in truth,
More ragged than need was! O'er pathless rocks,
Through beds of matted fern, and tangled thickets,   15
Forcing my way, I came to one dear nook
Unvisited, where not a broken bough
Drooped with its withered leaves, ungracious sign
Of devastation; but the hazels rose
Tall and erect, with tempting clusters hung,   20
A virgin scene!—A little while I stood,
Breathing with such suppression of the heart
As joy delights in; and, with wise restraint
Voluptuous, fearless of a rival, eyed
The banquet;—or beneath the trees I sate   25
Among the flowers, and with the flowers I played;

1. Clothes.
2. Ann Tyson, with whom Wordsworth lodged while at Hawkshead grammar school.

A temper known to those, who, after long
And weary expectation, have been blest
With sudden happiness beyond all hope.
Perhaps it was a bower beneath whose leaves   30
The violets of five seasons re-appear
And fade, unseen by any human eye;
Where fairy water-breaks[3] do murmur on
For ever; and I saw the sparkling foam,
And—with my cheek on one of those green stones   35
That, fleeced with moss, under the shady trees,
Lay round me, scattered like a flock of sheep—
I heard the murmur and the murmuring sound,
In that sweet mood when pleasure loves to pay
Tribute to ease; and, of its joy secure,   40
The heart luxuriates with indifferent things,
Wasting its kindliness on stocks and stones,
And on the vacant air. Then up I rose,
And dragged to earth both branch and bough, with crash
And merciless ravage: and the shady nook   45
Of hazels, and the green and mossy bower,
Deformed and sullied, patiently gave up
Their quiet being: and, unless I now
Confound my present feelings with the past,
Ere from the mutilated bower I turned   50
Exulting, rich beyond the wealth of kings,
I felt a sense of pain when I beheld
The silent trees, and saw the intruding sky.—
Then, dearest Maiden, move along these shades
In gentleness of heart; with gentle hand   55
Touch—for there is a spirit in the woods.

1800

---

3. Places where rocks break a stream's flow.

The World Is Too Much with Us

The world is too much with us; late and soon,
Getting and spending, we lay waste our powers;
Little we see in Nature that is ours;
We have given our hearts away, a sordid boon!
This Sea that bares her bosom to the moon,   5
The winds that will be howling at all hours,
And are up-gathered now like sleeping flowers,
For this, for everything, we are out of tune;
It moves us not.—Great God! I'd rather be
A Pagan suckled in a creed outworn;   10
So might I, standing on this pleasant lea,[1]
Have glimpses that would make me less forlorn;
Have sight of Proteus rising from the sea;
Or hear old Triton blow his wreathèd horn.[2]

                                        1807

James Wright
1927–1980

> *In his poetry, Wright often grapples with the tension between two visions of midwestern America: the social forces that can cripple individuals and the natural forces that have a restorative power. Like many poems since the Romantic era, "A Blessing" describes a moment of heightened awareness or perception during which the things of the world seem to harmonize in unusual splendor. (Twilight seems to be the appropriate time for such moments.) What distinguishes Wright's poem is the comparison of the slender pony to a girl: what does this metaphor suggest about the speaker's relationship to the phenomena he perceives?*

1. I.e., open meadow.
2. In Greek myth Proteus, the "Old Man of the Sea," rises from the sea at midday and can be forced to read the future by anyone who holds him while he takes many frightening shapes. Triton is the son of the sea god, Neptune; the sound of his conch-shell horn calms the waves.

A Blessing

Just off the highway to Rochester, Minnesota,
Twilight bounds softly forth on the grass.
And the eyes of those two Indian ponies
Darken with kindness.
They have come gladly out of the willows   5
To welcome my friend and me.
We step over the barbed wire into the pasture
Where they have been grazing all day, alone.
They ripple tensely, they can hardly contain their happiness
That we have come.   10
They bow shyly as wet swans. They love each other.
There is no loneliness like theirs.
At home once more,
They begin munching the young tufts of spring in the darkness.
I would like to hold the slenderer one in my arms,   15
For she has walked over to me
And nuzzled my left hand.
She is black and white,
Her mane falls wild on her forehead,
And the light breeze moves me to caress her long ear   20
That is delicate as the skin over a girl's wrist.
Suddenly I realize
That if I stepped out of my body I would break
Into blossom.

1963

Sir Thomas Wyatt the Elder
1503–1542

> *Wyatt introduced the sonnet into English and first modified the Pe-*
> *trarchan or Italian rhyme scheme into the English scheme adopted*
> *and popularized by Shakespeare generations later. "My Galley" is*
> *a translation of one of Petrarch's sonnets. The speaker, as in most*
> *sonnets of the sixteenth and seventeenth centuries, is a male lover*

pining over his beloved's cold indifference. "They Flee from Me" introduces an interesting comparison between the speaker's lover and a wild animal in the first stanza. Part of this poem's continuing appeal is the range of emotions expressed: try to trace the speaker's vacillating attitudes toward this fickle woman, which are reflected in subtle changes in tone.

My Galley

My galley charged[1] with forgetfulness
   Thorough sharp seas in winter nights doth pass
'Tween rock and rock; and eke mine enemy,[2] alas,
   That is my lord, steereth with cruelness;
And every oar a thought in readiness,   5
   As though that death were light in such a case.
   An endless wind doth tear the sail apace
   Of forced sighs and trusty fearfulness.
A rain of tears, a cloud of dark disdain,
   Hath done the wearied cords[3] great hinderance;   10
   Wreathed with error and eke with ignorance.
The stars be hid[4] that led me to this pain;
   Drowned is reason that should me consort,
   And I remain despairing of the port.

They Flee from Me

They flee from me that sometime did me seek
   With naked foot stalking in my chamber.
I have seen them gentle tame and meek
   That now are wild and do not remember
   That sometime they put themselves in danger   5
To take bread at my hand; and now they range
Busily seeking with a continual change.

---

1. I.e., laden.
2. I.e., love. "Eke": also.
3. The worn lines of the sail, with a possi-
ble pun on the Latin for heart *(cor, cordis)*.
4. I.e., the lady's eyes.

Thanked be fortune, it hath been otherwise
   Twenty times better; but once in special,
In thin array after a pleasant guise,[5]   10
   When her loose gown from her shoulders did fall,
   And she me caught in her arms long and small;
And therewithal sweetly did me kiss,
And softly said, *Dear heart,*[6] *how like you this?*

It was no dream, I lay broad waking.   15
   But all is turned thorough my gentleness
Into a strange fashion of forsaking;
   And I have leave to go of her goodness
   And she also to use newfangleness.
But since that I so kindely[7] am served,   20
I would fain know what she hath deserved.

William Butler Yeats
1865–1939

> Born into an old Irish family, Yeats cherished "the ambition . . . of
> living in imitation of Thoreau on Innisfree, a small island in
> Lough Gill," a lake on Ireland's west coast. In his autobiography,
> Yeats tells us that once, on the streets of London, he saw in a shop-
> window a display with a little spout of water, and he thought of
> writing "The Lake Isle of Innisfree." "The Second Coming" was
> written just after World War I, and its apocalyptic images were pro-
> voked by the Bolshevik Revolution in Russia. Later, Yeats claimed
> that the poem foresaw the rise of fascism in Italy and Nazism in
> Germany. Some critics think he made this comment to distance
> himself from the nearly fascist politics he espoused in the 1920s. The
> image of the falcon and falconer symbolizes Yeats's view that history
> can be depicted by a gyre, or cone. The point of the cone is the birth
> of Christ, which initiated a two-thousand-year era of individual-

5. In a thin gown, made in a pleasing
fashion.

6. With a pun on "heart" and "hart" (as deer).

7. I.e., in the way typical of female na-
ture, or "kind"; with kindness (ironic).

ism that reached its best moment in the Renaissance and was now spinning out of control in the mass politics of the twentieth century: democracy and communism. At this widest point of the cone, a new era would be initiated, reversing the last. Yeats originally titled "Leda and the Swan" "The Annunciation." The poem's depiction of a god, who appears as a swan, raping a mortal woman deliberately insulted Catholic readers, who saw in the poem a comment on the Virgin Mary's impregnation. Yeats meant the violent and obscene imagery to defy the censorship laws of the increasingly conservative and Catholic government in Ireland. "Sailing to Byzantium" was published when Yeats was sixty-three years old and felt there was little place for old men like himself in the young country. The first stanza, though universalized, describes Ireland. Byzantium was, for Yeats, an admired place of timeless, unchanging culture.

The Lake Isle of Innisfree

I will arise and go now, and go to Innisfree,
And a small cabin build there, of clay and wattles made:
Nine bean-rows will I have there, a hive for the honey-bee,
And live alone in the bee-loud glade.

And I shall have some peace there, for peace comes dropping
    slow,   5
Dropping from the veils of the morning to where the cricket
    sings;
There midnight's all a glimmer, and noon a purple glow,
And evening full of the linnet's wings.

I will arise and go now, for always night and day
I hear lake water lapping with low sounds by the shore;   10
While I stand on the roadway, or on the pavements grey,
I hear it in the deep heart's core.

1892

The Second Coming

Turning and turning in the widening gyre
The falcon cannot hear the falconer;
Things fall apart; the centre cannot hold;
Mere anarchy is loosed upon the world,
The blood-dimmed tide is loosed, and everywhere   5
The ceremony of innocence is drowned;
The best lack all conviction, while the worst
Are full of passionate intensity.

Surely some revelation is at hand;
Surely the Second Coming is at hand: 10
The Second Coming! Hardly are those words out
When a vast image out of *Spiritus Mundi*
Troubles my sight: somewhere in sands of the desert
A shape with lion body and the head of a man,
A gaze blank and pitiless as the sun,   15
Is moving its slow thighs, while all about it
Reel shadows of the indignant desert birds.
The darkness drops again; but now I know
That twenty centuries of stony sleep
Were vexed to nightmare by a rocking cradle,   20
And what rough beast, its hour come round at last,
Slouches towards Bethlehem to be born?

1921

Leda and the Swan[1]

A sudden blow: the great wings beating still
Above the staggering girl, her thighs caressed
By the dark webs, her nape caught in his bill,
He holds her helpless breast upon his breast.

How can those terrified vague fingers push   5
The feathered glory from her loosening thighs?
And how can body, laid in that white rush,
But feel the strange heart beating where it lies?

A shudder in the loins engenders there
The broken wall, the burning roof and tower   10
And Agamemnon dead.
                              Being so caught up,
So mastered by the brute blood of the air,
Did she put on his knowledge with his power
Before the indifferent beak could let her drop?

1924

---

1. In Greek mythology, Leda, a human woman, was raped by the god Zeus, who appeared
in the form of a swan. Leda gave birth to Helen, who eventually married Menelaus, a Greek
king. When Paris of Troy kidnapped Helen, the Greeks, led by Menelaus's brother Agamem-
non (who was married to Helen's sister, Clytemnestra), banded together to invade Troy and
retrieve Helen. The long history of the Trojan War, including Clytemnestra's murdering
Agamemnon upon his return, was engendered by this rape. Yeats considered this story to be
an analogue of the Christian annunciation, when God, in the form of a dove, impregnated
Mary. In Yeats's idiosyncratic theory of history, the birth of Jesus initiated a two-thousand-
year epoch that culminated in the mass politics and wars of the twentieth century.

Sailing to Byzantium[2]

1

That is no country for old men. The young
In one another's arms, birds in the trees
—Those dying generations—at their song,
The salmon-falls, the mackerel-crowded seas,
Fish, flesh, or fowl, commend all summer long   5
Whatever is begotten, born, and dies.
Caught in that sensual music all neglect
Monuments of unaging intellect.

2

An aged man is but a paltry thing,
A tattered coat upon a stick, unless   10
Soul clap its hands and sing, and louder sing
For every tatter in its mortal dress,
Nor is there singing school but studying
Monuments of its own magnificence;
And therefore I have sailed the seas and come   15
To the holy city of Byzantium.

3

O sages standing in God's holy fire
As in the gold mosaic of a wall,
Come from the holy fire, perne in a gyre,[3]

2. Byzantium (now Istanbul) was for centuries the capital of the Eastern Roman Empire. Yeats saw in its mosaics the prototype of an artificial, symbolic art that made no attempt at realism. Byzantium became, in his imagination, a country of unchanging, undeveloping artifice, and this permanence he contrasted with the mutability of a young country, like Ireland, which had gained its independence just six years before he wrote this poem.

3. The speaker is asking the sages to come down as if out of the golden mosaics painted on the inside of a dome and inspire him. "Perne" is Yeats's coinage. It refers to thread pulled from a bobbin; the unwinding thread would appear to make a conical shape. In this comparison, the thread would be the sages, and the point of the cone would be the speaker into whom these sages are descending.

And be the singing-masters of my soul.   20
Consume my heart away; sick with desire
And fastened to a dying animal
It knows not what it is; and gather me
Into the artifice of eternity.

4

Once out of nature I shall never take   25
My bodily form from any natural thing,
But such a form as Grecian goldsmiths make
Of hammered gold and gold enamelling
To keep a drowsy Emperor awake;
Or set upon a golden bough to sing   30
To lords and ladies of Byzantium
Of what is past, or passing, or to come.

1927

*

Biographical Sketches

John Agard (*1949–*) Born and raised in Guyana, Agard moved to England in 1977. The rhythm of the West Indies—a special mixture of African and European styles—pervades Agard's poetry. Many of his poems were written to be performed, and he considers himself part of a movement that has rediscovered the oral roots of poetry. Agard calls himself a "poetsonian," playing on the term "calypsonian," which refers to a performer of calypso song and dance. He writes poems for adults and children alike, and also works as a playwright, performer, and anthologist. Together with the BBC and other organizations Agard has sought to increase the place of poetry in everyday British life. His books include *Man to Pan*, *Mangoes and Bullets*, *We Animals Would Like a Word with You*, and *From the Devil's Pulpit*.

Paul Allen (*1945–*) Allen teaches courses in writing poetry and in writing song lyrics at the College of Charleston in Charleston, South Carolina, where he is Associate Professor of English. His first book of poems, *American Crawl*, received the Vassar Miller Poetry Prize and was nominated for a Pulitzer and a National Book Award. In 2000, Glebe Street Records released Allen's *The Man with the Hardest Belly: Poems & Songs*. Forthcoming is another poetry collection, *The Clean Plate Club*.

Matthew Arnold (*1822–1888*)   Arnold was a sort of jack-of-all-trades: a preeminent poet of the Victorian era, a pioneer in the field of literary criticism, an educator, a government official, and an influential public figure. Arnold's father was the headmaster of Rugby, a prestigious English prep school, and Arnold grew up knowing many of the leading intellectual and literary men of his day. He was educated at Winchester, Rugby, and Balliol College, Oxford, later serving as fellow of Oriel College, Oxford. In 1851 he married Frances Lucy Wightman, and when the newlyweds visited Dover on their honeymoon, Arnold wrote the earliest drafts of "Dover Beach." Arnold was well known in his own day as an arbiter of culture, and his theories of literary criticism are still highly influential today.

Margaret Atwood (*1939–*)   Atwood spent the first eleven years of her life in sparsely populated areas of northern Ontario and Quebec, where her father, an entomologist, spent eight months of each year doing research in the forest. The Atwood family stayed in a cabin heated by a wood stove and lit by kerosene lanterns. One of Atwood's few sources of entertainment was reading, and she soon began to write, too, beginning with poems, plays, comic books, and an unfinished novel about an ant. By sixteen, she had decided that all she wanted to do was write. Atwood received her bachelor's degree from Victoria College at the University of Toronto and her master's degree from Radcliffe College. She also studied at Harvard University. Together with a friend Atwood published her first book of poems on a small flat-bed press and sold copies for fifty cents each. She has received numerous prizes for her poetry as well as for her fiction.

W. H. (Wystan Hugh) Auden (*1907–1973*)   Born to a medical officer and a nurse, W. H. Auden attended Christ Church College, Oxford, where he distinguished himself more as a poet than as a student. While at Oxford, Auden formed friendships with such writers as Stephen Spender, C. Day Lewis, and Christopher Isherwood. Not only was Auden the principal poet of his generation, but he was also a playwright, librettist, editor, and essayist. He is widely admired for his technical virtuosity, his success with diverse poetic forms and themes, and his encyclopedic intellectual range. Auden moved to New York City's Greenwich Village in 1939 and became an American citizen in 1946. For many years he was actively involved in politics, vigorously opposing fascism. But he shocked audiences on both sides of the Atlantic when he repudiated the political scene by publishing "In Memory of W. B. Yeats" in *The New Republic*. Auden received the Pulitzer Prize for his body of work and served as Chancellor of the Academy of American Poets.

Elizabeth Bishop (*1911–1979*) Bishop lost both of her parents early in her life. She was shuttled between her father's wealthy Massachusetts family and her mother's rural Nova Scotia family throughout her childhood. Bishop was educated at Vassar College, where she fell in with a group of young, talented writers. In 1935 she met Marianne Moore, whose work deeply impressed Bishop and whose friendship was to become a stabilizing force in her life. *The Partisan Review*'s March 1940 publication of "The Fish" launched Bishop's career, and from then on her work frequently appeared in magazines such as *The New Yorker*. Bishop went on to win virtually every poetry prize in the country. She served as a chancellor of the Academy of American Poets, a member of the American Academy of Arts and Letters, and a consultant in poetry to the Library of Congress in 1949–50. She taught at the University of Washington, Harvard, New York University, and, just prior to her death, the Massachusetts Institute of Technology.

William Blake (*1757–1827*) Though Blake is today considered one of the earliest and greatest figures of English Romanticism, at the time of his death he was a little-known artist and an entirely unknown poet. Having been apprenticed at the age of fourteen, Blake's only formal education was in art, and he was an accomplished painter and engraver. For most of his life he made his living illustrating books and magazines, giving drawing lessons, and engraving designs made by other artists. From childhood, though, he spent most of his spare time reading, and often tried his hand at poetry. By adulthood, he was dissatisfied with the reigning poetic tradition and was testing new forms and techniques. In 1789, the year that the French Revolution began, he published *Songs of Innocence*, a series of poems accompanied by his own illustrations. In 1794 he published a parallel series, *Songs of Experience*. Together, Blake wrote, these two series portray "the two Contrary States of the Human Soul." He was a devout Christian who saw a close relationship between his religion and his art, declaring that "all he knew was in the Bible" and that the "Old and New Testaments are the Great Code of Art."

Anne Bradstreet (*1612 or 1613–1672*) Bradstreet's father, Thomas Dudley, steward of the Earl of Lincoln's estate, took care to see that his daughter received a better education than most young women of her day. At sixteen she married Simon Bradstreet, a recent graduate of Cambridge University and assistant of her father. Bradstreet was soon appointed to assist in preparations of the Massachusetts Bay Company, and so the Bradstreets and Dudleys sailed with Winthrop's fleet to Massachusetts. In leaving

"Old England" for "New England," Anne Bradstreet gave up a life of relative comfort and culture for the wilderness of the New World. When visiting England in 1650, Bradstreet's brother-in-law published a volume of Bradstreet's poetry without her consent. This volume, *The Tenth Muse*, was the first book of poetry written by a resident of the New World and was widely read throughout England. The verses for which she is remembered today were not published until 1678 in a posthumous edition. Bradstreet was an ambitious poet whose work is firmly grounded in English religious, political, and cultural history.

Gwendolyn Brooks (*1917–2000*)   Born in Topeka, Kansas, and raised in Chicago, Brooks began writing poetry at the age of seven. After graduating from high school, she attended art school at the South Side Community Art Center. Her main interest, however, was poetry, and she soon demonstrated her talent by winning contests sponsored by *Poetry* magazine and various other organizations. She published her first book of poetry in 1945. Her second book of poems, *Annie Allen*, won Brooks the distinction of being the first African American to be awarded the Pulitzer Prize, which she received in 1950. Brooks's early works concentrate on what Langston Hughes called the "ordinary aspects of black life," but her later poetry deals more with issues of African American consciousness and activism.

Elizabeth Barrett Browning (*1806–1861*)   The eldest of twelve children, Barrett Browning was the first in her family to be born in England in over two hundred years, as the Barretts had lived in Jamaica for centuries. Though she lived at home under her father's strict rule, Barrett Browning began writing poetry at an early age, publishing her first volume when she was only thirteen and gaining a considerable following by the time she was in her thirties. Her 1844 collection, *Poems*, caught the eye of Robert Browning, and the two exchanged 574 letters over a period of twenty months. Her father did not want any of his children to marry, and so Elizabeth was forced to elope with Robert, who was six years her junior. The two settled in Italy, where Barrett Browning bore a son; saw her chronic lung condition improve; and published *Sonnets from the Portuguese*, a sequence of forty-four sonnets that record the stages of her love for Robert Browning. Critics have compared the imagery of the sonnet sequence to that of Shakespeare and the skillful use of form to that of Petrarch.

Robert Browning (*1816–1889*)   Born in a suburb of London, Browning spent much of his childhood in his father's extensive library. From early on his aim was to become a poet; he abandoned his schooling in order to dedicate all his energies to the realization of this goal. His parents supported him until he was in his thirties. Browning admired the poetry of Elizabeth Barrett and began to correspond with her in 1844. Two years later they were married. In 1849 they moved to Italy because the warm climate there helped Elizabeth's lung condition. After Elizabeth died in 1861, Browning returned to London and began to establish his literary reputation. Today he is recognized as one of England's most prolific poets.

Lynne Bryer (*1946–1994*) Bryer, a white South African, received her Master's in English from Rhodes University (South Africa) in 1969. She worked in the publishing industry in London and Cape Town before opening her own publishing house, Chameleon Press. As a publisher Bryer provided a venue for new and progressive writing in South Africa. She received the prestigious AA Life Vita/Arthur Nortje Poety Award in 1991. She died after a courageous battle with cancer.

Lewis Carroll [Charles Lutwidge Dodgson] (*1832–1898*) Charles Lutwidge Dodgson was the man behind the pen name of "Lewis Carroll." Dodgson was born in Daresbury, Cheshire, England, to an Anglican clergyman who eventually had eleven children. He was educated at Richmond School, Rugby, and Christ Church, Oxford. A man of diverse interests, Dodgson was actively engaged in many fields: mathematics, logic, photography, art, theater, religion, medicine, and science. In 1855 Dodgson finally attained a college Mastership at Oxford, a position that he was to hold until 1881. For some time he aspired to the priesthood, and he even went so far as to be ordained as a deacon in 1861. Dodgson was happiest in the company of children for whom he created puzzles, clever games, and charming letters. He was particularly close to the children of Henry Liddell, dean of Christ Church, and wrote most of his stories for their amusement. Alice Liddell was his favorite, and it is she who stars in *Alice in Wonderland* and *Through the Looking-Glass*.

Samuel Taylor Coleridge (*1772–1834*) Coleridge was born in the small town of Ottery St. Mary in Devonshire, England, the youngest of ten children. When his father died in 1781, Coleridge was sent to a London charity school for children of the clergy, Christ's Hospital, where he read widely and finished first in his class. Coleridge went on to attend Jesus College, Cambridge, though he was forced to leave without a degree after he fell into debt. After a brief stint in the army and an attempt at lecturing, he married Sara Fricker and tried to settle down. He became friends with Wordsworth and the two men collaborated on a number of literary projects, notably *Lyrical Ballads*. Coleridge spent two years in Malta trying unsuccessfully to recover from painful rheumatism. Upon his return he dissolved his unhappy marriage, which had been strained by his love for another woman. As the years passed, he became more estranged from his family and more addicted to opium to ease his pain. Coleridge was also a literary critic.

Billy Collins (*1941–*)   Collins lives in New York and is professor of English at Lehman College of the City University of New York. He has received fellowships from the National Endowment for the Arts and the Guggenheim Foundation, and his work has been published in such venues as *Poetry*, *American Poetry Review*, *American Scholar*, *Harper's*, *The Paris Review*, *The Atlantic Monthly*, and *The New Yorker*. Collins's collections include *Picnic, Lightning*; *The Art of Drowning*; *Questions about Angels*; and the CD *The Best Cigarette*. He has won numerous awards, among them the Pushcart Prize and the National Poetry Series publication prize.

E. E. (Edward Estlin) Cummings (*1894–1962*)   Cummings was born in Cambridge, Massachusetts, to particularly supportive parents who encouraged him to develop his creative gifts. His father was a former Harvard professor who had become a Unitarian minister, and Cummings received both his B.A. and his M.A. from Harvard University. While there, he wrote poetry in the pre-Raphaelite and metaphysical traditions and published it in *The Harvard Advocate*. Cummings joined the Ambulance Corps the day after the United States entered World War I. During the war, he spent three months in a French prison because his outspoken anti-war convictions led the French to accuse him of treason. He transmuted this experience into his first literary success, *The Enormous Room*. After the war he shuttled among New York City's Greenwich Village, Paris, and New Hampshire. He showed little interest in wealth or his growing celebrity.

Emily Dickinson (*1830–1886*)   Dickinson's grandfather founded Amherst College, and her father was a state senator and U.S. congressman. Dickinson attended Amherst Academy and spent a year at the Mount Holyoke Female Seminary (now Mount Holyoke College). She spent the rest of her life in her father's Amherst mansion. Visitors were scarce, and Dickinson herself rarely ventured out. Though Dickinson was a prolific poet, her talents were not recognized in her day: only ten of her poems were published in her lifetime. After her death over seventeen hundred poems were discovered bound neatly in booklets. Four years later, Thomas Wentworth Higginson, an editor for the *Atlantic Monthly*, with whom Dickinson had corresponded, smoothed and regularized some of her poems and published them in a book. Editors did not restore her idiosyncratic expressions and punctuation until the twentieth century.

John Donne (*1572–1631*)   The first and greatest of a group that came to be known as the "Metaphysical" poets, Donne wrote in a revolutionary style that combined highly intellectual conceits, or metaphors, with complex, compressed phrasing. Born into a Catholic family at a time when Catholics were a persecuted minority, Donne felt his religion was central to his identity and to much of his poetry. He studied at both Oxford and Cambridge Universities but took a degree from neither school because to do so he would have had to subscribe to the Thirty-nine Articles, the tenets of Anglicanism. From Oxford and Cambridge Donne went to Lincoln's Inn, where he studied law. Two years later he relented and joined the Anglican Church, motivated in no small part by the recent death of his brother, who had been imprisoned for his Catholicism. After he secretly married the daughter of an aristocrat, Donne was briefly imprisoned himself. This politically disastrous marriage dashed his worldly hopes and forced him to struggle for years to support a large and growing family. During this time, he wrote on the lawfulness of suicide (*Bianthanatos*). He eventually managed to reestablish himself and by 1615 was sufficiently well known that King James I appointed him dean of St. Paul's Cathedral in London. Most of his published works were sermons; Donne circulated his poetry among learned people, but it was not published until after his death.

Rita Dove (*1952– *)   Growing up in Akron, Ohio, Dove wrote stories and plays for her classmates to perform. After being named a President's Scholar, Dove went on to attend Miami University in Ohio, study for a year at Tübingen University in Germany as a Fulbright scholar, and receive an M.F.A. in creative writing from the University of Iowa. She was also awarded fellowships from the Guggenheim Foundation and the National Endowment for the Arts. She served as Poet Laureate of the United States between 1993 and 1995, the youngest person ever to do so. In 1987 Dove was awarded the Pulitzer Prize for Poetry. She has taught creative writing at Arizona State University and is currently the Commonwealth Professor of English at the University of Virginia and an associate editor of *Callaloo*, the journal of African American and African arts and letters.

T. S. (Thomas Stearns) Eliot (*1888–1965*)   T. S. Eliot was born in St. Louis, Missouri, into a New England family. His grandfather founded Washington University and the first Unitarian Church in St. Louis. Eliot traveled to New England for college, received his B.A. and M.A. from Harvard, but eventually abandoned his doctoral studies in philosophy. He went to England in 1914, read Greek philosophy at Oxford, and published "The Love Song of J. Alfred Prufrock" the next year, with Ezra Pound's help. Eliot became a British citizen in 1927, and, in that same year, he shocked many of his fellow modernists by declaring that he had become a "classicist in literature, royalist in politics, and Anglo-Catholic in religion." Accordingly, his later works explore religious questions in a quieter idiom. Working for the publishing house of Faber & Faber in London, Eliot helped publish a number of young poets and eventually became the director of the firm. His unhappy marriage to Vivienne Haigh-Wood ended in 1933, and he married Valerie Fletcher in 1956. Eliot was awarded the Nobel Prize for Literature in 1948.

Louise Erdrich (*1954–*)   Erdrich is the daughter of a French Ojibwa mother and a German-American father; the eldest of their seven children, she grew up in North Dakota near the Turtle Mountain Reservation. Both of her parents taught at a Bureau of Indian Affairs school in an era when the primary aim of these schools was to acculturate their Native American pupils. Erdrich recalls that while she was growing up her mother read stories out loud and her father regularly recited poetry. She attended public schools until she enrolled at Dartmouth College in 1972 as part of the school's first coeducational class. During her junior year, she published a poem in *Ms.* magazine and won the American Academy of Poets Prize. After graduating from Dartmouth, Erdrich taught poetry and writing to young people through a position at the State Arts Council of North Dakota. Later on, she devoted herself full time to her own writing, working to support herself until she was able to live on what she earned from her poems and novels. Erdrich is best known for her award-winning first novel, *Love Medicine*.

Carolyn Forché (*1950–*)   Born in Detroit, Michigan, Forché attended the Justin Morrill College at Michigan State University, where she studied five languages, creative writing, English literature, and international relations. Her first poetry collection, *Gathering the Tribes*, won the Yale Series of Younger Poets Award. In 1977, she traveled to Spain to translate the work of Salvadoran-exiled poet Claribel Alegría and, upon her return, received a John Simon Guggenheim Foundation Fellowship, which enabled her to work as a human rights activist in El Salvador for two years. Her experiences there informed her second book, *The Country Between Us*, which received the Poetry Society of America's Alice Fay di Castagnola Award and was the Lamont Selection of the Academy of American Poets. In March 1994, Forche's third book of poetry, *The Angel of History*, received *The Los Angeles Times* Book Award. Forché has worked as a correspondent in Beirut for National Public Radio's "All Things Considered" and as a human rights liaison in South Africa. She has held three fellowships from the National Endowment for the Arts. Forché teaches in the M.F.A. program in poetry at George Mason University in Virginia.

Robert Frost (*1874–1963*)   When Frost was eleven, his father died of tuberculosis and his mother moved the family from San Francisco to New England, where she raised him and his sister on her salary as a schoolteacher. Frost studied classics in high school, and he and his future wife, Elinor Miriam White, were the co-valedictorians of their class. Frost entered and dropped out of both Dartmouth and Harvard. He married White, and while Frost tried to make his name known in literary circles, the young couple taught in a private school Frost's mother had opened. After the death of Frost's first child, his grandfather bought a farm in Derry, New Hampshire, for Frost and his wife, and the growing family lived there for a decade. Still struggling to get his work into print, he journeyed across the Atlantic to meet Ezra Pound, T. S. Eliot, W. B. Yeats, and other literary figures in London. Under Pound's patronage, Frost's work soon appeared in *Poetry* magazine, and his first book followed. In 1961, well over eighty years old, Frost read a poem at John F. Kennedy's inauguration.

Allen Ginsberg (*1926–1998*)   Ginsberg's childhood in Paterson, New Jersey, was overshadowed by his mother's severe mental illness. Intent on following his father's advice to become a labor lawyer, Ginsberg enrolled at Columbia University in New York. He soon became friends with fellow students Lucien Carr and Jack Kerouac as well as locals William S. Burroughs and Neal Cassady. He and his friends experimented with drugs, took cross-country treks, and worked to develop a new poetic vision. Ginsberg eventually graduated from Columbia in 1948 and went to San Francisco, where he did some graduate work, performed odd jobs, and spent eight months in a psychiatric hospital. In 1956 his first book of poems, entitled *Howl and Other Poems*, was published with an introduction by his mentor William Carlos Williams. With the publication of *Howl*, Ginsberg was catapulted to fame as a member of the Beat generation and as a significant poet in his own right.

Thomas Gray (*1716–1771*)　Perhaps the most important years of Gray's life were those in which he attended Eton College. There he met two boys, Horace Walpole and Richard West, who would be his lifelong friends. Gray's feelings for them were homosexual, but there is no evidence that the feeling was mutual. Gray went on to Cambridge, where he studied Greek and history and led a fairly secluded life. At Cambridge, Gray shone academically, emerging as one of England's best scholars. When West died of tuberculosis in 1742, Gray began writing poetry, most of which was inspired by his grief for his beloved friend.

Thomas Hardy (*1840–1928*)　Hardy was the son of a master mason in Upper Bockhampton and was apprenticed to a local architect at the age of fifteen. He wrote novels in his spare time and managed to publish one in 1871, but continued to make his living as an architect until his thirty-third year, after which time he devoted himself entirely to literature. He spent the next quarter of a century writing novels. After his *Jude the Obscure* was harshly criticized, he abandoned fiction for poetry. Much of his writing is situated in or is about "Wessex," the fictional area of England centered in Dorset. In Hardy's later years, he wrote his autobiography, which he arranged to have published after his death under the name of a friend. Hardy took a pessimistic view of the human condition and held that indifferent forces—not any divine plan—circumscribe human lives. This perspective is evident in both his novels and his poetry. Hardy is buried in Westminster Abbey, though his heart was removed and lies at Stinsford Church near his former residence.

Robert Hayden (*1913–1980*)　Hayden was born Asa Bundy Sheffey in Detroit, Michigan. His childhood was tumultuous, as he was shuttled between the home of his parents and that of a foster family next door. His impaired vision kept him from participating in sports, and so he spent most of his free time reading. With the help of a scholarship, he studied at Detroit City College (now Wayne State University) and at the University of Michigan with W. H. Auden. He taught at Fisk University for over twenty years and at the University of Michigan for more than ten. Hayden produced ten volumes of poetry during his lifetime, though he did not receive acclaim for his work until late in his life. In the 1960s Hayden resisted pressure to express the activist sentiments that were growing stronger in the African American community and thereby alienated himself from a growing African American literary movement. In 1976, he became the first black American to be appointed as Consultant in Poetry to the Library of Congress (later called the Poet Laureate).

Seamus Heaney (*1939–*) Heaney was born on a farm in Mossbawn, County Derry, Northern Ireland. He was among the first to take advantage of reforms that allowed Catholics access to a top-notch education in that province of Great Britain, which traditionally discriminated against Catholics in favor of Protestants. Educated and subsequently appointed as a lecturer in English at Queen's University, Belfast, Heaney began to publish work in university magazines under the pseudonym "Incertus." Heaney produced his first volume, *Eleven Poems*, in 1965. After experiencing six years of civil strife in Northern Ireland, Heaney published *North*, his most political book of poems by far. He has held teaching positions at the University of California at Berkeley, Carysfort College in Dublin, and Oxford University, and has served as the Boylston Professor of Rhetoric and Oratory at Harvard University. He won the Nobel Prize for Literature in 1995.

Robert Herrick (*1591–1674*) Herrick was the seventh child of a Cheapside, London, goldsmith who committed suicide only fifteen months after the poet's birth. He was apprenticed to his goldsmith uncle, Sir William Herrick. Herrick eventually decided to leave business and pursue his education, so he went to St. John's College, Cambridge. There, he earned a B.A. in 1617 and an M.A. in 1620 and, perhaps more importantly, became the eldest of the "Sons of Ben," poets who idolized Ben Jonson. He would have liked nothing better than to live a life of leisured study, discussing literature and socializing with Jonson. For a number of reasons, though, he took religious orders and reluctantly moved to Dean Priory, Devonshire. In 1647 the Protectorate government expelled Herrick from his post for his support of Charles I. He fled to London, where in 1648 he published a volume of over fourteen hundred poems with two different titles: *Hesperides* for those on secular subjects and *Noble Numbers* for those on sacred subjects. These poems did not fare well in the harsh Puritan climate and went unnoticed until the nineteenth century. Herrick was eventually restored to his Devonshire post and he lived out his last years there quietly.

Gerard Manley Hopkins (*1844–1889*) Hopkins was the eldest of eight children of a marine-insurance adjustor (shipwrecks later figured in his poetry, particularly *The Wreck of the Deutschland*). While studying at Balliol College, Oxford, Hopkins was drawn to the religious revival that John Henry Newman was leading there. He followed in Newman's footsteps and, despite his family's opposition, converted from the Anglican to the Roman Catholic Church. He was twenty-two years old at the time. A few years later he joined the Jesuit order, burning all of his early poetry, which he considered "too worldly." From then on he asked the rector to approve the subjects of his poems, most of which were either devotional or occasional. Hopkins kept most of his later poetry to himself, only occasionally including poems in letters to his friends. Consequently, it was not until after his death that his work was published. Near the end of his life he was appointed professor of Greek at University College, Dublin. He died there of typhoid at age forty-four.

A. E. (Alfred Edward) Housman (*1859–1936*)　Housman was born in Fockbury, Worcestershire. His father was a solicitor from Lancashire; his mother was Cornish. He was raised in the High Church part of the Church of England, but converted to paganism at eight, became a deist at thirteen, and switched to outright atheism at twenty-one. Housman did well at school and won a scholarship to St. John's College, Oxford, where he studied classics, ancient history, and philosophy. "Oxford had not much effect on me," he said, "except that there I met my greatest friend." The friend in question was Moses Jackson, who was willing to be Housman's friend, although Housman wanted a more intimate relationship. Housman shocked his friends and teachers at Oxford by failing his final examinations. His biographers often attribute this failure to the psychological turmoil that resulted from his suppressed love for Jackson. Housman next obtained a job in the civil service and pursued his classical studies. In 1908 he was appointed the Chair of Latin at University College, London, and he served as professor of Latin at Cambridge from 1911 until his death. Most of his poetry came in a creative burst that lasted about a year in the mid-1890s. He published his first book, *A Shropshire Lad*, in 1896. Housman aimed to write poetry that was both compact and moving. His work was influenced by Greek and Latin lyric poetry, by the traditional ballad, and by German poet Heinrich Heine.

Langston Hughes (*1902–1967*)　Hughes, born in Joplin, Mississippi, was a major figure of the intellectual and literary movement known as the Harlem Renaissance. His parents separated when he was young and he grew up with his maternal grandmother, residing only intermittently with his mother in Detroit and Cleveland and with his father in Mexico. Hughes was elected Class Poet in high school and went on to attend Columbia University. After a year of college, he dropped out and began to travel and write and publish poetry. His work was included in important African American periodicals like *Opportunity* and *Crisis* and anthologies like *The New Negro* and *Caroling Dusk*. Hughes graduated from Lincoln University in 1929 and began to travel again, working as a correspondent and columnist. When the Great Depression brought the Harlem Renaissance to an abrupt end, he became involved in activist politics, including the American Communist Party. In addition to writing poetry and novels, Hughes also founded theaters and produced plays.

Randall Jarrell (*1914–1965*)   Jarrell was born in Nashville, Tennessee, but spent most of his childhood in California. At Vanderbilt University, he met the Fugitives, a group of poets, professors, and students who launched a conservative, modern, distinctly Southern movement in American letters. He studied psychology as an undergraduate student and English as a graduate student. John Crowe Ransom, one of Jarrell's professors, became his mentor, and Jarrell followed him to Kenyon College in 1937, where Jarrell began his career as an academic. From then on, he was always linked with a university: after Kenyon, the University of Texas; Sarah Lawrence College; and from 1947 until his death, the Women's College of the University of North Carolina, Greensboro. Jarrell spent World War II in the Army, and during these years he published the critically acclaimed *Little Friend, Little Friend*. Jarrell sought to infuse his poetry with what he called the "dailiness of life" and wished to keep its tone familiar, even colloquial.

Ben Jonson (*1572–1637*)   Poet, playwright, actor, scholar, critic, translator, and leader of a literary school, Jonson was born the son of an already deceased clergyman and the stepson of a master bricklayer of Westminster. He won a scholarship to a prestigious London grammar school where he learned from the great scholar William Camden. He had an eventful early career, serving in the army at Flanders, killing an associate in a duel and narrowly escaping the death penalty, and converting to Catholicism. In the middle of all this, Jonson managed to write a number of plays, including *Every Man in His Humor* (in which Shakespeare played the lead role), *Volpone*, *The Alchemist*, and *Bartholomew Fair*. Jonson was a favorite of King James I, who made him England's Poet Laureate and granted him a substantial pension in 1616. In the same year Jonson published *The Works of Benjamin Jonson*, and by doing so made it clear that he considered writing his profession. This gesture broke with the Elizabethan tradition of circulating poems only among the aristocracy until the poet's death, at which point the author's poems were made available to the general public.

John Keats (*1795–1821*)   Keats's father was head ostler at a London livery stable and inherited the business after marrying his employer's daughter. Keats was sent to the Reverend John Clarke's private school at Enfield, where he was a noisy, high-spirited boy. His teacher, Charles Cowden

Clarke, took Keats under his wing, encouraging his passion for reading, poetry, music, and theater. After both his parents died, his uncle took him out of school and apprenticed him to an apothecary and surgeon. He subsequently studied at Guy's Hospital, London. After qualifying to practice as an apothecary, he abandoned medicine for poetry, over his guardian's vehement protests. The decision was influenced by Keats's friendship with Leigh Hunt, then editor of *The Examiner*, and a leading political radical, minor poet, and prolific critic and essayist. Keats was one of Hunt's protegés, and Hunt introduced him to great poets such as Hazlitt, Lamb, and Shelley. In February 1820 Keats coughed up blood and realized that he had caught tuberculosis, which had already claimed the lives of his mother and brother. He died at the age of twenty-five, with his third book just barely off the press.

Galway Kinnell (*1927–*)   Kinnell was born in Providence, Rhode Island. He earned his B.A. from Princeton, where he and classmate W. S. Merwin read each other their poems, and earned his M.A. at Rochester. But the process of writing poetry has for him been largely a process of de-education. He views all poetry as an attempt at self-transcendence, and he consequently dramatizes the process by which he steps out of himself and into other things and creatures. Kinnell has fused a life of poetry with one of politics: he has run an adult education program in Chicago, lived as a journalist in Iran, and worked in the field registering voters for the Congress of Racial Equality in Louisiana. He also served in the Navy in 1945 and 1946 and has taught at over twenty colleges and universities. He has earned various awards, including the 1983 Pulitzer Prize, and grants, including those from the Rockefeller Foundation and the National Endowment for the Arts.

Yusef Komunyakaa (*1947–*)   Yusef Komunyakaa was born in Bogalusa, Louisiana, in 1947, the eldest of five children. He graduated from Bogalusa's Central High School in 1965 and later joined the United States Army to serve in Vietnam. While in Vietnam he began to write, serving as a correspondent and later as managing editor of *The Southern Cross*. For his work with the paper Komunyakaa received the Bronze Star. Upon leaving the army in the early 1970s he enrolled at the University of Colorado. Before graduating with his B.A. in 1975, he took a creative writing course and discovered that he had a talent for poetry. He went on to take his M.A. in creative writing at Colorado State University in 1978, eventually leaving Colorado for the University of California, Irvine, where he received his M.F.A. He has published thirteen books of poems, among them

Neon Vernacular, a Pulitzer Prize winner, and *Thieves of Paradise*, a National Book Award finalist. Komunyakaa is interested in the influence that jazz music has had on poetry and was, along with Sascha Feinstein, the co-editor of *The Jazz Poetry Anthology*. Komunyakaa is a professor in the Creative Writing Program at Princeton.

Maxine Kumin (*1925–*) Born in Philadelphia and educated at Radcliffe College, Kumin settled in the suburbs of Boston to raise a family and write poetry. There, Kumin "workshopped" many of her poems with her close friends Anne Sexton, John Holmes, and George Starbuck. Over the years she has published twelve books of poetry, including *Up Country: Poems of New England*, which was awarded the Pulitzer Prize in 1973. She is also the author of five novels, a collection of short stories, more than twenty children's books, several books of essays, and a memoir. Kumin has served as a Consultant in Poetry to the Library of Congress as well as Poet Laureate of New Hampshire. She has received grants from such prestigious foundations as the National Endowment for the Arts, the National Council on the Arts, and the American Academy of Poets. She has taught at many colleges and universities, among them Princeton, Columbia, Tufts, Washington University, Randolph-Macon, and the University of Massachusetts.

Philip Larkin (*1922–1985*) Larkin was born in Coventry, England, and after being deemed unfit for military service, he attended Oxford University during World War II. The misery of his undergraduate years is depicted in *Jill*, the first of his two novels. At Oxford, Larkin belonged to the group of writers that came to be known as "the Movement." Members of this group refused to employ rhetorical excess in their poetry, opting instead to use more even-tempered, conversational idioms. Though his first book of poetry was strongly influenced by W. B. Yeats, his later works were more like those of Thomas Hardy, Wilfred Owen, and W. H. Auden. Larkin believed that to these people, technique mattered less than content; the same might be said of Larkin himself. After taking his Oxford degree, Larkin went to work as a university librarian for a number of universities, though mainly at the University of Hull. When Sir John Betjeman died in 1984, it was widely assumed that Larkin would succeed him as Poet Laureate. However, Larkin died before a successor to Betjeman could be appointed, and so the author of such colorful poems as "This Be the Verse" and "High Windows" never penned a Royal Birthday Ode.

Li-Young Lee (*1957–*) Lee's great-grandfather was president of China from 1912 to 1916, and his family was wealthy and well-connected, even after the communist revolution. His father was once Mao-Tse-tung's doctor. In the midst of political upheaval, the family fled to Indonesia, and Lee was born in Jakarta in 1957. Oppression of the Chinese minority in that city set the family on an odyssey that ended in the mid-1960s in a small Pennsylvania town, where Lee's father became pastor of the Presbyterian church. Lee studied at the University of Pittsburgh, the University of Arizona, and the State University of New York at Brockport. He has published *The Rose* and *The City in Which I Love You*, both books of poetry, and *The Winged Seed*, a critically acclaimed memoir.

Robert Lowell (*1917–1977*)   Lowell came from a well-established New England family. He took a dim view of his family, though, and published an unattractive portrait of it in one of his later books, *Life Studies*. Lowell's life was turbulent, in great part because he suffered from manic depression. He attended St. Mark's School, then enrolled in Harvard where he studied English literature for two years before abruptly transferring to Kenyon College so that he could study the classics, logic, and philosophy under John Crowe Ransom. He then attended Louisiana State University to work with Robert Penn Warren and Cleanth Brooks. He converted to Catholicism and also became a great pacifist, opposing both World War II and the Vietnam War.

Susan Ludvigson (*1942–*)   Ludvigson was born in Rice Lake, Wisconsin, and is the author of seven books of poetry and two chapbooks. Her work appears regularly in such magazines and journals as *The Atlantic Monthly*, *The Nation*, *The Ohio Review*, and *Antioch Review*. She has received a writer's Fulbright Fellowship as well as grants and fellowships from the Guggenheim Foundation, the Rockefeller Foundation, the National Endowment for the Arts, and the North and South Carolina arts commissions, as well as other institutions. Ludvigson represented the United States at the First International Women Writers Congress in Paris. She is professor of English and Poet-in-Residence at Winthrop University.

Archibald MacLeish (*1892–1982*)   MacLeish grew up in Glencoe, Illinois. He described his father as a "devout, cold, rigorous man of very beautiful speech," and his mother, who had taught at Vassar College before becoming his father's third wife, as having come of a "very passionate people with many mad among them." He attended Hotchkiss School in Connecticut and then earned his B.A. from Yale and his J.D. from Harvard. He went to France to serve in World War I. In the years following the war, MacLeish worked as a lawyer in Boston. In 1923, having found that his work distracted him from poetry, he moved to France to participate in the modernist movement and published four books of poetry. He returned to America in 1928 and retraced by foot and mule-back the route that Cortez's conquering army took through Mexico. The literary product of this journey, *Conquistador*, won the Pulitzer Prize for 1932. As World War II approached, he served as Librarian of Congress, Director of the Office of Facts and Figures, and Assistant Secretary of State. In 1949 he returned to Harvard, where he served as Boylston Professor of English Rhetoric until 1962.

Christopher Marlowe (*1564–1593*)　Marlowe was born to a shoemaker in Canterbury, only two months before the birth of William Shakespeare. Marlowe attended Corpus Christi College in Cambridge, holding a six-year scholarship ordinarily awarded to students preparing for the ministry. At the end of his studies he did not take holy orders, but began to write plays. He won fame at age twenty-three with his tragedy *Tamburlaine*, but lived for only six more years. During this time he managed to write five more plays: a sequel to *Tamburlaine*; *The Massacre at Paris*; two major tragedies, *The Jew of Malta* and *Dr. Faustus*; and a chronicle history play, *Edward II*. Marlowe's productivity was remarkable considering his tumultuous and short life. He was killed with a dagger during an argument over a bill in a tavern when he was only twenty-nine.

Andrew Marvell (*1621–1678*)　Marvell was born in Yorkshire, England, and was educated at Cambridge University. He completed his B.A. in 1638, just a few years before the start of the English Civil War. What he did after his years at Cambridge is uncertain, though it is well known that he supported the Puritan cause during the Civil War. In 1650 he served as the private tutor of the daughter of the Lord-General of the Puritan troops and in 1657 he was appointed to assist Oliver Cromwell's blind Latin secretary, the poet John Milton. Beginning in 1659, Marvell represented his hometown of Hull in Parliament. He survived the Restoration and even managed to save Milton from imprisonment and possible execution.

Edna St. Vincent Millay (*1892–1950*)　Millay was born in the small coastal town of Rockland, Maine. Her parents divorced when she was a child, and her mother, Cora, supported herself and her family of four by working as a nurse. Millay wrote her first poem at age five and as a child submitted her poetry regularly to various magazines. She attended Vassar College through the generosity of a benefactor who was impressed by her writings. She graduated when she was twenty-five years old, and her first book of poetry was published that same year. Millay then moved to Greenwich Village in New York City, where she fell in with the literary and political rebels who lived there. She seemed to embody all the qualities of the modern woman of the 1920s: she was talented, energetic, independent, and liberated. Of course, she was not completely typical: she was openly bisexual, and even when she did marry, hers was a "sexually open" marriage. In the same year that she married and moved to the Berkshires, Millay was also awarded the Pulitzer Prize.

John Milton (*1608–1674*)   Milton was the eldest son of a self-made London businessman. As a child, he exhibited unusual scholastic gifts: he had already learned Latin and Greek and was well on his way to mastering Hebrew and most of the European languages before he entered Cambridge University. After graduation, Milton retired to his father's house, where he read for six years. His father then sent him abroad for a year of travel and study. After returning to England, Milton became embroiled in political controversy. He wrote pamphlets defending everything from free speech to the execution of Charles I. When the monarchy was restored, Milton found himself impoverished and imprisoned. And he had lost his sight. Still, he spent his later years writing the masterpieces for which he is known today: *Paradise Lost, Paradise Regained*, and *Samson Agonistes*.

Marianne Moore (*1887–1972*)   Moore was born in Kirkwood, Missouri, a suburb of St. Louis. When she was young, her father abandoned her family. Moore was raised in the home of her grandfather, a Presbyterian pastor, until his death, after which Moore's family lived at first with other relatives in Missouri and then on their own in Carlisle, Pennsylvania. She graduated from Bryn Mawr College in 1906, and went on to work as a schoolteacher at the U.S. Indian School in Carlisle. She and her mother moved to New York City in 1918, and Moore began to work at the New York Public Library. In New York she met such influential poets as William Carlos Williams and Wallace Stevens and began to contribute her poetry to *Egoist, Poetry, Others*, and *Dial*, the prestigious literary magazine Moore eventually came to edit. In 1921, Hilda Doolittle published Moore's first book of poetry without her knowledge. Moore was widely recognized for her work: her *Collected Poems* won the Bollingen Prize, the National Book Award, and the Pulitzer Prize. Moore lived with her mother and brother in Brooklyn for most of her life.

Sharon Olds (*1942–*)   Olds was born in San Francisco and raised, as she puts it, "a hellfire Calvinist." She received her B.A. from Stanford and her

Ph.D. in English from Columbia. Olds recalls standing on the steps of the Columbia University library and vowing to become a poet at all costs. In her poetry Olds deals with such personal topics as her father's alcoholism and abusiveness and her own miscarriage and abortion. She has received grants from the National Endowment for the Arts and the Guggenheim Foundation and has won numerous awards, including the Lamont Poetry Selection and the National Book Critics Circle Award. Her books include *Blood, Tin; Straw; The Gold Cell; The Wellspring; The Father; The Dead & the Living;* and *Satan Says.* Olds lives in New York City and was the New York State Poet Laureate for 1998–2000. She teaches poetry workshops at New York University's Graduate Creative Writing Program and at Goldwater Hospital on Roosevelt Island in New York.

Wilfred Owen (*1893–1918*) The oldest of four children in a working-class Shropshire family, Owen left school in 1911 after he failed to win a scholarship to London University. For some time he assisted the vicar of a parish church, but abandoned his position after losing his faith. In 1913, he went to France to teach English at a Berlitz school in Bordeaux. He returned to England in 1915, enlisted in the army, and was immediately sent to the front in France. Two years later he was evacuated to Craglockhart War Hospital for treatment of shell shock. There he met the poets Siegfried Sassoon and Robert Graves. Once he had recovered, he returned again to the front, was caught in a German machine gun attack, and was killed just seven days before the signing of the armistice, at age twenty-five. Owen's poems, poignant and technically refined, portray the horror of trench warfare and satirize the unthinking patriotism of those who cheered the war from their armchairs. His poems were published posthumously after his friend Sassoon brought a collection of Owen's poems back from France.

Marge Piercy (*1936– *) Piercy grew up in Detroit, Michigan, in a working-class neighborhood. She won a full scholarship to the University of Michigan; when she received her B.A. in 1957, she became the first person in her family to graduate from college. She won a fellowship to Northwestern University and earned her M.A. the next year. Piercy began writing during the movement against the war in Vietnam, and since then she has primarily been concerned with the relationship between the sexes. Believing that she voices the rage of women who are dominated by men, Piercy has said, "I imagine that I speak for a constituency, living and dead." Piercy has given workshops, readings, and lectures at over 350 institutions. She lives in Massachusetts, on Cape Cod.

Sylvia Plath (*1932–1963*)   Plath's father, Otto, left Poland for the United States and eventually became a professor at Boston University, where he met his future wife, Aurelia Schoeber. Plath was born in Boston and raised in the suburbs. Her father died when she was eight, and her mother assumed responsibility for the family. As a child, Plath wrote poems and published them in local and national magazines. She went on to graduate *summa cum laude* from Smith College and win a Fulbright scholarship to Newnham College, Cambridge. In 1956 she married the British poet Ted Hughes. They returned to America after Plath completed her studies at Cambridge, living for a time in Northampton, Massachusetts, while Plath taught at Smith, moving back to England soon thereafter. They settled in Devonshire with their two children, Frieda and Nicholas. In 1960 Plath published her first book of poems, *The Colossus*, which was well received. Plath's marriage to Hughes slowly began to deteriorate, and Plath moved to London with her two young children. There, she slipped into a deep depression and committed suicide at the age of thirty. Multiple volumes of Plath's poetry were published posthumously, and her *Collected Poems* won the Pulitzer Prize in 1982. Plath is also the author of a novel, *The Bell Jar,* as well as many short stories.

Edgar Allan Poe (*1809–1849*)   Poe's mother, Elizabeth Arnold, was an actress and a teenage widow when she married his father, David Poe, an alcoholic actor who soon abandoned his family. Poe was born in Boston, and his mother died not two years afterward. A young merchant named John Allan took Poe in and educated him in England and Virginia. After a quarrel with Allan, Poe went to find his paternal relatives in Baltimore and ended up joining the army. Poe and Allan reconciled, and Allan helped Poe get admitted to West Point. There, he ruined any chance he might have had of becoming Allan's heir by getting expelled for missing classes and roll calls. After leaving West Point he went to live in poverty with his relatives. He soon fell in love with and secretly married his cousin Virginia when she was only thirteen years old. Desperate for income, he took a position at the *Southern Literary Messenger*. There and at other publications, his prospects as a writer and an editor flourished. But drinking and depression eventually ruined his career, and he was unable to resurrect it.

Ezra Pound (*1885–1972*)   Pound was born in Hailey, Idaho, but he was raised in Philadelphia. At the age of sixteen Pound enrolled as a "special student" at the University of Pennsylvania to study, as he put it, "whatever he thought important." There he met William Carlos Williams and Hilda Doolittle. He enrolled at Hamilton College in 1903 and took a degree from that institution in 1905, returning to the University of Pennsylvania for his M.A. in 1906. He moved to Europe in 1908 and ended up spending most of his life there, living in Ireland, England, France, and Italy. In 1912, Pound, along with Hilda Doolittle, Richard Aldington, and F. S. Flint, founded the Imagist group in order to sanction experimentation in verse form. Pound advised and assisted such authors as W. B. Yeats, T. S. Eliot, William Carlos Williams, James Joyce, and Robert Frost. He served as a propagandist for Mussolini during World War II, and when the United States captured him in 1943 he was indicted for treason. In 1945 he was remanded to St. Elizabeth's, an institution for the criminally insane, and he remained there until the indictment was dismissed in 1958. He retired with his daughter and longtime companion to Italy, where he spent the rest of his life.

John Crowe Ransom (*1888–1974*)   Ransom was born in Pulaski, Tennessee. He received a B.A. from Vanderbilt University in 1909 and as a Rhodes scholar received a B.A. from Christ Church, Oxford. He served as a lieutenant in World War I and then returned to Vanderbilt to teach. During his lifetime, he published three volumes of critically acclaimed poetry, but, after 1927, he dedicated himself primarily to literary criticism. In 1937 he made a surprise move to Kenyon College, where he founded and edited the *Kenyon Review*. He remained at Kenyon until his retirement in 1959. Ransom guided a group of writers known as the Fugitives who were wary of the social and cultural changes sweeping the South and who sought to preserve a traditional aesthetic ideal rooted in classical values and forms. Many of the Fugitives championed the New Criticism, whose methods of close reading are still taught in many English departments today.

Edwin Arlington Robinson (*1869–1935*)   Robinson grew up in the small, bleak town of Gardiner, Maine. It was here that he situated much of his poetry. The third son of a family in decline, he had a difficult childhood and a rather unhappy life. In 1890 he recognized that he was "doomed, or elected, or sentenced for life," as he put it, "to the writing of poetry." Robinson attended Harvard University as a special student, rather than a degree candidate, between 1891 and 1893. His years at Harvard increased his commitment to literature. He published his first book at his own expense in 1896, and his second in 1897. His third book, which he published in 1903, came to the attention of President Theodore Roosevelt, who wrote a magazine article in praise of Robinson and found him a position in the New York Custom House. Between 1910 and 1920 Robinson published the three books that established his literary reputation. During the 1920s he was awarded the Pulitzer Prize three times.

Theodore Roethke (*1908–1963*)   Roethke was born in Saginaw, Michigan. At six foot two and over two hundred pounds, Roethke was an imposing figure. But he was not as solid on the inside as he was on the outside: he suffered from alcoholism and frequent breakdowns. He earned his B.A. and M.A. from the University of Michigan and then spent a year studying at Harvard. He subsequently taught at several colleges and universities, including the University of Washington, where he taught from 1948 until his death. Roethke wrote little poetry, but took great care with what he did write. His first book, *Open House*, attracted considerable attention upon its publication in 1941. His collected poems appeared under the title *Words for the Wind* in 1959, only four years before his death. He earned a Guggenheim Fellowship, Ford Foundation grants, a Fulbright grant, the Pulitzer Prize, the Bollingen Prize, and two National Book Awards.

William Shakespeare (*1564–1616*)   Shakespeare was born in the English town of Stratford-on-Avon. His father was a tradesman and a prominent citizen who sat on the Town Council for many years and served as bailiff, or mayor, in 1568. His parents had eight children, three of whom died in childhood. Shakespeare attended a Stratford grammar school, and married Anne Hathaway, the daughter of a local farmer, in November 1582, when he was eighteen and she was twenty-six. Their first child was born in May of the next year, and in early 1585 Anne bore twins. By 1592, Shakespeare had established his reputation in London as an actor and playwright. He was a founding member of the Lord Chamberlain's Men, a highly popular repertory theater company, and wrote approximately two plays a year for the company to perform. When city officials closed theaters to prevent the plague from spreading, Shakespeare wrote poetry, including *Venus and Adonis* and *The Rape of Lucrece*, his first two published works, and his *Sonnets*, which circulated privately until a London printer published them without Shakespeare's consent in 1609. Upon ascending to the throne, James I granted royal patronage to the Lord Chamberlain's Men, which thus became the King's Men. After 1611 Shakespeare seems to have retired from the London theatre scene to Stratford. Six years after his death in 1616, the *First Folio*, the first collected edition of his plays, was published.

Percy Bysshe Shelley (*1792–1822*)   Shelley was born in Sussex; his father was a wealthy baron who later became a member of Parliament. Shelley was educated at Eton and Oxford and was expected to inherit his father's baronetcy and seat in Parliament. Not long after being expelled from Oxford for publishing a pamphlet entitled "The Necessity of Atheism," Shelley eloped with Harriet Westbrook, enraging the elder Shelley so much that he disinherited his son. Shelley and Harriet had two children, but their marriage was unhappy. Within three years Shelley had abandoned his wife and eloped with Mary Wollstonecraft Godwin, the daughter of his mentor, William Godwin. More than two years after Shelley left her, Harriet committed suicide. Her family arranged for Shelley to be found unfit to raise his children by Harriet, and so, after marrying Godwin, Shelley moved with her and their children to Italy. There he wrote some of his most famous works, including *Prometheus Unbound* and "Ode to the West Wind." His life in Italy was plagued by misfortune: already ostracized by his family and friends, he also lost all but one of his children to disease and suffered almost constant financial difficulty. Shelley remained in Italy with his wife until he drowned in a storm at sea.

Bruce Springsteen (*1949–*)   Springsteen was born in Freehold, New Jersey. During high school he began playing the guitar and joined a succession of small bands before settling down with the Bruce Springsteen Band. He signed with CBS Records as a solo artist and released his first album, *Greetings from Asbury Park, N.J.*, in 1973. Though the album sold poorly, it received a good deal of praise from critics in the U.S. and U.K. Soon thereafter he released *The Wild, the Innocent, and the E Street Shuffle*, which also sold poorly. Slowly, word about Springsteen spread, and when *Born to Run* came out in 1975, it shot to the top of the charts. The album received rave reviews, and Springsteen appeared on the covers of *Newsweek* and *Time*. Since then, he has recorded numerous albums and won numerous awards.

William Stafford (*1914–1993*)   Stafford was born in Hutchinson, Kansas, to a family that loved to read. He earned two degrees from the University of Kansas, working his way through school by waiting tables. He was drafted in 1940 and, as a conscientious objector, spent World War II in the "alternative service," working in forestry and soil conservation in Arkansas and California. In 1948, Stafford published his master's thesis, a book about conscientious objectors entitled *Down in My Heart*. He went on to earn a Ph.D. from the creative writing program at the University of Iowa, and taught at Lewis and Clark College in Portland, Oregon, from 1948 until his retirement thirty years later. He published his first book of poems at age forty-six. Stafford won numerous awards and honors, including the National Book Award, and served as Consultant in Poetry for the Library of Congress and Poet Laureate of Oregon.

Wallace Stevens (*1879–1955*)   Stevens spent three years at Harvard before leaving school to pursue a literary career. But he was determined never to "make a petty struggle for existence." After receiving a law degree from New York Law School, he went to work as an executive at Hartford Accident and Indemnity Company, becoming a vice president in 1934 and working there until his death. Having started to write poetry in 1904, ten years later he began to publish his work in various magazines and to attend literary gatherings in New York City. But he had little interest in the causes artists tended to espouse, and so after his move to Hartford, he abandoned his old literary circles. Stevens's first book, *Harmonium*, came out in 1923. Before his death, he received the Pulitzer Prize, the Bollingen Prize, and the Gold Medal of the Poetry Society of America.

Leon Stokesbury (*1945–*)   Stokesbury earned his M.F.A from the University of Arkansas in 1972 and his Ph.D. from Florida State University in 1984. He is currently at Georgia State University, where he serves as an associate professor and director of the M.F.A. program. His poems have appeared in many journals, including *Partisan Review, The Kenyon Review, The New Yorker, The Georgia Review*, and *The New England Review*. His first book of poems, *Often in Different Landscapes*, won the first Associated Writing Programs Poetry Competition. He recently edited the second edition of *The Made Thing: An Anthology of Contemporary Southern Poetry*. A popular public performer, Stokesbury has given poetry readings at more than one hundred colleges and universities.

Alfred, Lord Tennyson (*1809–1892*)   Tennyson was born the fourth of twelve children to a family in Somersby, Lincolnshire, England. He was educated at home by his father, a bitter man who had been the heir to a large estate before being disinherited. Drawn to poetry from an early age, Tennyson composed a six-thousand-line epic poem at the age of twelve. The same year that he entered Cambridge University, he and his brother Charles published a volume entitled *Poems by Two Brothers*. At Cambridge, he found himself in a secret society of promising intellectuals who called themselves "The Apostles," and published a second book of poetry. When one of his books was harshly reviewed in 1832, Tennyson was so demoralized that he hid from the public eye until 1842. Then he published a volume called simply *Poems*, which was such a success that Tennyson was soon named England's Poet Laureate and eventually even made a baron. By the middle of the nineteenth century, he was the most popular poet in the English language.

Dylan Thomas (*1914–1953*) Thomas was born in Swansea, Wales, in what he called the "smug darkness of a provincial town." His father, a schoolteacher, encouraged him to enroll at a university, but Thomas began writing poetry early in his life: his style was formed by the time he was seventeen, and he published his highly successful first book, *18 Poems*, when he was twenty. He proceeded to move to London, where, in 1936, he met Caitlin Macnamara, an Irishwoman whose temperament was almost as volatile as his own. The couple married the next year and together had three children. Thomas had a successful, though turbulent, literary career. He published poetry, short stories, and plays.

Walt Whitman (*1819–1892*) Whitman was born on Long Island and moved to Brooklyn, where he quit school at the age of eleven to work in a lawyer's office, then a printer's. He spent most of his youth in the printing business, then in newspapers, as a compositor and a writer. He burst on the literary scene with the first edition of *Leaves of Grass* in 1855. The eminent American writer Ralph Waldo Emerson told him in a letter, "I greet you at the beginning of a great career," and indeed, Whitman's career was launched not without Emerson's help, since his endorsement was printed as a preface to the second edition of *Leaves of Grass* in 1856. During the Civil War, he visited military hospitals and worked in the army's Paymaster Office, and two of his most famous poems commemorated Abraham Lincoln after his assassination. Few American poets have created such a public voice as Whitman, so that the speaker in his poems (for better or for worse) is often taken to be the poet/prophet speaking to his nation.

Richard Wilbur (*1921–*) Wilbur was born in New York City and raised in rural New Jersey. He graduated from Amherst College in 1942 and, after serving in World War II, received an M.A. from Harvard in 1947. He was elected to Harvard's prestigious Society of Fellows and used his three years as a fellow to write verse. After teaching at Harvard, Wellesley, Wesleyan, and Smith, he succeeded Robert Penn Warren and became the second Poet Laureate of the United States. In addition to writing five volumes of poetry, he has translated French literature; written lyrics for the comic opera based on Voltaire's novel, *Candide*; and written two children's books and a collection of prose pieces. Two of his volumes, *New and Collected Poems* and *Things of This World*, won the Pulitzer Prize, and the latter also won the National Book Award. Wilbur has received a number of other prestigious awards, including the Bollingen Prize, two Guggenheim fellowships, and a Ford Foundation award.

William Carlos Williams (*1883–1963*)   Williams was born in Rutherford, New Jersey, where he practiced obstetrics and pediatrics for most of his life and where he finally died. Though he studied abroad—in Paris and Leipzig—Williams was the most rooted of the modern American poets. His first book of poems was published in 1909, and he then published two more volumes under Ezra Pound's tutelage. But the publication of *Spring and All* (1923) announced his break with the other modernists: he gave up the erudite, philosophical, and cosmopolitan poetry of writers such as T. S. Eliot and championed a new poetry ignorant of forms, stripped of ideas, and rooted in "local conditions." In addition to his lyric poems, Williams wrote essays and novels and edited a literary magazine. A long poem, *Paterson*, crowned his career. When he died, he was working on the sixth book of that American epic.

William Wordsworth (*1770–1850*)   Wordsworth was born and raised in a modest cottage in Cockermouth in West Cumberland, on the northern fringe of England's Lake District. When he was eight, his mother died, and he and his three brothers were sent to school at Hawkshead, near Esthwaite Lake. After studying at St. John's College, Cambridge University, he spent a year in France in order to witness the French Revolution. There he became involved with a French woman of Catholic and Royalist sympathies. Financial difficulties forced him to return to England, and he had to leave behind his lover and their child, with whom he never reunited. Living with his sister Dorothy in Dorsetshire, Wordsworth began to devote himself exclusively to poetry. There he became close to Samuel Taylor Coleridge, with whom he wrote *Lyrical Ballads* in 1798. The two revolutionized English poetry with their use of colloquial diction and simple subjects. By the time Wordsworth was forty he had written most of his great work, including his masterpiece, *The Prelude*. In 1843 Wordsworth was made England's Poet Laureate.

James Wright (*1927–1980*)   Wright grew up in Martins Ferry, Ohio, a poor town that the Great Depression only made poorer. Upon graduating from the local high school, he joined the United States Army and served in Japan during the American occupation. In 1948 he left the military and returned to Ohio to attend Kenyon College on the GI Bill. At Kenyon he studied with John Crowe Ransom, and at the University of Washington he and his close friend Richard Hugo studied with Theodore Roethke. He earned an M.S. and a Ph.D. and won a Fulbright Scholarship to continue his studies at the University of Vienna. He taught at the University of Minnesota, Minneapolis, between 1957 and 1964 and at Hunter College in

New York City between 1966 and 1980. His first book, *The Green Wall*, won the Yale Younger Poets competition, and his *Collected Poems* won the 1971 Pulitzer Prize.

Sir Thomas Wyatt the Elder (*1503–1542*)   Wyatt was born at Allington Castle in Kent and educated at St. John's College, Cambridge. He spent most of his life as courtier and diplomat in the service of King Henry VIII, for whom he acted as Clerk of the King's Jewels and as ambassador to Spain and to the Emperor Charles V. His life was not calm: he was arrested and imprisoned twice, once after quarreling with the Duke of Suffolk and once after officials suspected him of treason. He managed to regain the king's favor and received a pardon after each of these incidents. It is hardly surprising that he should write in praise of a quiet life in the country and make cynical comments about court life after such experiences as these. Though Wyatt intended to publish a collection of his poems, he never did, and most of his verse was collected only after his death.

William Butler Yeats (*1865–1939*)   Yeats was born into an artistic family that divided its time between bohemian London and rural Sligo on the west coast of Ireland. He attended high school and art school in Dublin, but soon gave up painting and threw himself into literary work and began publishing poetry. In 1889 he fell in love with Maud Gonne, a nationalist and a beauty, and he later remarked that it was then that "the troubles of [his] life began." In 1903 Gonne married Major John MacBride, and as her politics became more extremist, she and Yeats grew further apart. He married an Englishwoman, Georgie Hyde-Lees, in 1917, and with her had a son and daughter and lived in a Norman tower called Thoor Ballylee near Coole. Yeats avidly pursued two occultist movements, the Theosophical movement and the Golden Dawn. His occultism came to form the basis of his complicated and esoteric symbolism. His poetry was also informed by his politics, and, fittingly enough, many of his poems were first published in newspapers. Yeats founded Ireland's national theater (the Abbey Theatre), joined a paramilitary organization committed to freeing Ireland from England (the Irish Volunteers), and served as a senator in the Irish Free State. Yeats won the Nobel Prize in 1923 and is generally recognized as Ireland's national poet.

Glossary

alliteration   the repetition of words with the same consonants within a line of poetry. For example: "In what distant deeps or skies" (Blake, "The Tyger").

allusion   a reference within one literary work to another literary work. For example, the following lines allude to the New Testament account of John the Baptist's beheading:

> Though I have seen my head (grown slightly bald) brought
>   in upon a platter,
> I am no prophet—
> (Eliot, "The Love Song of J. Alfred Prufrock")

anapest   a metrical foot with two unstressed syllables followed by a stressed syllable. For example: "of the night."

assonance   the repetition of words with the same vowel sounds within a line of poetry. For example: "Has found out thy bed" (Blake, "The Sick Rose").

audience   the character within a poem who is listening to the speaker, or the readership for which a poet writes a poem.

ballad   a lyric poem that tells a story in quatrains; some but not all ballads use the standard ballad stanza. For example: "Sir Patrick Spens."

ballad stanza　a quatrain in which the first and third lines are iambic tetrameter, and the second and fourth lines, which rhyme, are iambic trimeter. For example:

> Because I could not stop for Death—
> He kindly stopped for me—
> The Carriage held but just Ourselves—
> And Immortality.
>
> (Dickinson)

blank verse　unrhymed lines of iambic pentameter.

canon　a list of literary works approved by some body of evaluators; this process may be formal, as in the books of the Bible, or informal and debatable, as in the canons of Western literature or American literature.

carpe diem　literally, "seize the day." It is a philosophy of life that values taking pleasure in the present for fear of not being able to in the future. Usually, the pleasures are sexual. *Carpe diem* is a genre of lyric poems in which the speaker invokes this ethic to seduce his or her audience. For example: Marvell, "To His Coy Mistress."

colloquial　informal or regional use of language. For example: Williams, "This Is Just to Say."

connotation　the nonliteral associations, often emotional, attached to a word.

convention　the use of some motif, situation, character, form, etc. that has become customary within a genre. For example: comparing a woman to a rose is a convention of love poetry.

conventional symbol　an object that carries symbolic meaning only within a particular culture. For example: in Blake's "The Lamb," a poem written within the Western, Christian world, the lamb represents Christ.

couplet　two consecutive rhymed lines of poetry. Usually a couplet contains a completed thought. For example:

> If this be error and upon me proved,
> I never writ, nor no man ever loved.
>
> (Shakespeare, Sonnet 116)

dactyl　a metrical foot with one stressed syllable followed by two unstressed syllables. For example: "willowy."

denotation   the literal (or "dictionary") meaning of a word.

diction   the type of words a writer or speaker uses. The style of words that educated people often use is called "high," while "low" diction may refer to the language of less-educated people. Diction might be artificial or "poetic." For example, when Keats says, "Oh for a draft of vintage!" he employs a poetic way of saying, "I wish I had a glass of good wine!" Note that diction does not mean "word choice." It is a style of language, not the use of a particular word. Paul Allen's "The Man with the Hardest Belly," for example, uses the diction of a Southern evangelical preacher. But Andrew Marvell's decision to describe his love as "vegetable" is not a matter of diction. "Vegetable," though unusual, does not indicate a manner of speech to which the speaker adheres.

dramatic monologue   a lyric poem that sounds like a speech lifted from a play; the speaker is talking to someone in the midst of a scene that might be dramatized on stage. Usually, dramatic monologues tell stories, and often they are ironic. For example: Robert Browning, "My Last Duchess."

elegy   a melancholic lyric poem meditating on something, usually a death. For example: Gray, "Elegy Written in a Country Churchyard."

end rhyme   rhymes at the end of lines in poetry. For example, couplets share an end rhyme:

> This thou perceiv'st, which makes thy love more strong,
> To love that well which thou must leave are long.
> (Shakespeare, Sonnet 73)

English sonnet [also, **Elizabethan sonnet** or **Shakespearean sonnet**]   a lyric poem of fourteen lines divided by its rhyme scheme into three quatrains and a concluding couplet. For example: Shakespeare, Sonnet 73.

enjambment   the continuation of the sense and grammatical construction beyond the end of a line of verse. For example:

> But oh! that deep romantic chasm which slanted
> Down the green hill athwart a cedarn cover!
> (Coleridge, "Kubla Khan")

explication   an interpretation that closely discusses a poem's figurative and literal meaning, often line by line.

extended metaphor   a metaphoric comparison that extends beyond a single line of poetry. For example: Keats's "On First Looking into Chapman's Homer" metaphorically compares traveling to reading through the sonnet's first eight lines.

feminine rhyme   end rhymes of two syllables with the accent on the second-to-last syllables. For example:

> Then be not coy, but use your time,
>   And, while ye may, go marry;
> For having lost but once your prime,
>   You may forever tarry.
>   (Herrick, "To the Virgins, to Make Much of Time")

"Marry" and "tarry" are feminine rhymes.

figurative language   expressions that communicate beyond their literal meanings and therefore must be interpreted in some other way. For example: metaphor, irony, hyperbole, and symbol.

figurative level   meaning generated by a poem's figurative language.

figure of speech   see **figurative language**.

foot   see **meter**.

free verse   poetry with no metrical pattern or set line lengths and usually no rhymes; its rhythms are often established by grammatical repetitions and parallelisms. For example: Whitman, "When I Heard the Learn'd Astronomer."

genre   a grouping of literary works usually based on similar formal structures; works within a genre will share conventions. For example: the sonnet.

hyperbole   a figure of speech in which what is literally said overstates the meaning. For example:

> An hundred years shall go to praise
> Thine eyes, and on thy forehead gaze;
> Two hundred to adore each breast,
> But thirty thousand to the rest . . .
>   (Marvell, "To His Coy Mistress")

iamb   a metrical foot with one unstressed syllable followed by a stressed syllable. For example: "the book."

image   a sensation—visual, tactile, auditory, olfactory, or gustatory—conveyed by language. Anything you see, hear, feel, smell, or taste in a poem is an image.

internal rhyme   rhyme between a word within a line and another word at the end of the same line or within another line. For example:

> Look left, look right, the hills are bright . . .
> (Housman, "1887")

irony   a figure of speech in which what is literally said is different from (and often the opposite of) what is meant. For example: The last two lines of Piercy's "Barbie doll" read: "Consummation at last. / To every woman a happy ending." The speaker means that this ending is not happy.

   Irony may be more complex. For example, the carved words on the pedestal in Shelley's "Ozymandias" that say, "Look on my Works, ye Mighty, and despair!" certainly were meant to be taken at face value. But in their present context, on the pedestal of a ruined statue surrounded by desert, they communicate Ozymandias's impotence rather than his might.

   "Irony" is also used to describe poems in which the poet disapproves of or disagrees with the speaker. For example: the speaker in Browning's "My Last Duchess" voices despicable things that Browning means for us to disapprove.

Italian sonnet   [also **Petrarchan sonnet**]   a lyric poem of fourteen lines divided by its rhyme scheme into an octet and a sestet. For example: Keats, "On First Looking into Chapman's Homer."

literary symbol   an object that carries symbolic meaning only within the context of a particular literary work. For example: in Blake's "The Tyger," the tiger represents evil, sin, experience, etc. But these meanings are invented by Blake. In another context, an image of a tiger would suggest none of these meanings.

litotes   a figure of speech in which what is literally said understates the meaning.

lyric   a relatively short poem. Every poem in this volume is a lyric poem.

metaphor   a figure of speech that compares one thing to another; the expression will literally make no sense; its meaning can be understood only by applying one term's connotations to the other. For example:

> That time of year thou may'st in me behold
> When yellow leaves, or none, or few, do hang . . .
> (Shakespeare, Sonnet 73)

The age of the speaker is compared to the season of late autumn.

meter　the measurement of poetry's rhythms based on stressed and unstressed syllables. The basic unit of meter is a "foot." Each foot consists of two or three syllables. The most common feet and their notations are

iamb: [˘ ´] unstressed, stressed syllables

trochee: [´ ˘] stressed, unstressed syllables

spondee: [´ ´] stressed, stressed syllables

pyrrhic: [˘ ˘] unstressed, unstressed syllables

anapest: [˘ ˘ ´] unstressed, unstressed, stressed syllables

dactyl: [´ ˘ ˘] stressed, unstressed, unstressed syllables

Meter also describes line lengths. For example, a line with

one foot is monometer;
two feet is dimeter;
three feet is trimeter;
four feet is tetrameter;
five feet is pentameter;
six feet is hexameter; and
seven feet is heptameter.

The rhythm of a line can be described by combining these two notations. For example, a five-foot line with mostly iambs is called "iambic pentameter."

motif　a recurring feature of a literary work or genre, usually an image, idea, situation, or theme. For example, sexual seduction is a motif of *carpe diem* poems.

natural symbol　an object that carries symbolic meaning that is suggested by its own nature and, therefore, is the same in various cultures. For example: the sunrise symbolizes new beginnings.

occasional poem　a poem written to commemorate or interpret a particular public event. For example: Hardy's "Convergence of the Twain" was written on the sinking of the *Titanic*.

octave   an eight-line stanza.

ode   a usually long lyric poem, often irregular in form, on an occasion of public or private reflection in which personal emotion and general meditation are united. For example: Keats's "Ode to a Nightingale" is a personal meditative ode.

off rhyme   a rhyme in which the sounds are similar but not exact. For example: "stopped" and "wept," "home" and "come."

onomatopoeia   a word or phrase that mimics the thing it literally means. For example: "splash" sounds like an explosion of water.

oxymoron   a paradoxical phrase linking two contrary terms. For example: "waking dream" in Keats's "Ode to a Nightingale."

paradox   a figure of speech in which the literal meaning seems to contradict itself but really expresses a higher truth. For example:

> Except you enthrall me, never shall be free,
> Nor ever chaste, except you ravish me.
>   (Donne, Holy Sonnet 14)

paraphrase   a translation of a poem or a part of a poem into the style of everyday, common prose. A critic will paraphrase a passage to be sure he or she understands its literal meaning.

parody   a work that makes fun of the conventions of a particular genre, usually by exaggerating them. For example: Collins's "Sonnet" is a parody of the sonnet form.

pastoral   a poem that uses shepherds as characters; or the use of pleasant images from the country.

personification   a type of metaphor in which some nonhuman object or abstraction is compared to a human being. For example, in this line from Donne's Holy Sonnet 10, Death is compared to a tyrannical ruler: "Death, be not proud, though some have callèd thee / Mighty and dreadful[.]"

Petrarchan sonnet   see **Italian sonnet**.

prose poem   a short piece of writing in paragraph form rather than in meter, but which in other ways resembles a poem. The subject matter and treatment are like poetry, and the sentences, despite the lack of meter, create a strong sense of rhythm. For example: Forché, "The Colonel."

prosody   the study of meter.

quatrain   a four-line stanza.

rhetorical situation   the fictional scene that encompasses a poem: who the speaker is; who the audience is; the setting surrounding them; the occasion that has prompted the speaker to speak. Sometimes the rhetorical situation is impossible to define.

rhyme   the repetition of sounds. For example: "forever" rhymes with "never."

rhyme scheme   a notation used to describe the rhymes of a poem. For example, the rhyme scheme of the following lines is *aabcc:*

> Let us go then, you and I,
> When the evening is spread out against the sky
> Like a patient etherised upon a table;
> Let us go, through certain half-deserted streets,
> The muttering retreats . . .
>   (Eliot, "The Love Song of J. Alfred Prufrock")

rhythm   the musical quality of a poem usually established by a pattern of stressed and unstressed syllables.

satire   a literary work that tries to correct social institutions or human behavior by making fun of them.

scansion   a description of a poem's meter that marks feet (/) and stressed (´) and unstressed (˘) syllables. For example, here is a scanned line from Keats's "On First Looking into Chapman's Homer":

> ˘   ´   ˘   ´   ˘   ´   ˘   ´   ˘   ´
> And man / y good / ly states / and king / doms seen

sestet   a six-line stanza.

sestina   a poem of six sestets plus a concluding tercet. The end words of each line in the first stanza are used as end words (in varying order) in the following five stanzas. The concluding tercet uses the end words in the middle and at the end of each line. For example: Bishop, "Sestina."

Shakespearean sonnet   see **English sonnet.**

simile   a metaphor that introduces its comparison with the word "like" or "as." For example:

> Here and there
> his brown skin hung in strips
> like ancient wallpaper.
>   (Bishop, "The Fish")

The skin of the fish is compared to old wallpaper.

sonnet   a fourteen-line poem, usually in iambic pentameter. The two main types of sonnets are English and Italian. Often they are written in cycles, or sequences, of many poems, and they typically explore the theme of love.

speaker   the person who is uttering the words in a poem. Unless you have evidence to the contrary, you should assume that the speaker is *not* the poet—that the speaker is a fictional persona.

spondee   a metrical foot with two consecutive stressed syllables. For example: "bookcase."

stanza   a division of lines within a poem. Usually a stanza is indicated by white space on the page; often stanzas are indicated by repeated patterns in a rhyme scheme (each unit that is repeated is a stanza).

subgenre   a genre within a genre. For example: the lyric poem is a subgenre of poetry, and the sonnet is a subgenre of the lyric poem.

symbol   an object that carries meaning on the literal level and also stands for something else on a figurative level. Sometimes, one object might symbolize another object. When you say, "Give me a hand," the "hand" represents the whole person from whom you are requesting help. More often, a symbolic object will represent an abstraction (or a range of abstractions). For example: the American flag symbolizes (among other things) the United States and those qualities commonly associated with it, such as political freedom and prosperity. To some individuals and cultures the same flag might represent cultural imperialism.

symbolic action   that which happens to the symbols in a poem: do they change? are they acted upon? For example: the jar in Stevens's "Anecdote of a Jar" represents, among other possibilities, human civilization. The "action" of the jar is to take dominion over the wilderness; so, *symbolically,* human civilization also takes dominion over the wilderness.

syntax   the order of words to form phrases and sentences. Syntax in poetry is often more complex than the syntax we use in our everyday language, and occasionally it violates Standard English. Such violations are called "poetic license." Paraphrase helps to untangle difficult syntax.

tercet   a three-line stanza.

theme   the abstract subject of a poem; what the poem is about. For example, some themes in Shelley's "Ozymandias" are "mutability," "ambition," "art," and "nature."

tone the verbal indication of a speaker's (and a poet's) attitude toward the poem's subject. For example, Arnold's "Dover Beach" begins with a light, even hopeful tone, but quickly becomes melancholic.

trochee a metrical foot with a stressed syllable followed by an unstressed syllable. For example: "hover."

universal symbol symbols that seem to carry the same meanings in many cultures. For example: sunrise as a symbol for birth, or the crown as a symbol of monarchy.

villanelle a poem of five tercets and a quatrain using just two rhymes. The first and third line of the first tercet are repeated throughout the other stanzas. For example: Thomas, "Do Not Go Gentle into That Good Night."

*

Permissions Acknowledgments

John Agard: "Palm Tree King" from *Mangoes and Bullets*, published by Pluto Press 1985. Reprinted by kind permission of the author and Caroline Sheldon Literary Agency.

Paul Allen: "The Man with the Hardest Belly" from *American Crawl*, University of North Texas Press, 1997. Reprinted by permission of the author.

Margaret Atwood: "You Fit into Me" from *Power Politics*. Copyright © 1971 by Margaret Atwood. Reprinted by permission of House of Anansi Press Limited.

W. H. Auden: "In Memory of W. B. Yeats" and "Musée des Beaux Arts" from *W. H. Auden: Collected Poems,* edited by Edward Mendelson. Copyright © 1940 & renewed 1968 by W. H. Auden. Reprinted by permission of Random House, Inc., and Faber and Faber Ltd.

Elizabeth Bishop: "One Art," "Sestina," and "The Fish" from *The Complete Poems 1927–1979*. Copyright © 1979, 1983 by Alice Helen Methfessel. Reprinted by permission of Farrar, Straus and Giroux, LLC.

Gwendolyn Brooks: "The Bean Eaters," "the mother," and "We Real Cool" from *Blacks*. Reprinted by permission of the author.

Lynne Bryer: "The Way" from *Illuminations*. Reprinted by permission.

Billy Collins: "On Turning Ten" from *The Art of Drowning* by Billy Collins, © 1995. "Picnic, Lightning" from *Picnic Lightning* by Billy Collins, © 1998. Reprinted by permission of the University of Pittsburgh

Press. "Sonnet" from *Poetry*, Vol. CLXXIII, No. 4 (February 1999), copyright © 1999 by The Modern Poetry Association. Reprinted by permission of the Editor of *Poetry* and by the author.

E. E. Cummings: "in just-" and "Buffalo Bill's" from *Complete Poems:1904–1962* by E. E. Cummings, edited by George J. Firmage. Copyright 1923, 1951, © 1991 by the Trustees for the E. E. Cummings Trust. Copyright © 1976 by George James Firmage. Used by permission of Liveright Publishing Corporation.

Emily Dickinson: "After great pain, a formal feeling comes" from *The Poems of Emily Dickinson*, Thomas H. Johnson, ed., Cambridge, Mass.: The Belknap Press of Harvard University Press, Copyright © 1951, 1955, 1979 by the President and Fellows of Harvard College. Reprinted by permission of the publishers and Trustees of Amherst College.

Rita Dove: "Daystar" from *Thomas and Beulah*, Carnegie Mellon University Press, © 1986 by Rita Dove. "The House Slave" from *The Yellow House on the Corner*, Carnegie Mellon University Press, © 1980 by Rita Dove. Reprinted by permission of the author.

T. S. Eliot: "The Love Song of J. Alfred Prufrock" from *Collected Poems 1909–1962*. Reprinted by permission of Faber and Faber Ltd.

Louise Erdrich: "Captivity" and "Indian Boarding School: The Runaways" from *Jacklight* by Louise Erdrich, © 1984 by Louise Erdrich. Reprinted by permission of Henry Holt and Company, LLC.

Carolyn Forché: "The Colonel" from *The Country Between Us*. Copyright © 1981 by Carolyn Forché. Originally appeared in *Women's International Resource Exchange*. Reprinted by permission of HarperCollins Publishers, Inc.

Robert Frost: "Design" and "Stopping by Woods on a Snowy Evening" from *The Poetry of Robert Frost*, edited by Edward Connery Lathem. Copyright 1936, 1951, by Robert Frost, © 1964 by Lesley Frost Ballantine, copyright 1923, 1969 by Henry Holt and Company. Reprinted by permission of Henry Holt and Company, LLC.

Allen Ginsberg: "A Supermarket in California" from *Collected Poems 1947–1980* by Allen Ginsberg. Copyright © 1955 by Allen Ginsberg. Copyright renewed. Reprinted by permission of HarperCollins Publishers, Inc.

Robert Hayden: "Those Winter Sundays" from *Collected Poems of Robert Hayden*, edited by Frederick Glaysher. Copyright © 1966 by Robert Hayden. Used by permission of Liveright Publishing Corporation.

Seamus Heaney: "Digging" and "Punishment" from *Open Ground: Selected Poems 1966–1996* by Seamus Heaney. Copyright © 1998 by Seamus Heaney. Reprinted by Permission of Farrar, Straus and Giroux, LLC, and by permission of Faber and Faber Ltd.

Langston Hughes: "Harlem," "The Negro Speaks of Rivers," and "Theme for English B" from *Collected Poems* by Langston Hughes. Copyright © 1994 by the Estate of Langston Hughes. Reprinted by permission of Alfred A. Knopf, Inc., a Division of Random House, Inc.

Randall Jarrell: "The Death of the Ball Turret Gunner" from *The Complete Poems* by Randall Jarrell. Copyright © 1969, renewed 1997 by Mary von S. Jarrell. Reprinted by permission of Farrar, Straus and Giroux, LLC.

Galway Kinnell: "Blackberry Eating" from *Three Books* by Galway Kinnell. Copyright © 1993 by Galway Kinnell. Previously published in *Moral Acts, Mortal Words* (1980). Reprinted by permission of Houghton Mifflin Company. All rights reserved.

Yusef Komunyakaa: "Facing It" and "We Never Know" from *Dien Cai Dau*, © 1988 by Yusef Komunyakaa and reprinted by permission of Wesleyan University Press.

Maxine Kumin: "Woodchucks" from *Selected Poems 1960–1990* by Maxine Kumin. Copyright © 1972 by Maxine Kumin. Used by permission of W. W. Norton & Company, Inc.

Philip Larkin: "Aubade" from *Collected Poems* by Philip Larkin. Copyright © 1988, 1989 by the Estate of Philip Larkin. Reprinted by permission of Farrar, Straus and Giroux, LLC, and by Faber and Faber Ltd.

Li-Young Lee: "The Gift" and "Visions and Interpretations" from *Rose: Poems* by Li-Young Lee, copyright © 1986 by Li Young Lee. Reprinted with the permission of BOA Editions Ltd.

Robert Lowell: "Skunk Hour" from *Selected Poems* by Robert Lowell. Copyright © 1976 by Robert Lowell. Reprinted by permission of Farrar, Straus and Giroux, LLC.

Susan Ludvigson: "After Love" from *Everything Winged Must Be Dreaming*. Reprinted by permission of the author.

Archibald MacLeish: "Ars Poetica" from *Collected Poems 1917–1982*. Copyright © 1985 by The Estate of Archibald MacLeish. Reprinted by permission of Houghton Mifflin Company. All rights reserved.

Edna St. Vincent Millay: Sonnet XXX of *Fatal Interview* and "What lips my lips have kissed" from *Collected Poems*. Copyright © 1923, 1931, 1951, 1958 by Edna St. Vincent Millay and Norma Millay Ellis. All rights reserved. Reprinted by permission of Elizabeth Barnett, literary executor.

Marianne Moore: "Poetry" from *The Complete Poems of Marianne Moore*. Copyright 1935 by Marianne Moore; copyright renewed © 1963 by Marianne Moore and T. S. Eliot. Reprinted with the permission of Simon & Schuster.

Sharon Olds: "Sex Without Love" and "The One Girl at the Boys' Party" from *The Dead and the Living* by Sharon Olds. Copyright © 1983

William Carlos Williams: "Spring and All, section I," "The Red Wheelbarrow," and "This Is Just to Say" from *Collected Poems: 1909–1939*, Volume I, copyright © 1938 by New Directions Publishing Corp. Reprinted by permission of New Directions Publishing Corp.

James Wright: "A Blessing" from *Above the River* © 1990 by Anne Wright, Wesleyan University Press. Reprinted by permission of University Press of New England.

W. B. Yeats: "Leda and the Swan" and "Sailing to Byzantium" from *The Collected Poems of W. B. Yeats*, edited by Richard J. Finneran. Copyright © 1928 by Macmillan Publishing Company, renewed 1956 by Georgie Yeats. Reprinted with the permission of Scribner, a Division of Simon & Schuster. "The Second Coming" from *The Poems of W. B. Yeats*, edited by Richard J. Finneran. Copyright © 1924 by Macmillan Publishing Company, renewed 1952 by Bertha Georgie Yeats. Reprinted with the permission of Simon & Schuster.

Every effort has been made to contact the copyright holders of each of these selections. Rights holders of any selections not credited should contact W. W. Norton & Company, Inc., 500 Fifth Avenue, New York, NY 10110, in order for a correction to be made in the next reprinting of our work.

Index

WELL I USTO WAKE THE MORNEN
BEFORE THE ROOSTER CROWED
SEARCHIN FOR SODA BOTTLES
TO GET MYSELF SOME DOUGH

BROUGHT EM DOWN TO THE CORNER
DOWN TO THE COUNTRY STORE
CASH EM IN AND GIVE MY MONEY
TO A MAN NAMED CURTIS LOWE

OLD CURT WAS A BLACK MAN
WITH WHITE CURLY HAIR
WHEN HE HAD A FIFTH OF WINE
HE DID NOT HAVE A CARE

HE USTO OWN AN OLD DO-PRO
USTO PLAY ACROSS HIS KNEE
WHEN HE HAD A DRINK OF WINE
THEN HE'D PLAY ALL DAY FOR ME

HE LIVED TO BE 60
MABE I WAS 10
MAMA USTO WOOP ME
BUT I'D GO SEE HIM AGAIN

I'D CLAP MY HANDS STOMP MY FEETS
TRY TO STAY IN TOWN
BUT ON THE DAY OLD CURTIS DIED
NOBODY CAME TO PRAY